THE SOCIOLOGY OF NATIONALISM

Nationalism is fast becoming the social and political ideology of our time, in a world where every continent, economic system or level of development has to come to terms with its main concepts. This book analyses the many manifestations of nationalism in the wider context of the social sciences, bringing together sociology, social anthropology, politics and history in the course of its analysis. Among the topics covered are:

*   Classical and contemporary theories of nationalism
*   Nationalism and ethnicity
*   Nationalism and the construction of history
*   Nationalism and the nation-state
*   Colonial and post-colonial nationalisms
*   Neo-nationalism and post-communist nationalism.

It concludes with a look to the future and asks why nationalism is growing when its goal, the 'nation-state', seems to be going out of business.

Clear and concise in its presentation of key concepts and theories as well as in its arguments and analysis, *The Sociology of Nationalism* can be seen as a significant new addition to the literature already available on the subject and will be essential reading for students across a wide range of disciplines, including sociology, history, politics and anthropology.

David McCrone is Professor of Sociology, and Convener of the Unit for the Study of Government in Scotland, at Edinburgh University. His previous publications include *Understanding Scotland: The Sociology of a Stateless Nation*, also published by Routledge.

INTERNATIONAL LIBRARY OF SOCIOLOGY

SOCIOLOGY

Founded by Karl Mannheim

Editor: John Urry

Lancaster University

THE SOCIOLOGY OF NATIONALISM

Tomorrow's ancestors

David McCrone

London and New York

First published 1998
by Routledge
11 New Fetter Lane, London EC4P 4EE

Simultaneously published in the USA and Canada
by Routledge
29 West 35th Street, New York, NY 10001

© 1998 David McCrone

Typeset in Baskerville by Routledge
Printed and bound in Great Britain by Clays Ltd, St Ives PLC

British Library Cataloguing in Publication Data
A catalogue record for this book is available from the British Library

Library of Congress Cataloging in Publication Data
McCrone, David.
The sociology of nationalism: tomorrow's ancestors/
David McCrone.
(International library of sociology)
Includes bibliographical references and index.
1. Nationalism. 2. Political sociology. 3. Sociology.
4. Ethnicity. I. Title. II. Series.
JC311.M392 1998
320.54 – dc21   98–9523

ISBN 0–415–11459–4 (hbk)
ISBN 0–415–11460–8 (pbk)

CONTENTS

PREFACE

What kind of book is this? Inevitably it is a book of its time and place. Fifty – even thirty – years ago it would have been hard to imagine such a book being written, indeed adding to a long list of books which have been published on nationalism in the last decade. It joins a burgeoning literature which spreads across the social sciences – sociology, social anthropology, politics, history – and into cultural and literary studies. Nor is it simply part of an intellectual fad. We struggle to keep up with, never mind to explain, the manifestations of nationalism wherever we look. There is no continent, no economic system, no level of development which does not have to come to terms with nationalism. If we had told our predecessors in the middle of this century that studying nationalism was not simply writing history but coping with its many modern manifestations, in all probability they would not have believed us. But then, we inhabit a late twentieth-century world in which many of the old nostrums and doctrines have withered. Socialism has gone; fascism has gone. Nationalism has survived and prospers.

This book is a sociologist's modest attempt to make sense of these different manifestations. It is not a history book, still less a revelation of a new, bright theory of nationalism. It reviews the literature on nationalism from a disciplinary perspective. It does not seek to claim that only sociologists can make sense of it, but, rather like the cobbler who thought there was nothing quite like leather, the author starts from the viewpoint of his sociological trade. Nationalism is above all a social and political movement. It manifests itself in rich and in poor countries; it has left-wing as well as right-wing variants; it works with, as well as against, movements of class and of gender.

This is a sociological book because it does not reduce nationalism merely to politics. It seeks to look at the social and economic interests which mobilise nationalism, without arguing that it is in any sense epiphenomenal. It is a cultural form of politics which is not simply reducible to material interests. We live in an age of nationalism, but one which spends a lot of its energies denying that nationalism exists. The orthodoxy is that it is a virus left over from an older more vicious age, which, as if mutating itself against all known antidotes, comes back to wreak its havoc on hapless victims. Centres of power employ the common-sense that they are patriotic while their enemies are nationalistic. If we look about us, we know that this simply cannot be true. The most powerful forms of nationalism are those which operate its power while denying its existence.

The study of nationalism is barely forty years old. To be sure, Hans Kohn's entry in *Encyclopaedia Britannica* in the 1940s marked out its intellectual territory for much of the following twenty years, but this standard source of universal particularism was addressing a world which had disappeared (with fascism) rather than one which was to come. What Kohn and others did not realise was that all the modern states of the post-war era were locked into an era of competitive nationalism 'in the national interest', while blaming it for the troubles of the 1930s and 1940s.

How does this book handle the subject? It is an attempt to lay out the arguments and debates around the key issues. The first chapter outlines the fall and rise of nationalism, the efforts to wrestle with what a 'nation' is, with the variants of nationalism, ethnic and civic, and with what we can cull from the classical writers of sociology. In the second chapter, we review the complex relationship between ethnicity and nationalism, arguing that one cannot reduce the latter to the former. There is also something deeply personal and intimate about nationalism; in Billig's felicitous phrase, it is 'banal'. This perspective is important because it helps us to escape from the orthodoxy that nationalism is a kind of political brainwashing, a sort of false consciousness. Nationalism is above all about 'history' in the sense that it writes its own, that it constructs an account of its origins and its past which legitimates the present and offers signposts for the future. That is why nationalists are 'tomorrow's ancestors'. This is the subject of chapter 3.

Standing at the heart of modern nationalism studies is Ernest Gellner, whose sociology of nationalism is examined in chapter 4. Gellner wrote, as John Hall put it, with 'devils at his back'. He represented so well the deliberately 'marginal man' whose positioning at the tangents of the great movements of our time gave him the unique perspective on nationalism. Much of the writing on nationalism in the last thirty years has been done with Gellner in mind. He has been an irritant and an inspiration.

In chapter 5 we examine the central orthodoxy of nationalism, that it was the handmaiden of state-building in the modern era. Its success is reflected in our equation of 'nation' with 'state'. The following chapter tackles what appeared at the time to be its 'last wave' – liberation nationalism against colonial regimes. Again, we were confounded as these post-colonial systems were themselves attacked for not being truly nationalist.

Usually at this point in history, the narrative ends. With state-building and the end of colonialism, nationalism seemed over. It wasn't. In the final quarter of the twentieth century a new variant emerged in the form of neo-nationalism which its opponents sought to counter by denying its existence. They have largely given up. In a world of limited and shared sovereignty, the self-styled nation-state finds itself squeezed from above and below. The fall of communism, so long predicted but ultimately unexpected, ushered in a new and more complex wave, and we are still struggling to make sense of this wave as the century draws to a close. These modern manifestations – neo-nationalism, and post-communist nationalism – are the subjects of chapters 7 and 8.

In the final chapter, the central conundrum is reviewed: why nationalism, when its goal the 'nation-state' seems to be going out of business? That is a good point to end with, as we cannot afford to draw a line under nationalism in all its mutations. Further variants will no doubt surface and demand our attention in the new millennium, for it is the sheer versatility of the phenomenon which is both its delight and exasperation.

Nationalism is a subject which attracts disciples and heretics. Much of what is written comes from those who either support it, or condemn it. It is therefore important for the current author to offer an insight into his own perspective. It is significant that this book is written by a Scot. It is not, however, a book about Scottish nationalism. To my generation, *les événements* of 1968 coincided with the rise of modern political nationalism in Scotland. It did not have a place in intellectual orthodoxy, which claimed to be cosmopolitan in its ideology, but which was riddled with the parochialisms of the centre. Just as women have to do, Scots learned to fillet out the in-built biases of conventional discourses, and to combat the complacent assumptions that people are men, and Britain a nation. Faced too with the particularistic accusation that the only way to explain nationalism in Scotland was in terms of what was perceived to be its own distorted and parochial history, it became important to study the many variants of nationalism, and to discover that they all had something in common. To the accusation that the author is a nationalist, one would have to reply that, since the British general election of 1997 at which the self-defined Unionist party in Scotland (and Wales) was wiped out, we are all nationalists now – to some degree or another.

Readers of this book will find, then, a commentary on nationalism which is informed by the fact that the author is both a sociologist and a Scot. Those are the key dimensions to bear in mind. This book is not a political tract, and it has no special axes to grind. It tries to be as dispassionate and analytical as possible. Whether or not the author succeeds is for the reader to decide. I owe particular thanks to fellow students of nationalism, and in particular to John Hall, Graeme Morton, Lindsay Paterson and Gianfranco Poggi who made such perceptive comments on earlier drafts. Tom Nairn's *Faces of Nationalism* (Verso, 1997) was published after this manuscript was written, but the reader will see that his influence has been profound. I have benefited greatly from sharing teaching with him. This book is dedicated to all those who have taken a part in the debate about a Scottish Parliament, but above all to Mary with whom I have had my own domestic debates on these matters, and without whom this book would certainly not have been written.

St Andrew's Day, 1997

1

THE FALL AND RISE OF NATIONALISM

Few social and political phenomena have attracted more attention in recent years than has nationalism, and yet few have been so much neglected. By the middle of the twentieth century much of social and political science had confined it to the dustbin of history. Nationalism was 'over'. It had ushered in the modern state in the nineteenth century, and had reached its deformed apotheosis in fascism in the twentieth. Its final purpose seemed to be to break up empires thereafter, as post-colonial regimes used it as a vehicle for state-building. For the rest, this observation by Dudley Seers on the conventional wisdom seemed to ring true:

> Nationalism was not merely of little and declining practical consequence: it was obviously evil. It had lain at the root of war. German chauvinism, in particular, had contributed to two terrible wars. Moreover, nationalist sentiment was still a menace in the second half of the twentieth century, getting in the way of the creation of a just, peaceful and prosperous world society, which modern technology had put within our reach – if only population growth could be controlled. Particularly silly and dangerous were the narrower nationalists who rebelled, often violently, against the state to which they belonged – the Basques, Welsh, Kurds, Matabele, Amerindians, French Canadians, to name a few out of scores of possible examples. They might have economic grievances, but these could be put right by some redistribution of income.
>
> (Seers, 1983: 10)

Writing this in the early 1980s, Seers was pointing to the failure of social scientists to see what was developing beneath their noses. His gentle sarcasm was aimed at their failure to take nationalism seriously. As the millennium approaches, this is no longer possible. In the West, regions and nations which seemed settled within their existing states for so long began to seek greater autonomy in the final quarter of the century just as new supra-national organisations such as the European Community/Union and the North American Free Trade Association were eroding the sovereignty of these states. In the Third World, liberation nationalism was judged to have done its work of breaking up empires, but was proving reluctant to leave the scene. By the 1990s 'ethnic' conflicts had broken out, and could be traced back with little difficulty to fairly arbitrary devices employed by colonialists for the purposes of divide and rule. The central African conflict between Tutsi and Hutu seemed to owe far more to the racist grid used to map the peoples of that territory than to any meaningful and long-standing cultural hatred between people so labelled. Finally, and to cap it all, the collapse of communism in 1989 ushered in a new wave of nationalism across the old Soviet empire which even the most reluctant of commentators could not ignore. A new vocabulary of 'ethnic cleansing' – a new word for an old idea – emerged in the tripartite war in the former Yugoslavia, attributed to a despairing UN official seeking a term for bouts of inter-ethnic killing which the textbooks told us was not meant to happen. Nationalism had joined the ranks of the Undead.

What did it all mean? The said textbooks were of little help. To be sure, there was a sizeable literature on 'nation-building', mainly on the nineteenth-century variety which shaped most modern European states. Liberation nationalism was also an important sub-literature, but little else was to hand. These things might have ushered in the twentieth century, but they were not meant to usher it out. Mid-century developments were deemed to have 'solved' the problem. Fascism was dead, and post-war states had evolved a safer form of economic nationalism where they sought to harness popular support for economic competition with other states in 'the national interest'.

By the 1980s, when it was no longer possible to ignore nationalism, the weight of 'informed opinion' was largely hostile. The British liberal newspaper, the *Guardian*, issued a leader – 'Don't put out more flags!' – on the premise, as Tom Nairn pointed out, 'if enough new flags were put out, the Old Demon would wreak havoc with the New World Order' (Nairn, 1993: 3), as if more flags would lead inexorably to ethnic cleansing. This new order was rapidly turning into a New World Disorder, and opinion educated in the binary divides of the Cold War translated easily into a new Manichean view: 'Armageddon has been replaced by the ethnic abyss' (ibid.).

By the 1980s and 1990s the political orthodoxies of the Right and Left were also uncomfortable with new forms of nationalism. The New Liberalism on the Right gave primacy to the market, which was gifted with the powers to reduce all conflicts to economic competition, and hence resolve them by recognisable means. An older form of Conservative thought which laid greater stress on national units as the core of economic, political and cultural relations was superseded by this neo-liberalism, only to be revived by the perceived threat of supra-state bodies like the European Union to 'national sovereignty'. The problem with its analysis is that it failed to resolve the contradiction between global markets and national self-determination; it assumed the triumph of economics over politics. The Right, certainly in the UK, had so firmly hitched its wagon to the neo-liberal horse in the 1980s that to belatedly dispute the direction in which it was going was not very convincing. In many ways the old nineteenth-century association of liberalism and nationalism – that national and social liberation went together – had been lost.

Reducing society to marketplace meant that there was little room in the intellectual canon of the New Right for the 'nation'.

The Liberal-Left too was ill-prepared to analyse new forms of nationalism. In
both its socialist and social democratic forms, nationalism was an ill-fitting
garment. In his monumental study of the history of socialism, Donald Sassoon
(1997) makes it plain that the social democratic state operated within a highly
organised and de facto nationalism, which was nevertheless usually implicit. Yet, at
an ideological level, it often defined itself over and against nationalism which was
associated with bourgeois or right-wing political parties. Before it finally imploded,
communism had put its faith in workers of the world (not nations) uniting. Social
democrats preferred the diffuse and eroding qualities of 'cosmopolitanism' to see
off nationalist particularism, and were especially ill-prepared when it emerged in
their own western backyards. (Scotland and Wales continue to cause political and
intellectual difficulties for the Labour Party.) A few brave souls have worked at
fusing socialism and nationalism – 'neo-nationalism' – but by and large the major
social democratic parties of Europe have found that this does not come naturally
to them.

Nationalism: what is it?

If political parties struggle to come to terms with nationalism, then the academy is
far less reticent. It is difficult to open a publisher's catalogue these days without
encountering another slew of books on the subject. (This one, of course, takes its
share of the blame.) Nationalism studies is a burgeoning subject, and scholarly
treatises on theories of nationalism sit alongside studies of new empirical instances
in all parts of the world. The student of nationalism can quickly become disillu-
sioned, for there are no neat definitions of the key concepts. There simply is no
agreement about what nationalism is, what nations are, how we are to define
nationality.

On reflection, why should there be? Like many/most concepts in social
sciences, conceptual definitions and differences are theoretically rooted. Just as we
would not expect social scientists to agree what 'social class' is, neither is it
surprising that they disagree about nations and nationalism. No single universal
theory of nationalism is possible, for as John Hall points out, 'As the historical
record is diverse, so too must be our concepts' (1993: 1). Like 'social class', the
'nation' is bound up with social praxis. In Rogers Brubaker's words:

> 'Nation' is a category of 'practice', not (in the first instance) a category of
> analysis. To understand nationalism, we have to understand the practical
> uses of the category 'nation', the ways it can come to structure percep-
> tion, to inform thought and experience, to organise discourse and
> political action.
>
> (Brubaker, 1996: 10)

Here, we are on familiar, if somewhat boggy, terrain in the social sciences. Are nations 'real', or are they simply terms of discourse which are caught up in political and social practice? Do we focus on historical events and processes in which the ideology of nationalism and nations operate, or do we stand outside and deconstruct them? We might follow Brubaker who argued that it is important to decouple the study of nationhood and 'nation-ness' from the study of nations as substantial entities, collectivities and communities. He comments: 'We should not ask "what is a nation?", but rather: how is nationhood as a political and cultural form institutionalised within and among states?' (ibid.: 16). This may seem to be sound advice, but if we think about it, it can be applied to almost any other social category we care to mention – social class, gender, ethnicity and so on – and can too often lead to an obsession with deconstruction which never actually gets down to analysing what happens 'on the ground'.

The question 'what is a nation?' has, of course, a particular resonance in nationalism studies. It is the title of a famous lecture by Ernest Renan in 1882 which has subsequently become an obligatory reference for all scholars of the subject. Taking as his starting-point nations with 'full national existence' such as France, England, Italy and Spain (but not Germany, for reasons we will come to), Renan was more interested in the problematic cases. For example, why is Holland a nation, and Hannover not? How did France continue as a nation when the dynastic principle which created it was swept away? Why is Switzerland, with three languages, three religions and three or four 'races', a nation when Tuscany is not? Why, he asked, is Austria a state but not a nation?

Renan examined in turn the 'objective' bases of nations. As regards 'race', it is plain that in modern nations blood is mixed whereas in the tribes and cities of antiquity it was not (or far less so). In a comment unwittingly loaded with the weight of future twentieth-century history, he ridiculed the blood definition: One does not have the right to go through the world fingering people's skulls and taking them by the throat saying: 'You are of our blood; you belong to us!' (Eley and Suny, 1996: 49). Renan died a decade after delivering his lecture, and did not live to see precisely such fingering and measuring in the first half of the twentieth century culminating in fascism. Just as race cannot define nations, neither can the usual suspects of language, religion, physical or material interests. For example, language 'invites people to write, but it does not force them to do so' (ibid.: 50). There are nations which speak the same language as their oppressors. Liberation movements in Latin America had, for instance, little difficulty in using Spanish as a linguistic means of mobilising their populations (Williamson, 1992), and English was the main language of nationalism in India and Ireland, despite the misgivings of some indigenous nationalists. Max Weber pointed out that in reality many states have more than one language group, and a common language is often insufficient to sustain a sense of national identity (Weber, 1978: 395–6). Neither can religion supply a sufficient basis for nationalism despite its ideological power and the powerful ways in which modern nationalism appeals to what Hayes called a 'religious sense' (Hayes, 1960). Despite this, there is no simple mapping of God onto nation.

Material factors cannot be discounted either, but self-contained trading patterns do not a nation make. In a comment resonant of the future European Community/Union, Renan observes: 'a Zollverein [customs union] is not a patrie' (Eley and Suny, 1996: 51), although he predicted that a European confederation would probably replace nations, a comment manifestly ahead of its time. While material and economic interests cannot be ignored, there is more to nationalism than these. To echo Chateaubriand's comment: 'Men [*sic*] do not allow themselves to be killed for their interests; they allow themselves to be killed for their passions' (quoted in Connor, 1994: 206). We should be careful here not to assume a dichotomy between 'interests' and 'passions', for to do so would be to ignore the significance of 'national' interest which is every bit as 'rational' (in a geo-political sense) as economic interests. Finally, nationalists may make great play of geography – rivers, mountains, soil – but such geo-politics ignores the fact that the nation 'is a spiritual family not a group determined by the shape of the earth' (Renan, in Eley and Suny, 1996: 52).

So, what is required, according to Renan? Speaking the language of the nineteenth century, he observes that the nation is in essence a 'soul', a spiritual principle, a kind of moral conscience. He concludes: 'A nation is therefore a large-scale solidarity, constituted by the feeling of sacrifices that one has made in the past and of those one is prepared to make in the future' (Eley and Suny, 1996: 53). This is very close to what Benedict Anderson meant by his now-celebrated definition of the nation as 'an imagined community', written a century after Renan's lecture. Much ink was wasted in the intervening period by scholars trying to distil the objective essence of the nation. What is less well-remembered about Renan's lecture is its purpose. He was making a political statement, not simply an academic one. He was a (French) liberal nationalist who was horrified at the defeat of France and the annexation of Alsace-Lorraine by Prussia on the grounds that this territory was 'objectively' part of the Reich. Renan was at pains to point out that people's day-to-day commitment to the territory in which they were governed was essential – what he memorably referred to as the 'daily plebiscite' of the nation's existence: 'a great aggregation of men [*sic*] with a healthy spirit and warmth of heart, creates a moral conscience which is called a nation' (ibid.: 53). Plainly his plea fell on deaf ears, and it was a point which took another sixty-odd years and two world wars to drive home.

By the 1990s, Benedict Anderson's definition of the nation as an 'imagined community' is undoubtedly the dominant one. Like Renan, he takes a 'spiritual' view of these things. His point of departure is:

> that nationality, or as one might prefer to put it in view of that word's multiple significations, nation-ness, as well as nationalism, are cultural artifacts of a particular kind. To understand them properly we need to consider carefully how they have come into historical being, in what ways

their meanings have changed over time, and why, today, they command such profound emotional legitimacy.

(Anderson, 1991: 4)

In essence, says Anderson, the nation is an imagined political community, in the following ways (ibid.: 6–7).

- 'It is *imagined* because the members of even the smallest nation will never know most of their fellow-members, meet them, or even hear of them, yet in the minds of each lives the image of their communion.'
- 'The nation is imagined as *limited* because even the largest of them, encompassing perhaps a billion living human beings, has finite, if elastic boundaries, beyond which lie other nations.'
- 'It is imagined as *sovereign* because the concept was born in an age in which Enlightenment and Revolution were destroying the legitimacy of the divinely-ordained hierarchical dynastic realm.'
- 'It is imagined as a *community*, because, regardless of the actual inequality and exploitation that may prevail in each, the nation is always conceived as a deep, horizontal comradeship.'

We should note, following Anderson, that the nation is 'imagined' not 'imaginary'. In his essay, he rebukes Ernest Gellner for the famous line that 'nationalism is not the awakening of nations to self-consciousness; it invents nations where they do not exist' (Gellner, 1964: 169). Anderson points out that Gellner confuses 'invention' with 'fabrication' and 'falsity' rather than 'imagining' and 'creation'; in other words, the nation is imagined rather than imaginary. This is an important but easily overlooked point, and will form the basis of this book. In counter-criticism of Anderson, we might say that he does not develop the ways in which this process of 'imagining' is carried out and sustained. For example, we would not have much difficulty showing that the *fons et origo* of a nation is false, but it is quite another matter to trace the institutional mechanisms which sustain and shape the belief in a people's distinctiveness. As we shall see in the next section, many of the key debates about nationalism are formed around this disputed point.

Kedourie's comment that 'nationalism is a doctrine invented in Europe at the beginning of the nineteenth century' (1960: 9) begs more interesting questions than it answers. Can we be sure, for example, that nothing like it predated the 'modern' era? And if not, why has it transformed itself into so many different forms, and will it last into the twenty-first century?

Nationalism is full of puzzles. It is a form of 'practice' rather than 'analysis' (Brubaker); it presents itself as a universal and global phenomenon, but is ineluctably particular and local (Anderson); it is a feature of the modern age, but has its roots in something much older (Smith); it is essentially about cultural matters – language, religion, symbols – but cannot be divorced from matters of economic and material development (Nairn).

We will use these conundrums to review the main disputes and debates about nationalism of recent years. Perhaps the most fundamental of these concerns the relationship between the cultural and the political or, to put it another way, between the 'nation' and the 'state'. So successfully have these two ideas been grafted on to each other, that our vocabulary struggles to distinguish between them. Put simply, the 'nation' is usually a synonym for the state. We talk for example of the 'British nation' while (usually) recognising that it is actually a multi-national state. Even historians of this problematic subject such as Linda Colley (1992) speak of how this 'nation' was forged in the eighteenth century. Sociologists too tend to equate nation and state. Anthony Giddens, for example, defines the nation as a 'bordered power-container' in the following way: 'a "nation", as I use the term here, only exists when a state has a unified administrative reach over the territory over which its sovereignty is claimed' (1985: 119), and a 'nation-state' is 'a set of institutional forms of governance maintaining an administrative monopoly over a territory with demarcated boundaries (borders), its rule being sanctioned by law and direct control of the means of internal and external violence' (ibid.: 121).

This (con)fusion of nation and state is a common one, and must be taken seri-ously. It is not simply a slip of Giddens' illustrious pen. What it signifies is that so closely allied have the cultural and the political become in the modern state that we usually treat nation and state as synonyms. In its conventional expression – the nation-state – it is implied that the cultural and the political are in alignment, that the 'people' who are governed by the institutions of the state are by and large culturally homogeneous in having a strong and common linguistic, religious and symbolic identity. Because the author of this book stands – in time – at the end of the twentieth century, and – in space – in a 'stateless nation', Scotland, where the lack of alignment is more and more obvious and increasingly problematic, the conventional wisdom seems misplaced. Perhaps we see more clearly than most the 'impending crisis of the hyphen' (Anderson, 1996b: 8). Some scholars such as Connor (1994: ch. 4) have pointed out that very few so-called nation-states are actually such (he claims less than 10 per cent in 1971), and historical sociologists like Charles Tilly are at pains to distinguish between 'nation-states' and 'national states' which are governed by common political and institutional structures. He comments that very few European states have ever qualified as nation-states (possibly Sweden and Ireland), and that 'Great Britain, Germany and France – quintessential national states – certainly have never met the test' (Tilly, 1992: 3).

Why we have allowed ourselves to treat nation and state as indistinguishable? Here we encounter one of the great fault-lines between Eastern and Western modes of thinking about nationalism. This distinction was crystallised by Hans Kohn in 1945, and has both ideological and analytical significance. That is, it helps to justify the 'superiority' of Western – political – forms of nationalism over Eastern – ethnic – forms. At the same time, it offers an explanatory account of the development of such forms in the light of political-economic development (see, for example, the discussion of 'zones' of nationalism by Gellner on pages 77–8).

'Western' nationalism arose, according to Kohn, in countries like England,

France, the Netherlands, Switzerland and the US as a response to the formation of the modern state. It was essentially political and territorial; the cultural nation coincided with the political territory governed by the state. Citizens were in essence members of the nation. However, 'Eastern' forms of nationalism (beginning significantly with Germany) allowed for no such correspondence. In Central and Eastern Europe and in Asia the frontiers of existing states and ethnic identity rarely coincided. Nationalism became largely a means of disrupting rather than reinforcing state boundaries, and sought to redraw them in line with ethnic demands. Hence, nationalism in the West was mainly political – people were defined as 'citizens' – while in the East it was cultural – people were 'the folk'. The Eastern form, according to Kohn, 'extolled the primitive and ancient depth and peculiarities of its traditions in contrast to Western nationalism and to universal standards' (Hutchinson and Smith, 1994: 164). In the West, nationalism had its origins in concepts of individual liberty and rational cosmopolitanism, whereas Eastern nationalism 'lacked self-assurance', had an 'inferiority complex' which was compensated for 'by over-emphasis and over-confidence'. Kohn's account seemed to square with the view that German nationalism with its influence of Herder's romanticism had to be replaced by something more rational and Western.

Kohn's account has been long-lasting and dominant in the second half of the twentieth century. In recent years, much of the debate has turned on distinctions between 'civic/territorial' forms of nationalism (good) and 'ethnic/cultural' forms (bad). Plamenatz (1976), for example, distinguished between the rise of 'Western' nationalism (in Germany and Italy) among those who felt themselves to be at a disadvantage, but who nevertheless were 'equipped culturally' in ways that favoured success and excellence; and 'Eastern' nationalism (among Slavs, in Africa, Asia and Latin America) which emerged among those recently drawn into an alien civilisation and whose culture was not adapted to new conditions, and which was frequently illiberal. The resurrection of what Gellner called the 'dark gods' theory of nationalism from the 1980s owes much to the fear in Western cosmopolitan circles that the Pandora's box of ethnic irrationalism has been reopened. The vocabulary used was frequently that of tribal feeling, kinship, religion, cultural traditions, attachment to land – all implying that nationalism belongs properly to pre-modern social formations, and that once the forces of modernism and consumerism get to work, all that will vanish. Nationalism is caricatured as 'thinking with the blood', and has drawn the ire of cosmopolitan intellectuals. Eric Hobsbawm, for example, has judged that 'the characteristic nationalist movements of the late twentieth century are essentially negative, or rather divisive' (1990: 164). Even much pro-nationalist opinion in the West (such as in Scotland or Catalunya) goes out of its way to stress how theirs is of the non-racist, non-threatening, civic variety, while not denying the 'ethnic' character of nationalism elsewhere, thereby accepting that nationalism can be divided into good (civic) and bad (ethnic) forms. Such is the power of orthodoxy.

While there is much which is ethno- and Euro-centric, about these accounts –

of the 'we-are-patriotic, you-are-nationalistic' variety – scholars have sought to show that nationalism has emerged at different historical conjunctures and has taken different forms in different parts of Europe and the world. Ernest Gellner, for example, has characterised the time-zones of Europe, from the westernmost zone I where dynastic realms created states which were by and large culturally uniform; to zone II (such as in Italy and Germany) which, though politically fragmented, were well-equipped with pre-existing and codified high cultures; through zone III (Central/Eastern Europe) in which the mix of diverse cultures in social and geographical terms failed to map on to cultural and religious boundaries; and finally to zone IV, the territories of the old Tsarist empire in which the old religious order was peremptorily replaced by the new secular communism (Gellner, 1994a).

The American sociologist Rogers Brubaker has also employed the distinction between 'civic' and 'ethnic' nationalism to useful analytical effect in his study of French and German models of nationalism (1992). He argues that in France citizenship came to be defined as a territorial community based on 'ius soli' – the law of the soil, that is, on a territorial jurisdiction. Whatever one's ethnic or geographical origins, all residents on French soil could in principle be citizens of the French state. By contrast, in Germany where the unitary state did not arrive until the 1870s, citizenship was formed on the basis of a community of descent, on 'ius sanguinis' – the law of blood. In other words, a child received German citizenship if the parent had it. Whereas the French model was state-centred and assimilationist, the German one was volk-centred and differentialist. This squares, Brubaker argues, with the different ways in which France and Germany were created. In the former, the state preceded the nation (the task was how to turn peasants into Frenchmen, in Eugene Weber's phrase); whereas in Germany, the nation preceded the state, and 'Germans' did not live necessarily on German soil, nor were those born there automatically German.

While the analytical value of the civic/ethnic distinction has been put to good use by both Gellner and Brubaker, it does lend itself to ethnocentric caricature – why can't *they* be more like *us*? It is also a distinction which can be criticised on analytical grounds. Is it, for example, possible to maintain such a distinction in practice? How is one to make sense of endemic racism against the 'Other' in Western societies which profess overwhelmingly civic definitions of citizens? Further, Chateaubriand's comment about people being willing to die for passions but not for interests is apposite here. How in practice can these be kept apart? Are 'blood' and 'soil' so distinct, and does not the latter imply the former? After all, *lebensraum* was a concept which connected both of these in Hitler's Germany. There is also the problem of caricaturing civic definitions in such a way that they imply order and good reason. Michael Herzfeld has pointed out that modern bureaucratically regulated societies are no more 'rational' or less 'symbolic' than 'traditional' societies. Bureaucratic practices rely heavily on symbols and language replete with moral boundaries between insiders and outsiders (Herzfeld, 1992). European nationalism, he argues, is a 'secular theodicy' which resembles religion in that both imply a transcendent status. 'Just as nationalism can be viewed as religion, bureaucratic actions are its most commonplace rituals' (ibid.: 37). Adam Seligman has also made this point in another way in his critique of 'civic republicanism' with its implication that morality is a public, communal enterprise, the outcome of the 'general will' which clearly has illiberal consequences (Seligman, 1995).

Nation: ancient or modern?

The debate about civic and ethnic nationalism is embedded in a broader one about the origins and character of 'the nation' itself. This is the debate sometimes labelled 'primordialist' versus 'modernist', and at other times 'essentialist' versus 'instrumentalist'. In essence, this is a debate about the origins of national sentiment. On the one hand, there is the view that nations are primordial entities embedded in human nature and history which can be identified through distinctive cultures expressed by way of language, religion, culture and so on. Primordialists tend to be nationalists themselves who adopt an essentialist view of the/their nation to justify why it is not only desirable but in the long run inevitable that it will achieve political self-determination. Nowadays there are few academic writers who would follow Herder, Fichte and the German Romantics in arguing this case, but we should remind ourselves of the role played by some Serbian academics who have provided, wittingly or unwittingly, ideological underpinning for ethnic cleansing (Silber and Little, 1995). A more refined version of the debate focuses on just how ancient or modern nationalism is.

The 'modernists' are in most respects in the ascendant these days. The essence of their case is that nationalism is a cultural and political ideology of 'modernity', a crucial vehicle in the Great Transformation from traditionalism to industrialism, and in particular the making of the modern state. Its proponents include Gellner, Deutsch, Anderson and Hobsbawm who view it as dating from the eighteenth century with its rationalist political philosophy (making the point that nationalism is not simply about 'passions'). Nationalism becomes the successor to religion as a secular glue which binds society together (Hayes, 1960). In Llobera's words: 'The nation, as a culturally defined community, is the highest symbolic value of modernity: it has been endowed with a quasi-sacred character equalled only by religion. In fact, this quasi-sacred character derives from religion' (1994: ix).

Modernists argue that there are major discontinuities between modern and pre-modern nationalism (Hutchinson, 1994). Its sacral quality derives from the Enlightenment period of the late eighteenth century; nationalism superseded a religious view of the world, and derived its legitimacy from the will of the people rather than from God. Second, nations have tended to take a different territorial shape from previous political units, most obviously in the break-up of empires (Austrian, Russian and Ottoman in particular), and the creation of new manageable political formations reflecting national markets and national polities. Third, the principles on which modern nations are founded are different insofar as there is a basic assumption that nation and state will coincide, reflected in a homogeneous linguistic culture with a distinctive vernacular. Fourth, and following Benedict Anderson's key argument, modern nations are artefacts of print capitalism: 'the convergence of capitalism and print technology on the fatal diversity of human language created the possibility of a new form of imagined community which in its basic morphology set the stage for the modern nation' (1983: 49). The daily newspaper through its use of the vernacular makes the nation imaginable and bounded. Finally, and this is the key point in Gellner's analysis, modern nations are industrial societies with a high degree of economic and cultural integration, which do not tolerate significant and abiding cultural inequalities (class inequalities are more easily handled unless they coincide with cultural markers). Gellner argued that modern societies require much higher degrees of social mobility, and hence more pervasive levels of literacy – in his words, 'everyone is turned into a cleric' (1983: 32).

Modernists *do* differ among themselves as regards the emphasis they give to different factors, but all agree that nationalism is in essence a modern construction. (We will return to the 'constructed' quality of the nation shortly.) We have seen how Anderson focuses on the importance of print capitalism in generating nationalism, while Gellner emphasises its role in the process of industrialisation. An important variant of this is the way in which nationalism exploits processes of uneven development so that waves of economic and social change generated by industrialisation wash over territories and in their wake instigate political demands for self-determination by social groups, notably the native bourgeoisie.

A further variant of the modernist perspective places greater emphasis on political rather than economic factors. Writers such as Breuilly (1982 and 1996) and Mann (1993a, 1993b and 1995) argue that nations and nationalism developed primarily in response to the making of the modern state. Says Mann, 'the nation is not so intimately related to capitalism or industrialism as is often argued' (1995: 47). Two sets of forces mattered more. On the one hand, warfare swallowed up more and more of the state budget from the eighteenth century (Mann argues that by 1810 the state was absorbing between 15 and 25 per cent of GNP for this purpose, virtually what it was to take in mass warfare in the twentieth century), and concomitantly the drive to democracy and political accountability required the state to develop an ideology of nationalist inclusion as a means of legitimating its actions. 'Popular sovereignty' was its most usual and obvious expression, as a means of rallying the citizens behind the new regimes.

In recent years, notably in the work of Anthony Smith, the 'modernist' thesis has come under attack. It is noticeable that, by and large, modernists are hostile to nationalism, and seek to show the 'invented', the 'constructed' quality of the nation. We have already alluded to Gellner's famous quotation that nationalism makes nations rather than the other way round, and that Anderson takes issue with Gellner's implication that nations are imaginary rather than imagined. Hobsbawm's general perspective on nationalism is hostile, and like many modernists he adopts a debunking mode. Smith takes issue with this, and while he rejects a crude primordialism, he points to many instances where nations predate modernisation. His view is shared by Llobera, who points out that the problem with modernist accounts is that they project the image of the nation as *ex nihilo* the creation of the post-Enlightenment period (Llobera, 1994). This, he implies, is the sociological equivalent of making bricks without straw. He concludes:

> The idea that nationalism is invented, so dear to Hobsbawm, Gellner and other contemporary observers, is patently untrue. Modern nationalisms are re-creations of medieval realities; in fact, they can only be successful if they are rooted in the medieval past, even if the links with it may often be tortuous and twisted.
>
> (Llobera, 1994: 86)

Smith identifies the set of myths, symbols and cultural practices – what he calls the 'ethnie' – as the key to making the modern nation. The nation is an ethno-cultural community shaped by a common myth of origins, a sense of common history and way of life. He comments: 'the modern nation, to become truly a 'nation', requires the unifying myths, symbols and memories of pre-modern ethnie' (Smith, 1988: 11). Having a territory, an economy, an education system and a legal code are not enough in themselves. Nations require passions, not merely interests, and the links with religion are obvious. Smith observes: 'To belong to a "community of history and destiny" has become for many people a surrogate for religious faith, over and above any individual worldly ends that the collective action it inspires may serve' (ibid.: 12). Above all, it is the sense of a common past and a shared destiny which is the ideological motor driving the modern state forward. How else is it to persuade more people to die for it in wartime, more or less willingly, than at any other time in history?

Smith argues that while there may be differences between modern and older ethnies, these are differences of degree not of kind. Similarly, modernism ignores the variety of ethnic polities for its own purposes. Ethnic identities are themselves much more durable over time despite major upheavals and conquests, and enforced state-making. Smith identifies two main types of ethnie which come to lay the foundations of modern states. These are, on the one hand, the lateral or aristocratic type which developed around a centralised and elitist state before filtering down (such as in England, Spain and France). On the other hand, there is the vertical or demotic type of ethnie which was normally generated in 'popular' opposition to an oppressive state and frequently sustained by religion and a secular intelligentsia which sought to reinterpret the religio-ethnic identity and harness it against the state (as in Ireland or Poland, for example).

In short, Smith and other 'ethnicists' such as Armstrong (1982) argue that the myth of the 'modern' nation greatly exaggerates the impact of industry, capitalism and bureaucracy in shaping the modern state. Modernism fails to locate the nation in a historical sequence of cultural shaping, and hence overdraws the distinction between 'tradition' and 'modernity', frequently missing the deep roots which nations have in an ethnic substratum.

Support of a historical kind for Smith's thesis comes from Leah Greenfeld (1992) who argues that the original modern idea of the nation emerged in sixteenth-century England, and was in turn inherited by the American colonies who refined the individualistic civic version of nationalism which so characterises the West. She argues that, in England, national consciousness grew out of a shared awareness of people's dignity as individuals, which in turn generated ideas of individual liberty and political equality, confluent with the Protestant Reformation. Protestantism stimulated literacy through the coincidence of the translation of the Bible into the English language and the Reformation itself. Hence, the consciousness of belonging to the English nation was reinforced by reading the Bible (in English). According to Greenfeld: 'Though Protestantism cannot be said to have given birth to the English nation, it did play the crucial role of a midwife without whom the child might not have been born' (1992: 63). In other words, while Englishness was not defined strictly in ethnic terms, this was achieved by the religious and political values which converged on the rational individual (in opposition, of course, to the 'Popish' nations).

For Greenfeld, the American case illustrates the essential independence of nationality from ethnic and geo-political factors, and underscores its conceptual and ideological nature. She comments:

> Since nationality is the original identity of the American population, which preceded the formation of its geo-political and institutional framework, the analysis of American nationalism does not focus on the conditions of its emergence, which is unproblematic, but rather on its effects, which can in this case be observed in an almost pure form.
>
> (Greenfeld, 1992: 23–4)

Greenfeld tends to take an almost utopian view of American nationalism, seeing it as the closest realisation of the principles of individualistic, civic nationalism. The American student of nationalism, Carlton Hayes, took a more pessimistic view of his fellow citizens. Writing in the 1930s, he commented: 'integral nationalism is far advanced among us. We are peculiarly intolerant of any domestic dissent, of all foreigners and minorities in our midst' (Hayes, 1948: 320). The American case is an interesting one as it seems to contradict the view that nationalism requires at least some 'primordial' roots. Anthony Smith overcomes this objection by pointing out that while the US became a prime example of the territorial national type of political community and of the power of territorial nationalism, it had its roots in Anglo-American Protestant traditions deriving from the Puritan forefathers who proclaimed the unique destiny for the 'chosen people' in a North American New Jerusalem. He concludes: 'This Anglo-American myth of Puritan election was reinforced by the secular Romanising myths of the revolution, the Constitution and the heroic age of the Founding Fathers' (Smith, 1991: 150).

Such evidence that national consciousness predated what we have learned to call 'modernisation' even in its prototype, England, would seem to contradict the modernist accounts that nationalism only emerged in the wake of this process, at least a century after the Protestant Reformation. The counter to this view is put by Sami Zubaida who argues, *contra* Smith, that a shared ethnie was the product not the cause of nation-ness. In other words, ethnic homogeneity in societies with a long history of centralised governments, such as England and France, was not a cause but an effect precisely of those political processes which facilitated centralisation. Englishness and Frenchness were constructed by the state itself after the event. Zubaida argues:

> 'Common ethnicity' and solidarity are not the product of communal factors given to modernity, but are themselves the product of the socio-economic and political processes which, in the West, were institutionalised into state and civil society. These became the genealogical antecedents of modernity.
>
> (Zubaida, 1989: 330)

The 'ethnie' is itself a cultural construction of nationalism, rather than its cause. Primacy, claims Zubaida, should be given to socio-economic and political processes which mould the nation into the shape of the state. Where these processes are most successful, it comes to appear that the ethnie itself brings the nation-state into being. There is a methodological issue here. Where states are successful, they mobilise their ethnies. Where they do not, they cease to exist. We are, then, left mainly with a set of self-selected successful cases rather than an array of all those which are possible.

Smith's co-editor, John Hutchinson (1994), has argued that while there is some common ground between the modernists and the ethnicists – most notably that both camps recognise the qualitative difference in the nature of the modern state – there are important points of disagreement. First, there is the extent of this difference. Modernists argue that the modern state, as a political community, is essentially national rather than local in generating its allegiances. Ethnicists argue for the continuity of language, folklore and common consciousness, and seek to restore the importance of ethnicity in history.

Second, there is a dispute over the idea of a transition to modernity. Hutchinson argues that modernists claim an unprecedented shift to a qualitatively different kind of society associated with nationalism. The problem with this view, he comments, is that many nation-states predate the process of industrialisation and, further, that there is no causal link between this process and the development of mass education on which nationalism depends. For example, in England, mass education was introduced only in the 1870s, at least a century after the process of industrialisation had begun, and (if Greenfeld is correct) several centuries after national consciousness had taken root. Further, 'industrialisation' is a weak explanation for the rise of nationalism because it ignores the fact that often nationalism was a reaction against industrialisation rather than its complement, and because it

14

fails to explain why nationalism and ethnicity show no signs of ebbing away once industrialisation has occurred.

Third, there is a dispute about the extent to which nations should be seen as inventions on the one hand, or as reconstructions shaped by earlier ethnic sentiments on the other. While modernists argue that ethnicity is a fluctuating instrument shaped to serve social interests, ethnicists point out that nationalism must have a resonance and cannot be explained in socially reductionist terms. In other words, the national past is not a *tabula rasa* which can continually be reinvented, but a crucial means of connecting the present to the past.

In late 1995, a few months before his sudden death, Ernest Gellner met with Anthony Smith at Warwick University to debate the modernist and ethnicist positions (reprinted in *Nations and Nationalism* 2(3) 1996). Smith repeated his view that the modernist account tells only half of the story, namely that the nation is a product of specifically modern economic, social and political conditions, but that at root it suffers from the fact that the account is ineluctably materialist. Modernists are then led, as a result of their deconstructionism, to debunk cultural aspects of nationalism. However, Smith argues, nations and nationalisms are also the products of pre-existing traditions and heritages which have coalesced over generations. Modernist theories explain everything and nothing, and cover too much, from rich Quebec to poor Eritrea. In essence, Smith argues that modern political nationalisms cannot be understood without reference to earlier ethnic ties and memories, what he calls the ethno-symbolic base. This base is crucial in accounting for the deep and abiding emotional appeal of nationalism, whereas modernist accounts handle these aspects uneasily, falling back on the equivalent of 'false consciousness' arguments derived from materialist accounts with which they have so much in common. 'Civic' or state nationalism may be the nationalism of order and control, but ethnic nationalism becomes an important weapon against the state. 'Theirs', says Smith, 'is the politics of cultural revolt' (1996a: 363), which helps to explain the deeper, inner source of so many ethnic and national conflicts today.

Gellner's reply to Smith was typically engaging. 'Do nations have navels?', he asked. The analogy here is with the philosophical argument about the prototypical Adam. If he did not have a navel, then God created him. The ethnic, the cultural national community, is like the navel. Some nations have it and others don't, said Gellner, but having a navel is not essential. He characterises Smith as an 'evolutionist', implying that all nations have a navel in contradistinction to his own 'creationist' views. Half a story accounting for nationalism is good enough, Gellner says, for the other – cultural – bits of the story are redundant. Take the Estonians, he argues. At the beginning of the nineteenth century they didn't have a name for themselves – no ethnonym – but subsequently did create a vibrant culture and a past as reflected in their national museums. Gellner uses this as a good example of the way in which, in the modern world, the role of culture has been totally transformed by the economic and scientific changes since the seventeenth century. He concludes: 'There is a certain amount of navel about but not everywhere, and on the whole it's not important . . . the cultural continuity is contingent, inessential' (Gellner, 1996c: 369).

Smith's reply to Gellner was succinct: *nihil ex nihilo* – nothing from nothing. He disputes Gellner's characterisation of him as an 'evolutionist' because he accepts that nations are 'modern' while connected with earlier ethnic communities. He comments:

> there is considerable evidence that modern nations are connected with earlier ethnic categories and communities and are created out of pre-existing origin myths, ethnic cultures and shared memories; and that those nations with a vivid, widespread sense of an ethnic past, are likely to be more unified and distinctive than those which lack that sense.
>
> (Smith, 1996a: 385)

Smith argues, *contra* Gellner, that no general theory of nationalism is possible, for the differences across time-periods and spaces are too great. As regards the 'navel' question, his view is that nations must have navels; if they don't, they must invent them.

The debate between Smith and Gellner has been reproduced in some detail because it typifies probably the key dispute within nationalism studies. In essence, both sides have strengths and weaknesses. Modernists are able to show how the ideologies of nationalism connect with processes of social and economic change, and especially with the political and material interests generated by 'modernisation'. The weaknesses of this approach are that it does not handle cultural matters well, being too deconstructionist. It is also fairly crude in its working definition of 'culture'. One would want, for example, to include the institutional carriers of culture (such as the education system) which also have their own capacity to shape beliefs and values. Second, as we shall see in chapter 4, its focus on the transformation to industrial capitalist society makes it less able to handle what we might call post- or late-modern expressions of nationalism. If nationalism was a potent ideology which ushered in 'modern' society, how are we to account for its salience now that this society seems to be passing away, or at least transforming itself in turn?

The strength of the ethnicist argument is that it is able to trace the cultural dimensions of nationalism, especially the ways in which the mythical past or ethnie is mobilised. This is important because of the undoubted emotional power of the 'nation's' history, something which the modernist accounts tend to play down or dismiss. On the other hand, ethnicists have to struggle with the undoubted discontinuities between the past and the present. Even Smith in his reply to Gellner is reduced to admit that if nations have no cultural 'navels', they must invent them. The issue, then, seems to come down to how much invention; to matters of degree rather than of kind. To paraphrase, how little cultural straw does one need to make political bricks? If the answer is 'not much', then the modernists and the ethnicists are possibly closer together than they like to pretend.

The sociology of nationalism

Given the involvement of sociologists in the study of nationalism, we might ask whether there is a systematic theory generated by the discipline. We would ask largely in vain. This is in part because the discipline grew up with another agenda, namely to explain the Great Transformation from pre-industrial, pre-modern to industrial, modern society, and to develop a more general theory of 'society'. The founding figures of sociology – Marx, Durkheim and Weber – each had a perspective on nationalism, but it was not central to their endeavours. However, all three were caught up in the socio-political issues of their day, mainly as these focused around the two great continental powers, France and Germany.

Marx (1818–83) lived through the economic and political upheavals of the nineteenth century, including the unification of Germany out of the myriad statelets. He thought Germany more backward than France or Britain, and took a critical view of 'nationality' as a fraud, a device of the ruling bourgeoisie to further its interests: 'this community of interest, which is directed against the proletariat inside the country, is directed against the bourgeoisie of other nations outside the country. This the bourgeoisie calls nationality' (Guibernau, 1996: 15). Again, in the *Communist Manifesto*: 'the working men have no country . . . national differences and antagonisms between peoples are daily more and more vanishing' (ibid.: 15–16). He was, of course, wrong in his prediction, but it gave voice to his view that nationalism was an expression of bourgeois interests.

After 1848, and under the influence of Engels, Marx modified his views to distinguish between support for the national causes in 'historic' nations – especially where these furthered the development of the motor of history by aiding and abetting a proletarian revolution in the longer term – and 'non-historic' nations such as the smaller Slavic nations, especially the Czechs, which had no such claim on Marx's approval. Like Weber after him, he adopted at times a fairly pro-German stance towards nationalism and its culture. Despite his well-known views on nationalism, Marx did not formulate an explicit theory, preferring to articulate the views that, in class societies, the prevailing ideas are the ideas of the ruling classes, that class struggle was aimed at the overthrow of the state not its entrenchment as a bourgeois device, and that nothing, especially an ideology of nationalism, should obstruct proletarian liberation.

The conventional wisdom that Marx's interest in nationalism began after 1848, and was influenced by Engels, has been taken to task by Roman Szporluk (1988) who argues that, in 1845, Marx began an essay on 'the national system of political economy' written as a critical response to Friedrich List. Szporluk maintains that nationalism was not a product of the Industrial Revolution as Marxism was, but occurred prior to it, influenced by the conjuncture of the French Revolution (also an important influence on Marxism), German Romanticism and developments in Eastern Europe, especially the Polish question. List, a contemporary of Marx, had preached class co-operation and solidarity in building the nation's power, and argued that the community of the nation, defined by cultural criteria, was the real basis of a political community. (The revival of interest in the writings of Friedrich List is reflected in the article by David Levi-Faur (1997) who has applied his thoughts on political economy to the role of the state under globalisation.) This theme of building a strong nation/state, especially in Germany, was a belief shared with Max Weber as we shall see below. The point of Szporluk's study 'Communism and Nationalism' is to show that Marxism was as much a critique of nationality as of capitalist political economy, and that nationalism cannot be subsumed either under capitalism or under communism. He concludes: 'That nationality and class are recognised now as essential components of individual identity and political legitimacy is a proof of how profoundly our modern outlook has been shaped by the ideologies of nationalism and Marxism' (Szporluk, 1988: 240).

Despite the historic hostility of socialism and nationalism, as Guibernau observes, there were points of similarity as well as difference. Both were 'salvation movements', in the first instance against bourgeois capitalism, in the second, against the alien coloniser. Despite the millenarian aspects of the movements, both found the proper arena for struggle, class or national, in the modern state. In practice, socialism and nationalism were to make common cause notably in anti-colonial movements, especially in the twentieth century. Marx and Engels' support in the 1870s for Irish liberation from Britain was an early forerunner of this alliance. In Russia, argues Szporluk, nationalism came to live with 'socialism in one country' insofar as Stalin russified Soviet communism, and Lenin can be seen as the 'first National Communist' (ibid.: 232). Nationalism in the Third World established itself as a third force, sometimes an ally, sometimes a rival, of communism and capitalism alike.

The other two classical founders of sociology, Émile Durkheim (1858–1917) and Max Weber (1864–1920), overlapped in their life spans from the 1860s until the second decade of the twentieth century. Each was influenced by his own nationality and its geo-politics in this crucial period of European history. Durkheim, like Marx and Weber, had no explicit theory of nationalism, but his views can be distilled from his writings on religion, and the *conscience collective*. In essence, as Llobera points out, Durkheim was a 'nation-builder', who made a vibrant contribution to the making of modern France, and has been called the 'theologian of the French civil religion' (1994: 157). Durkheim, like his compatriot Renan, was influenced by the events of the Third Republic (1870–1914), notably the defeat by Prussia in 1870, the Paris Commune and the Dreyfus Affair. He did not approve of nationalism, denouncing it as an extreme and morbid form of patriotism. The essence of his case was that while religion had been eroded in modern societies, its eternal qualities had been transformed into the 'sacrilisation of the secular', with rituals and symbols of patriotic nature. In other words, both religion and nationalism have the ideological power to instil cohesion into the political community. Durkheim's concept of the *conscience collective* was closer to Rousseau's *volonté générale* (Seligman, 1995), and as such he can be considered an illiberal thinker 'wishing to cage individuals morally because convinced that they could not manage their lives on their own' (Hall, 1995: 26).

Patriotism Durkheim defined as 'a sentiment that joins the individual to political society insofar as those who get to make it up feel themselves attached to it by a band of sentiment' (Guibernau, 1996: 28–9). Nevertheless, he did not see it as enduring, as there was an inherent tension between the 'national' ideal and the 'human' ideal (he favoured an eventual European *patrie*). However, until such time, the 'patrie' is the highest organised society that people are likely to know. In his later essay, 'L'Allemagne au-dessus de tout' (1915), Durkheim was highly critical of what he saw as the morbid character of the German '*mentalité*'. The German idea of the state was an extreme interpretation of the idea of sovereignty. 'The *Deutschland über alles* meant that there was nothing above the German state: no ideal, no morality' (Llobera, 1994: 154).

In this regard, Durkheim would have put himself at odds with his contemporary Max Weber. Guibernau argues that 'Weber did not formulate a theory of nationalism but adopted a "nationalist" attitude throughout his life' (1996: 36). This view of Weber as a German nationalist owes much to Wolfgang Mommsen's book *Max Weber: und die deutsche Politik*, published in 1959 (Beetham, 1985: 119). The view that nationalism was the driving force of Weber's politics can be seen as too simplistic; it was a highly complex affair melding economic, political and ideological and communal elements (ibid.: 121). Viewing Weber as a nationalist believer also owes something to Perry Anderson's more recent essay in which he juxtaposes Weber and Gellner in the following way: 'Whereas Weber was so bewitched by the spell of nationalism that he was never able to theorise it, Gellner has theorised nationalism without detecting its spell' (1992: 205). Like many aphorisms of this sort, it does violence to both Weber and Gellner, as we shall see when examining the latter's riposte in chapter 4.

Stargardt, who includes this quotation from Anderson in his essay on Gellner, argues that while Weber was, in his view, 'an outspoken German nationalist' (1996: 180), he in fact rejected theories of nationalism which took as their starting point a *Volk* or *Volksgeist*, and instead adopted a 'constructivist' view of the nation. His aim, like that of Otto Bauer, was to show by what contingent means national identity could aspire to the non-contingent status of *Gemeinschaft* (Stargardt, 1995). While cultural identifiers, such as language, were crucial, as we have already seen in this chapter, Weber accepted that nation and state were of different orders. Nevertheless, Weber regarded 'nation' as in essence a political concept which could only be defined in relation to a state, but was not identical to it. He argued that a nation was a 'community of sentiment which would find its adequate expression only in a state of its own, and which thus normally strives to create one' (ibid.: 122). At the same time, a nation is also a subjective phenomenon, rooted usually in race, language, religion, customs or political experience, each and any of which can generate national sentiment. Of these, Weber thought race the least important, and language the most important. For a nation to exist, (1) there had to be some common factor between people, distinguishing them from others; (2) this factor had to be regarded as a source of value and a basis for solidarity; and (3) this solidarity found its expression in autonomous political institutions co-extensive with the community in question (Beetham, 1985: 122).

Weber singled out '*Kultur*', those characteristics which distinguished one group of people from another, as crucial in the formation and maintenance of national communities. As Beetham points out: 'He drew a clear distinction between "*staats-politisch*" questions, which concerned the power and integrity of the state, and national or "*kulturpolitisch*" questions, which concerned the maintenance and promotion of national individuality' (1985: 130). The promotion of '*Kultur*', national distinctiveness, in Weber's view, was one of the chief aims of the political system. This fusion of politics and culture in Weber's writing is what convinces Mommsen that 'he remained a convinced nationalist, never questioning his German nationalism or submitting it to critical examination. The nation and its power in the world remained the ultimate political value for him' (Guibernau, 1996: 38).

There is, however, a counter-argument. Like List, Weber took the view that the most important task for Germany in the late nineteenth/early twentieth centuries was to unite against advanced powers like Britain so that it might surpass them not only economically, but also politically and culturally. Seeing Germany as *machstaat* – a great power state – was not, as Mommsen argues, an end in itself, but a means of meeting the economic demands of a growing working class, and encouraging among them a degree of social unity and common consciousness. Weber argued that, compared to its counterparts in Britain and France, the German working class was politically immature, and he saw nationalism as the means for their participation in national culture. Similarly, being a world power like their European neighbours would have a marked effect on the character of German life and values.

While war was a cement for the nation, Weber viewed the Great War as a disaster for Germany, something not reconcilable with Mommsen's interpretation. Military power, thought Weber, was simply a means to an end – political influence. Similarly, far from being a disciple of German expansionism for its own sake, Weber viewed the war as a means of cementing the nation internally, containing the power of Tsarist Russia and defending the autonomy of smaller nations such as Poland. Beetham comments: 'In a world of power states, the independence of small nations could only be guaranteed by the tension of one great power against another. It was in this sense that Germany had a *duty* to be a "*Machstaat*"' (1985: 142).

If we locate Weber in his time-frame, we can see that he shared many of the left-liberal views of his day. Like Karl Renner and others in liberal and social democratic circles, he was suspicious of the absolutist aspirations of Russia, a consequent believer in the cultural superiority of Western European values, as well as being sceptical of the proposal to disband the Austro-Hungarian empire into independent nation-states as opposed to some kind of democratic federation of nationalities, as the Social Democrats had tried to do at the turn of the century (Stargardt, 1995).

In general terms, then, all three founders of sociology made nationalism central to their way of seeing the world, yet none of them set out an explicit theory. For Marx, the theory of the state draws on the history of society as a history of class struggle. For Durkheim, the state is the organ of moral discipline, and patriotism is its ideology. For Weber, the state is essentially a political instrument, but one which both requires a distinctive national ideology, and is required in turn to make its protection its main aim.

Conclusion

The intellectual maps which sociology has passed down to us for making sense of nationalism are of limited value. Essentially they were designed to explain something else – the emergence of 'modern' society – and were creations of another age. In the late twentieth century, we have a different manifestation. As Benedict Anderson comments: 'Portable nationality, read under the sign of "identity", is on the rapid rise as people everywhere are on the move' (1996b: 9).

In this book, we will review the main manifestations of nationalism: in its classical form of nineteenth-century state-building; twentieth-century liberation nationalism; but also its more recent formulations – neo-nationalism or autonomism in Western societies, and post-communist nationalism. Before doing this, it is necessary to complete our review of the analytical building blocks of nationalism: its relationship with ethnicity; the personal 'power' of nationalism; and its role in historical construction and invention.

2

TRIBE, PLACE AND IDENTITY

Ethnicity and nationalism

The late twentieth century, with its language of 'ethnic cleansing', is an epoch in which ethnicity and nationalism have come into their own. In a recently published anthology on ethnicity, the editors write: 'Ethnicity, far from fading away, has now become a central issue in the social and political life of every continent. The "end of history", it seems, turns out to have ushered in the era of ethnicity' (Hutchinson and Smith, 1996: v). Whether we look at the Balkans, Chechnya, Nagorno-Karabakh, Central Africa or closer to home in Northern Ireland and Euskadi (the Basque Country), some of the most emotionally charged and seemingly intractable political disputes appear to be 'ethnic' in origin. The 'dark gods' theorists of nationalism who accuse it of releasing and mobilising ethnic hatreds would seem to have a point.

Students of nationalism also argue that ethnicity and nationalism are closely linked. For example, Walker Connor begins his collection of essays on 'Ethnonationalism' by justifying why he did not simply call it 'nationalism'. The answer he gives is that 'there is no difference if nationalism is used in its pristine sense' (1994: xi). Unfortunately, he continues, this is rarely the case. Why it should be 'unfortunate' is debatable, but it is a fairly widespread sentiment. Nationalism without ethnicity is judged not to be quite the right thing.

The analysis of nationalism in Scotland provides a good, apparently negative, instance of this. In recent years, much has been made of the fact that what underlies Scottish nationalism is a 'sense of place' rather than a 'sense of tribe' (Smout, 1994). In other words, Scottishness is based on living in a common territory despite clear and abiding social, religious and geographical differences. The nationalist party, the SNP, prides itself on the 'mongrel' character of the Scots, and has argued that residence in Scotland, not blood-line, will confer citizenship if and when political independence is achieved.

Some writers have drawn the implication of this 'territorial' sense of nationality that it is a second-best definition, in the absence of a strong sense of ethnicity, the sense of tribe. Steve Bruce, for example, has drawn lessons about Scotland from his work on Northern Ireland to argue that it is precisely the lack of a single identity of a 'people' with common ancestors, common language, shared religion and a glorious history which prevented nationalism emerging in Scotland when it was doing so elsewhere in the nineteenth century. 'There is no modern demotic myth-ical history . . . and certainly nothing to compare to the shared history which informs the thinking of the majority of Ulster Protestants' (1993: 11). As a result, 'If Scotland's intellectuals in the nineteenth century had wanted to promote Scottish nationalism, they would have been unable to do so' (ibid.: 11–12). The country has long been divided linguistically, geographically and religiously, which, coupled with Scotland's participation in British imperialism as a 'junior partner' rather than as a 'colony', has made nationalism a late, and not very convincing, developer. Bruce concludes that territoriality – civic nationalism – is too weak a base on which to erect the kind of atavistic passions generated by a sense of belonging to a 'community of the blood', as witnessed in the Balkans, Africa and, indeed, Northern Ireland. While he accepts that, for example, religious divisions between Catholics and Protestants, or geo-linguistic ones between highlanders and lowlanders, are far less significant than previously, he maintains that there does not seem to be enough of a common ethnicity for a full-blown nationalism worthy of the name to emerge in Scotland at the end of the twentieth century, which, anyway, is a time in which the nation-state appears to be losing its powers. There are echoes here of Hobsbawm's comment that the nationalist owl of Minerva flies at the dusk of the nation-state (1990: 83).

It is not our task at this stage to set up the counter-view; this will be summarised towards the end of this chapter. The value of Bruce's account is that it spells out clearly the orthodox relationship between ethnicity and nationalism, making the case that the latter without the former is an insubstantial and transient phenomenon. It provides a useful benchmark against which to examine what we mean by ethnicity vis-à-vis the rise of nationalism. In her study *Nationalism: Five Roads to Modernity*, Leah Greenfeld comments:

> In ethnic nationalisms, 'nationality' became a synonym of 'ethnicity', and national identity is often perceived as a reflection or awareness of possession of 'primordial' or inherited characteristics, components of 'ethnicity', such as language, customs, territorial affiliation, and physical type.
>
> (Greenfeld, 1992: 12)

Such identifiers of ethnicity, however, do not automatically generate an 'identity', because the key will be how an individual chooses to identify with these character-istics. 'Identity is perception. If a particular identity does not mean anything to the population in question, this population does not have this particular identity' (ibid.: 13). This is a key point. The argument in this chapter will be that issues of identity provide the key to understanding both ethnicity and nationalism in such a way that 'history' is a poor guide to conditions of the late twentieth century.

'Ethnicity' requires some definitional elaboration. The consensus is that it appeared as a term in the social sciences only in the mid-twentieth century, commonly attributed to Lloyd Warner in 1941 and David Riesman in 1953, before making an official appearance in the *Oxford English Dictionary* as late as the 1970s. This might seem hard to believe, given that ethnic divisions clearly existed as key characteristics of pre-industrial societies, but we are referring here to its usage as a social scientific concept. The American references indicate that social scientists were using it to describe and explain distinctive patterns of settlement in US cities by 'ethnic groups'. The students of the Chicago School in the 1920s and 1930s would have recognised the phenomenon of differential racial and ethnic mixing and segregation. However, Robert Park's classic essay *The City* (1925) which contains the key extracts from the Chicago urban school contains no index reference to 'ethnicity' at all.

By and large, to be 'ethnic' in this context was to be 'other' – Black, Hispanic, Jewish, Polish, Irish and so on. Powerful groups are not defined as 'ethnic', and Digby Baltzell's famous WASPs – white Anglo-Saxon Protestants – were the implicit 'us' against which the explicit 'them' were defined. As Michael Banton observed, WASPs are 'minus-one' ethnics, for 'members of that groups perceive themselves not as ethnic but as setting the standard by which others are to be judged' (1983: 65). In other words, 'ethnics' are 'not-us', but others who are different and usually inferior in key respects. In the previous chapter, we alluded to Greenfeld's view that the population of the US is 'national' but not 'ethnic' insofar as it is not an ethnic community as such. Be that as it may, some ethnic groups are clearly more equal than others and, as Anthony Smith observes, the dominant myth and culture of the US might be described as 'vernacular ancestralism' given its ideological roots in Anglo-American Protestantism of the eighteenth century. In recent years, the linguistic challenge to the hegemony of English by Hispanic-Americans helps to lay bare these roots. Defenders of the status quo like Edward Shils (1995) argue that multiculturalism is destroying the 'national spirit' and the 'nation as a unity', because civil society is an expression of the nation, and this in turn is an articulation of core cultural values. Change the language, for example, and everything downstream changes too, Shils implies.

The modern usage of the terms ethnicity, ethnic and so on has a linguistic history. The word 'ethnic' is from the ancient Greek word *ethnikos*, meaning a pagan or a heathen. *Ta ethne* means 'foreigners', and the term found its way into descriptions of non-chosen people, outsiders, like non-Jews (*amamim* – Greenfeld, 1992: 4), or later non-Christians. On the Roman side, the term *natio*, meaning a breed, a stock or race, usually referred to foreigners as opposed to citizens (of Rome) who were 'civilised' or organised people. Only later did 'nation' come to mean a distinct group of people characterised by common descent, language or history. Greenfeld argues that it was in sixteenth-century England that 'nation' was translated to become a synonym for 'the people': 'This semantic transformation signaled the emergence of the first nation in the world, in the sense in which the word is used today, and launched the era of nationalism' (Greenfeld, 1992: 6).

The lesson of this brief etymological history is that we have to be careful with the complex taken-for-granted taxonomy in which 'ethnicity' is embedded. The language of ethnicity, as Anthony Cohen points out, 'refers to a decision people make to depict themselves or others symbolically as the bearers of a certain cultural identity' (1993: 197). Ethnicity has to do with the politicisation of culture. 'Thus, it is in part a claim to a particular culture, with all that entails. The statement made ... in Northern Ireland, "He's a Prod" – is clearly not merely descriptive: it has an added value, either negative or positive, depending on who is speaking to whom' (ibid.). This is an appropriate point to refer back to Steve Bruce's observations. Labels like 'Catholic' or 'Protestant' (or for that matter, 'Scots' and 'English') are not neutral, descriptive labels but are to be interpreted in the context of the social and cultural claims which are being made.

A similar point is made by Stuart Hall when he argues for the unpacking of 'ethnic' categories in the British context. Precisely what 'ethnicity' means is the contested issue, as the debate over which labels to use on the British census form indicates. It is not a question of wording, but of the power-laden symbolism which lies behind the categories. The ideological contestation around the term ethnicity which has been generated should not, Hall argues, allow it to be an uncontested carrier for racial stereotyping.

> We still have a great deal of work to do to decouple ethnicity, as it functions in the dominant discourse, from its equivalence with nationalism, imperialism, racism and the state, which are the points of attachment around which a distinctive British, or more accurately English ethnicity have been constructed.
>
> (Hall, 1996c: 162)

In this respect, everyone is ethnically placed, but not conditioned by that location. The task for black people, he says, is to work out a politics of ethnicity predicated on difference and diversity. Paul Gilroy's book *There Ain't No Black in the Union Jack* requires, says Hall, an answer to the question, 'why not?'. While it is not our task here to give an answer, it does raise the puzzle which is obvious in the literature: why, in the British context at least, do the literatures on 'ethnicity' and 'nationalism' rarely if ever connect?

Ethnicity, race and nationality

Ethnicity is a term which helps to describe what used to be called 'race relations' before the term 'race' was edged out of the vocabulary. Writers like Robert Miles have argued that 'race' is not an analytical concept and does not have an independent existence apart from 'racism'. Similarly, by implication, 'nations' have no independent existence outwith the discourse of nationalism. Both 'race' and 'nation' are deemed to be socially constructed and reproduced in a tainted form, that is, as imagined communities located in theories which imply that differences are 'natural'. Miles does permit that, while doctrines of nationalism are usually constructed on a racial basis, within the UK there are differences: 'in Scotland, the "national question" has partially displaced (although not eliminated) the influence of racism in constructing the political agenda in this period [the 1960s and 1970s], suggesting that racism is not as central to nationalism as in England' (1993: 78).

Miles is one of the few writers who engage with nationalism, 'race' (he uses inverted commas as a sign of renunciation) and ethnicity. His suspicion of 'race' is also carried over, one suspects, to ethnicity, as it appears only once in his index, to refer to an official census category. The counter-view is that 'pronouncements renouncing race as an ideological or social construction are frequent, yet it is not clear why the social nature of "race" makes it any less authentic' (Rodkin, 1993: 644). Many writers on ethnicity do not share Stuart Hall's view that the term should be recovered as a means of understanding and promoting a politics of difference and diversity. While Hall admits that much needs to be done to uncouple ethnicity from its racial-imperial-nationalist discourse, he does not believe that the term should be permanently colonised in this context.

A more positive view of 'ethnicity' and 'race' is also taken by social anthropologists such as Michael Banton (1983) and Thomas Eriksen (1993). Banton argues that while 'race' as a biological category has no influence on people's behaviour, it does serve as a role sign. In other words, what people see is not race but the phenotypical variations to which they attribute social meaning, just as other biological categories like age and sex are significant in the cultural interpretations which they carry. Similarly, the use of 'race' in sociology focuses on the ways physical characteristics like skin colour are used as the basis of group identity. 'Ethnicity' implies that cultural characteristics like language, customs, religion and so on operate as important cultural markers. He comments that no-one can hear, see, smell, taste or touch ethnicity; we can only know it through its signs. 'Racial' and ethnic differences are then mapped on to socio-economic differences in different societies in different ways. In Latin American societies, finer and more complex gradations are used reflecting more complex economic and cultural niches than in, for example, the (southern) US where a simpler 'racial' dichotomy is in use. Banton argues that social scientists do not buy into 'racism' by being interested in how actors use and mobilise racial and ethnic categories in their behaviour:

> 'Race' relations are distinguished not by the biological significance of phenotypical features but by the social use of these features as signs identifying group membership and the roles people are expected to play. The long-run 'problem' of 'race' relations is that of explaining how groups identified by such signs come to be created, how they are maintained, and how they are often dissolved.
>
> (Banton, 1983: 76)

Thomas Eriksen largely agrees with Banton over the use of ethnicity. He says that it 'emerges and is made relevant through social situations and encounters, and through people's ways of coping with the demands and challenges of life' (1993: 1). While 'race' may be of dubious descriptive value, its significance lies in the fact that it is a cultural construct which does not imply its 'objective' significance. It would be possible to have 'redhead studies' if influential people had a similar theory about the character traits of persons with red hair.

As regards the relationship between ethnicity and nationalism, these are sufficiently distinct in the minds of both Banton and Eriksen. The former argues that national differences are essentially political, defined in relationship to the state: 'The English, Welsh and Scots are accounted nations comprising the British state, not as ethnic divisions of a British nation or race' (Banton, 1983: 64). Similarly, Eriksen defines nationalism as a political ideology which holds that the boundaries of the state should be coterminous with cultural ones, whereas many/most ethnic groups do not demand control over their own state. Hence, black people in the US may well define themselves as an ethnic group (even more than one), but have not sought to map these cultural differences onto political boundaries. That is what Smith means by saying that in the US ethnic aspirations are communal rather than territorial (1991: 149). If and when cultural differences come to be expressed territorially, then the ethnic movement becomes a nationalist one.

Eriksen points out that the key to both ethnic and national identity is self-identification, and he uses the distinction between 'emic' and 'etic' categories to make the point: the former refers to the native's self-definition, whereas the latter is the analyst's concept. The process of creating, maintaining and dissolving ethnic and national groups is also worthy of study, according to Banton. Ethnic groups are often immigrant minorities seeking either to protect their identity or, more often, to derive differential advantage from acculturation. In like manner: 'national groups have often ended when their more influential members come to a similar conclusion [being unable to offer members the same benefits as those offered in the wider society], as did the Scots with the Act of Union of 1707' (Banton, 1994: 15). Presumably, Banton would also have to say that the perceived loss of advantage to the Scots within that Union has led to an amplification of Scottishness. This is an important point, because it implies that ethnicity/nationality is not lost and found in a linear way, but is constructed and mobilised within a wider and more discursive context.

The key perspective here is that of the Norwegian social anthropologist Fredrik Barth, whose 1969 paper 'Ethnic groups and boundaries' is among the most influential and most cited in ethnic and national studies. Barth took issue with the conventional way of imagining how ethnic groups are formed:

> We are led to imagine each group developing its cultural and social form in relative isolation, mainly in response to local ecologic factors, through a history of adaptation by invention and selective borrowing. This history has produced a world of separate peoples, each with their own culture and each organised in a society which can legitimately be isolated for description as an island to itself.
>
> (Barth, 1981: 200)

The point here is not that nationalism, for example, is the mobilisation of objective and long-standing differences in ethnicity, but that it is the mobilisation of those which actors deem to be salient. In other words, cultural differences like language, religion, even skin colour, are not primary and definitional characteristics, but are social identifiers which are the result, the product, of struggles in the first place. Being able to show that there is ethnic homogeneity in a given territory – or, rather, that people living there believe themselves to be homogeneous – is the outcome of political and social processes, not their explanation or their cause. Writers on the Balkans, for example, tell how neighbours who lived in a fair degree of harmony for decades, even centuries, suddenly developed great hatred for each other on the grounds that they were Serb, or Bosnian or Croat. This activity cannot be explained in terms of long-standing and deep-seated ethnic rivalries, but only in those which the combatants choose to remember, construct or activate as a result of the changing political context.

In Barth's words: 'To the extent that actors use ethnic identities to categorise themselves and others for purposes of interaction, they form ethnic groups in this organisational sense' (1981: 202–3). The key point here is that there is no one-to-one relationship between ethnicity and cultural identifiers. What matters is which ones key actors regard as significant, for which purposes and under which conditions. Barth continues: 'some cultural factors are used by the actors as signals and emblems of differences, others are ignored, and in some relationships radical differences are played down and denied' (ibid.: 203).

Related to the variation in the potency of cultural markers is the issue of boundaries. It is the social boundary which defines the group in question, not the cultural stuff which the boundary contains. Where social interaction is defined as taking place within or across these boundaries, then the group's identity will be maintained, reinforced or dissipated. It will not be necessary for the cultural content of two adjacent groups to alter significantly – indeed, they may grow more similar. What matters is the interaction across a meaningful boundary (not only geographical, but also social and cultural) which may weaken or strengthen. For example, it is not difficult to show that in most respects the people who live in Scotland and England have grown more similar in economic, social and cultural terms. What matters sociologically, however, is how they define themselves *vis-à-vis* each other. Again, before the outbreak of war in the Balkans in 1991, it was supposed that the different peoples of the region living quite literally side by side had nothing to fight about. As Eriksen observes:

> Ethnic boundaries, dormant for decades, were activated; presumed cultural differences which had been irrelevant for two generations were suddenly 'remembered' and invoked as proof that it was impossible for the two groups to live side by side. It is only when they make a difference that cultural differences are important in the creation of ethnic boundaries.
>
> (Eriksen, 1993: 39)

Barth advocates a relational and processual approach to ethnicity; a group's culture may change without removing the ethnic boundary, and as we have seen, groups may become culturally more similar at the same time as the boundaries are strengthened. If we are trying to define ethnic or national identity, then what matters is what the boundaries are, especially people's self-descriptions of themselves *vis-à-vis* others.

Barth's perspective has been very influential in the study of ethnicity and identity. It is, however, not without criticism. Despite Barth's relational and processual approach to ethnicity, Abner Cohen (Eriksen, 1993) accuses him of treating ethnicity as having an imperative, primordial status. That is, Barth's treatment of ethnic categories as organisational vessels, as more-or-less constants which can be called upon as and when necessary, means that they appear to become a priori categorical ascriptions of a static quality (Eriksen, 1993: 54–5). Barth's 'transactionalism' means that ethnic groups are treated as units of ascription where social boundaries ensure the persistence of the group. The boundaries themselves are 'policed' by symbolic border guards such as language, religion and culture which help to perpetuate the community internally. This implies a degree of fixity about the boundaries (and hence of bounded ethnic identities), and possibly underplays variations in types of and conditions for ethnic allegiances.

Anthony Cohen comments that Barth's view also rests on the assumption that ethnicity is simply generalised to group members – as bearers of a given ethnic identity – without being implicated in their own self-perceptions (Cohen, 1996: 120). Hence, although Barth adopts a subjectivist view of identity, self-consciousness is actually down-played, as is the importance of the symbolic expression of identity. Treating ethnicity as largely a tactical identity patrolled by cultural border guards underplays the self-conscious and symbolic expression which people themselves negotiate actively about.

Who are we? Constructing identity

The missing link here is 'identity'. We find that we cannot discuss ethnicity and nationality without focusing on the process of identification, on the active negotiation in which people take part as they construct who they are and who they want to be. In Stuart Hall's words:

> Identity is not as transparent or unproblematic as we think. Perhaps instead of thinking of identity as an already accomplished fact, with the new cultural practices they represent, we should think instead of identity as 'production', which is never complete, always in process, and always constituted within, not outside, representation. This view problematises the very authority and authenticity to which the term 'cultural identity' lays claim.
>
> (Hall, 1990: 222)

While it is true that identities are constructed by participants in the course of social and political action, they are not entirely of their own making. We work within cultural representations, as Hall points out: 'We only know what it is to be "English" because of the way "Englishness" has come to be represented, as a set of meanings, by English national culture. It follows that a nation is not only a political entity but something which produces meanings – a system of cultural representation' (1992: 292).

Hall argues that national culture is a discourse, a way of constructing meanings which influences and organises our actions and our conceptions of ourselves. The idea of the nation is a 'narrative' (Bhabha, 1990) whose origin is obscure, but whose symbolic power to mobilise the sense of identity and allegiance is strong. We will return to Hall's point that identities are cultural representations or discourses which both facilitate and restrict choice. However, by looking at national identity in this way, as multifaceted and plural, we begin to see that it cannot be taken for granted, that it will reflect social power, and that competing identities will emerge and challenge each other. In Peter Worsley's words: 'Cultural traits are not absolutes or simply intellectual categories, but are invoked to provide identities which legitimise claims to rights. They are strategies or weapons in competitions over scarce resources' (1984: 249).

Nor are national cultures and identities fixed and immutable. They are subject to processes of translation and change. Hall's term 'cultures of hybridity' refers to the ways in which identities are subject to the play of history, political representation and difference, and are very unlikely to be pure or unitary. He cites the writer Salman Rushdie's description of his controversial book *The Satanic Verses*, as 'a love-story to our mongrel selves' (Hall, 1992: 311).

Edward Said has also made this point central to his writings on Orientalism, and Culture and Imperialism. He points out that imperialism and resistance to it are inextricably linked, defining and competing with each other. There is no meaningful 'us' and 'them'. 'Gone', he says, 'are the binary opposites dear to the nationalist and the imperialist enterprise' (1993: xxviii), although each has a vested interest in their defining separateness. He elaborates as follows:

> If you know in advance that the African or Iranian or Chinese or Jewish or German experience is fundamentally integral, coherent, separate, and therefore comprehensible only to Africans, Iranians, Chinese, Jews or Germans, you first of all posit as essential something which . . . is both historically created and the result of interpretation, namely the existence of Africanness, Jewishness or Germanness or for that matter Orientalism and Occidentalism.
>
> (Said, 1993: 35–6)

The point is that the codification of difference is a vital part of the strategy of identity-politics, and ought not be taken for granted by the social scientist or historian. In practical terms, as Said says, today no-one is merely one thing. Such stereotypes are part of the polemic batteries of discourse, especially in a rapidly changing world in which state formations are coming under attack from below and above. What we are confronting here is a shift in how we approach issues of identity. In practice, there is a dialectic between what is laid out before us and our capacity to choose. We seem to have reached a point in the late twentieth century when we believe ourselves, rightly or wrongly, to have more choice about our nationality and ethnicity than hitherto. How are we to explain this?

Challenges to existing states in the late twentieth century have grown more, not less, common. Alternative political identities have been emerging, different from those laid down by existing state structures. Late twentieth-century challenges to the social, economic and cultural jurisdiction of the modern state – what we might call processes of state re-formation – began to have implications for national identity. Suddenly identity issues are back on the political agenda. In Mercer's words: 'Identity only becomes an issue when it is in crisis, when something assumed to be fixed, coherent and stable is displaced by the experience of doubt and uncertainty' (Mercer, 1990: 43). From this angle, the eagerness to talk about identity is symptomatic of the postmodern predicament of contemporary politics and sociology.

In many respects, 'identity' has taken over from 'postmodernism' as the intellectual fashion-accessory of the second half of the 1990s. There is good reason for this, as the fluidity and plurality of identities is part and parcel of the postmodern condition. Zygmunt Bauman has pointed out that identity issues have taken on a new form:

> if the modern 'problem of identity' was how to construct an identity and keep it solid and stable, the postmodern 'problem of identity' is primarily how to avoid fixation and keep the options open. In the case of identity . . . the catchword of modernity was creation; the catchword of postmodernity is recycling.
>
> (Bauman, 1996: 18)

Identity, he says, has become fashionable because people are not sure as to who they are. The uncertainty of (post)modern life generates both bewilderment and freedom. Identity becomes the name for that escape from uncertainty. Bauman's way of expressing this is to say that just as 'modernity' had the 'pilgrim', postmodernity has the '*flâneur*' (stroller). In other words, the pilgrim had a route to follow and a goal to reach. The *flâneur* practices the 'as-if' life, with a considerable amount of playful detachment, and pursues identities in the likes of shopping and tourism (where, following Umberto Eco (1987), 'appearance' matters less than 'reality').

Until recently, sociology had little new to say about identity. The term had largely migrated into the reserve of micro-sociology, where it was inextricably bound up with social psychological notions of 'self'. In the rest of sociology, it became quite unproblematic. As Stuart Hall (1992) has pointed out, echoing Bauman, the implicit model of modernity which underpins contemporary sociology assumes that the key social identities in the modern world were long-formed by the process of modernisation. Political, social, occupational, class and even gender identities were assumed to have been formed in this process, and nothing new needed to be said.

The sociological concept of identity, Hall argues, was formed as a reaction to the orthodox notion that identity was an individual characteristic, that 'the essential centre of the self was a person's identity' (Hall, 1992: 275). Sociology, in dispute with this orthodoxy, argued that identity was formed in relation to significant others, in the interactions between self and society. In Hall's metaphor, identity 'sutures' the subject into relevant social structures, thereby making social interaction unified and predictable. Once this orthodoxy took hold, identity became uncontentious, the product of processes of primary and secondary socialisation. There was little need to ask who we were, because the social structures we lived in allowed us to read off our identities in an unproblematic way.

Plainly, however, this notion of identity has in recent times begun to come apart. The 'crisis' of self has entered the discourse, not simply as a theme of social psychology, but in response to radical change in the social structures which maintained a fairly consistent sense of self – family, marriage, occupation. Self appears to have become more fragmented, composed of several competing identities, and the generic process of identification has become more problematic and contentious. Increasing rates of social change help to destabilise traditional social structures, opening up new anxieties as well as new possibilities. To be sure, such rates of social change are not new. The whole process of industrialisation and what we term modernisation – political, cultural, social – also disrupted older identity-frames, and ushered in new ones, which the discipline of sociology (as well as the rest of the social sciences) were designed to explain. And so they did.

It is this fairly recent mode of analysis which has restored the concept of identity to problematic status. Simply put, we can no longer assume that there is much fixed, essential or immutable about identity, but that individuals assume different identities at different times which may not even be centred around a coherent sense of self. The sociologist who insinuated this new perspective back into sociology was Erving Goffman whose concern with the 'presentation' of self implied that identity was basically a badge with little real substance (Goffman, 1973). Goffman was following a line of thought out of symbolic interactionism in which identity was a tactical construction designed to maximise advantage for the player.

Although Goffman was writing about self in the 1950s and 1960s, he was the precursor of what became essentially a postmodern concept of identity. Postmodernism argues that late or postmodern societies are impelled by constant and rapid social change which makes a fixed and immutable sense of self redundant. The result of this discontinuity and fragmentation is that social life is increasingly 'open', to use Giddens' term, offering opportunities and choices for individuals in a rapidly changing world. His formulation of the issue (Giddens, 1991) is that lifestyle choice becomes more important in the constitution of identity, and, as a result, a new kind of 'lifestyle' politics emerges from the shadow of 'emancipatory politics'.

In parallel to this, no 'master-identity' [*sic*] is possible, and, especially, people can no longer identify their social interests mainly or entirely in terms of social class, the classical mode of emancipatory politics in 'modernist' society. In Hall's words, 'Class cannot serve as a discursive device or mobilising category through which all the diverse social interests and identities of people can be reconciled and represented' (1992: 280). What occurs, Hall argues, is a politics of 'difference' – defined by new social movements such as feminism, Black struggles, nationalist and ecological movements – which supersedes a politics of class identity.

The other manifestation of this collapse of 'modernist' social identities is the reassertion of individualism in both philosophical and economic forms. We might interpret the political success of New Right liberalism in Western countries as one version of this process of deconstruction. After all, saying that 'there is no such thing as society, only individuals and their families', as Mrs Thatcher did in the 1980s, is to assert that individuals are free to construct their identities as they please. Its economic expression – I buy, therefore I am – is the supremacy of the consumer. Bauman observes:

> it is the consumer attitude which makes my life into my individual affair; and it is the consumer activity which makes me into the individual. . . . It seems in the end as if I were made up of the many things I buy and own: tell me what you buy and in what shops you buy it, and I'll tell you who you are. It seems that with the help of carefully selected purchases, I can make of myself anything I may wish, anything I believe it is worth becoming. Just as dealing with my personal problems is my duty and my responsibility, so the shaping of my personal identity, my self-assertion, making myself into a concrete someone, is my task and mine alone.
>
> (Bauman, 1992: 205)

Bauman is articulating here the postmodern, even the post-sociological construction of identity. Just as sociology in its modernist form reacted against methodological individualism by asserting the ways in which individuals were social beings whether they realised it or not, so lifestyle and consumerist conceptions of identity have returned to a highly individuated and economically liberating sense of identity. The demise of overarching or meta-identities appears to have allowed a plurality of new ones to emerge from under the corpse. These are not simply individualist *tout court*, but reflect the possibility of playing out what one wants to be, selecting from an array of choices, and with greater control over the messages and signs given off. Essentially, the politics which emanates from this process is indeed personal, a feature recognised by social movements like feminism, for example, which adopted the slogan that 'the personal is political'. When it comes to nationality, the old certainties and fixtures have also come in for scrutiny. The focus on 'personal nationalism' (A.P. Cohen, 1994 and 1996; Billig,

1995) – how individuals construct a sense of who they are in terms of national identity – is a manifestation of the same sets of issues. In many ways, what we are seeing is the replay of the classical sociological issue, the relationship of structure and action. To translate in terms of nationality: is our identity conveyed by the social and political structures which are the frames within which we operate, or do we have greater capacity to choose these frames and move between them?

Problematising identity in the late twentieth century suggests that identity should be considered less as a categorical self-concept, and more as a process. In Stuart Hall's words:

> Though they seem to invoke an origin in a historical past with which they continue to correspond, actually identities are about using the resources of history, language and culture in the process of becoming rather than being; not 'who we are' or 'where have we come from' so much as what we might become, how we have been represented and how that bears on how we might represent ourselves. Identities are therefore constituted within, not outside representation.
>
> (Hall, 1996a: 4)

In other words, identities should be seen as a concern with 'routes' rather than 'roots', as maps for the future rather than trails from the past. To put it another way, identity, as Bauman points out, should be treated as a verb not as a noun, 'albeit a strange one to be sure: it appears only in the future tense' (1996: 19). Identity, he says, is a name given to the escape from that uncertainty.

The discussion about national identity, then, properly belongs to a much broader debate about identity generally. Rapidly changing social structures have an effect on all forms of social identity, including the ones which interest us here – national, political identity. By the 1990s, the old agenda had changed. New political structures, and the concomitant decline of older ones, seem to have focused the issue of identity. The discontinuity, fragmentation and dislocation of social arrangements mean that no meta-identity seems possible, and that how different identities relate to each other is quite unpredictable. In Giddens' words, 'The more tradition loses its hold, the more daily life is reconstituted in terms of the dialectical interplay of the local and the global, the more individuals are forced to negotiate lifestyle choices among a diversity of options' (1991: 5).

National identities become more problematic as conventional state-identities are corroded by forces of globalisation which shift the classical sociological focus away from the assumption that 'societies' are well-bounded social, economic and cultural systems. What replaces conventional state-identities is not 'cultural homogenisation' in which everyone shares in the same global postmodern identity because they consume the same material and cultural products. Rather, as Stuart Hall observes, 'We are confronted by a range of different identities, each appealing to us, or rather to different parts of ourselves, from which it seems possible to choose' (1992: 303).

Hence, the argument goes, globalisation leads to the creation or strengthening of local identities, as well as to the emergence of strong counter-ethnicities. These may simply be the reproduction of traditional ones, devoted to defending and restoring the purity of the original, or 'translating' new identities into the spaces created by new social forces. That these may employ the rhetoric of tradition might mask their novelty and adaptability to new social circumstances. These 'cultures of hybridity', as Hall calls them, are more likely to try to assimilate different identities without asserting the primacy of one in particular. The examples he gives are derived from the experiences of people of Afro-Caribbean and Asian backgrounds in Britain today who produce new identities which 'translate' between different cultures.

Some identities gravitate towards (re)constructing a single, unified culture expressing one true self, 'reflecting common historical experiences and shared cultural codes which provide us as "one people" with stable, unchanging and continuous frames of reference and meaning beneath the shifting divisions and vicissitudes of our actual history' (Hall, 1990: 223). This view of identity is to be found in ethnic as well as national forms, among subordinate as well as dominant groups. Recovering the 'real history' of a people is a common project, which seeks to restore what has been lost. This Hall characterises as recourse to 'tradition', which usually takes a fundamentalist and purist form.

On the other hand, and with greater force in a rapidly changing world, there are cultures of 'translation' which recognise that identity is subject to the play of history and difference, and is unlikely to be pure or unitary. By inference, this approach to cultural identities is better adapted to the conditions of the modern world:

> It belongs to the future as much as to the past. It is not something which already exists, transcending place, time, history and culture. Cultural identities come from somewhere, have histories. But like everything which is historical, they undergo constant transformation. Far from being eternally fixed in some essentialised past, they are subject to the continuous 'play' of history, culture and power.
>
> (Hall, 1990: 225)

Hall's focus here is on subordinate and 'ethnic' cultures, and their 'translation' into larger and more dominant ones. Their hybridity is not a sign of weakness but of adaptation to changing realities and contexts. All cultures are products of this process of hybridity, and all seek to construct narrative unities. Hybridisation of this sort has in practice always occurred, but its relationship to power structures is what matters. 'Unified' cultures are those which have told themselves the right kind of story, and have the power to impose it on listeners. Identity becomes an effective story which people tell themselves but one which is written across differences. The subordination of less powerful cultures is often explained in terms of their internal differences, and becomes an important weapon for the powerful to disparage other cultures. We recognise here that identity involves a positioning in relation to what Foucault called the power/knowledge couplet.

> We should admit that power produces knowledge . . . that power and knowledge directly imply one another; that there is no power relation without the corrective constitution of a field of knowledge, nor any knowledge that does not presuppose and constitute . . . power relations.
>
> (Foucault, 1980: 27)

Hall speaks, for example, of black Caribbean identities as framed by twin axes: one of similarity and continuity (with a grounding in the past), and the other of difference and rupture (experiences of profound discontinuity). The former is experienced as internal; the latter as the result of external and alien forces. In practice, however, the two are intermingled. Further, there is no significant difference between the self and the other.

Following Said, we can see that who 'we' are and who 'they' are are inextricably linked. The 'West' is defined in terms of the 'Orient', as well as vice versa. Hall provides the link between 'ethnic' and 'national' identities with which we began. In an English context, for example, the other actually defines who 'we' are: 'The English are racist not because they hate the blacks, but because they don't know who they are without the blacks' (1996c: 345). In other words, they have to know who they are not in order to know who they are. 'The other is not outside but also inside the self, the identity. So identity is a process; identity is split. Identity is not a fixed point but an ambivalent point. Identity is also the relationship of the other to oneself' (ibid.). Nor is this process unique to ethnic/national identity. 'Constructing difference' with regard to gender, class, and so on involves a relational opposition (but not necessarily antagonism) to the other. Hence, constructing an essential, and exclusive, sense of cultural self cannot avoid embedding the 'other', whether one is talking about Black/White, Scottish/English, and so on. The 'difference' involves the 'same'.

Ethnic and national identities in the UK

We can now return to the earlier question: why 'ethnic' and 'national' questions in the UK by and large talk past each other's shoulders. As we have seen, identities of 'Englishness' are common to both. In ethnic terms, it means not being 'black'; in national terms it means not being Scottish, Welsh or Irish, but above all not French, German and so on. On top of this, there is the conundrum of Britishness. In Robin Cohen's helpful metaphor (1994), it is 'fuzzy', that is, blurred and opaque. (Cohen is making the analogy with 'fuzzy logic' in mathematics by which a solution is reached by way of eliminating the uncertain edges to a problem.) If the conventional essence of nationality is 'citizenship', then Britain is an awkward case.

The making of citizenship in these islands is instructive. The inhabitants of the UK attained citizenship by a legislative sleight of hand under the 1948 Nationality

Act as 'citizens of the UK and the colonies'. Prior to 1948 the inhabitants of the British Isles and the British Empire were formally 'subjects' of the Crown. The 1914 British Nationality and Aliens Act was a consolidation of the law relating to British nationality over the centuries (Goulbourne, 1991). This act did not refer to Britain as a geographical entity; it was perceived in terms of those who owed allegiance to the Crown, reflecting the pre-modern and dynastic origins of the 'Kingdom'. In this regard, there was something pre-modern about the relationship between the state and its inhabitants.

The post-1945 crisis arose because independent states such as Canada and India wished to redefine citizenship for immigration purposes, and so a separate status was necessary for the remaining inhabitants of the UK. The preferred position of the British Government was that people in Commonwealth countries were British subjects first, and citizens of individual states second, but it quickly became obvious that newly independent countries baulked at this constraint on their sovereignty. The British political parties reflected the confusion. In the post-imperial age, the Labour Party sought to encourage a 'traditional' (i.e. non-ethnic) definition of 'Britishness' to encompass the Commonwealth while supporting colonial peoples in their liberation struggles (Goulbourne, 1991). This helps to explain Labour's opposition in the 1960s and 1970s to Scottish and Welsh nationalism as a betrayal of the multinational, non-ethnic identity of Britain. The Conservative Party for its part developed an 'ethnic' definition – 'those groups which consider themselves to be British, and also the indigenous and/or white population' (ibid.: 245). This was reflected in the 1962 Commonwealth Immigration Act, the 1971 Immigration Act, and the 1981 Nationality Act (which embedded the 'patriality' clause), and an ethnic definition was reinforced ideologically under the influence of Enoch Powell and Margaret Thatcher. The politicisation of ethnic identity has helped to highlight the racial context of the debate over the last thirty years. By the 1981 Act, patriality ushered in the law of blood (*ius sanguinis*) rather than the law of territory (*ius soli*), so that ethnic definitions of Britishness are at least as important as civic ones.

This brief overview of how 'Britishness' has come to be redefined in the post-colonial age provides a context for important shifts in national identities within the UK itself, notably in Scotland. If British identity is externally fuzzy, so also is its meaning within these islands. Goulbourne argues that until Ireland became a republic in 1948, its citizens remained formal 'subjects' of the British Crown (reinforced by the new republic leaving the Commonwealth a year later, largely to break finally with this colonial legacy). A number of other key confusions remained, notably that between 'Britain' and 'England', a distinction which was rarely made in the UK's largest country as well as overseas. It was the norm to describe the UK as a 'nation-state', an extension of England. For example, in his exploration of *The English Tribe*, Stephen Haseler comments: 'Great Britain was always a misnomer; "Greater England" would have been better' (1996: 30). Although the Scots and the Welsh worked within a more logical model whereby their national identities were nested in the broader British state identity, the unitary nature of that state with a single, sovereign parliament seemed to reinforce the equation of Britain and England. In recent years an important debate has started south of the border about whether or not black people can be 'English' rather than simply 'British'. In many ways this is a debate about ethnic (being English by lineage or 'blood') versus civic definitions (being British by residence and citizenship).

The debate north of the border is more explicit and seemingly more clear-cut. Broadly speaking, if asked to choose, around three-quarters of people living in Scotland opt for 'Scottish' and only one-quarter 'British'. This prioritising of Scottishness over Britishness is also reflected when a scale is used in survey research asking people to choose from 'Scottish not British' at one end, to 'British not Scottish' at the other (named the Moreno scale after its author). Generally, six out of every ten people living in Scotland give priority to their Scottishness over their Britishness (either 'Scottish not British', or 'More Scottish than British'). Nevertheless, well over half claim some version of dual nationality, being both Scottish and British in some degree, albeit with a clear emphasis on the former. These results are fairly robust over time, and correlate well with social characteristics. Young people, the working class, and SNP and Labour voters are more likely to emphasise their Scottishness, although all social groups do so by significant majorities.

We have, then, in these islands a complex set of national political identities. Adapting Robin Cohen's idea of 'fuzzy frontiers', we might identify the following: that between the English (the largest nationality) and the Scots – who were jointly responsible for founding the 'Great Britain' in 1707; the relationship between the English/Scots and the other Celtic peoples – the Welsh on the one hand, and the Irish on the other (most of whom are citizens of an independent republic, but with voting and residence rights in the UK – and leaving aside the complications in Northern Ireland); the (white) Dominions – which are politically independent, but genealogically, culturally and legally linked (via 'patriality' rights of settlement); the (black) Commonwealth, with the history of post-war settlement (defining 'ethnicity' in the UK); European links via (but not exclusively with) the European Union, which also implies rights of settlement and residence to 'non-British' people; Anglophones (especially via cultural and historical links with the US). The result, in Robin Cohen's words, is:

> British identity shows a general pattern of fragmentation. Multiple axes of identification have meant that Irish, Scots, Welsh and English people, those from the white, black and brown Commonwealth, Americans, English-speakers, Europeans and even 'aliens' have had their lives intersect one with another in overlapping and complex circles of identity-construction and rejection. The shape and edges of British identity are thus historically changing, often vague and, to a degree, malleable – an aspect of the British identity I have called 'a fuzzy frontier'.
>
> (R. Cohen 1994: 35)

The issues of ethnicity and nationality, then, in the UK are especially 'fuzzy' for reasons outlined above. Britishness is a political identity, roughly equated with citizenship but, as we have seen, growing out of a pre-modern prior definition of people as 'subjects' of the Crown, even those who do not live in these islands. As the sense of Britishness declines (after all, those entering pensionable age in 1997 were barely into their early teens when the Second World War ended), it is tempting to over-emphasise its demise. After all, British 'stateness' (to borrow Juan Linz's (1992) concept) has helped to create a sense of cultural and political identity for people in the UK.

One would imagine that more 'modern', that is, republican states would have a less fuzzy concept of nationality. This is true of the US, but there the history of settlement has left a complicating legacy of 'hyphenated' Americans, in terms of their ethnic origins and citizenship (as in African-Americans, Hispanic-Americans, etc.), and there is some evidence from US census data that the proportion of such self-defining Americans has grown in recent years if census results are anything to go by (Portes and MacLeod, 1996). The other founding republic, France, has, as Brubaker pointed out, an apparently more straightforward territorial definition of who is French. However, the very lack of fuzziness has caused problems for the political system in recent years as it does not easily cope with those, such as Muslims, who wish to express their ethnic as well as their state identity. Wearing the *Hijeb* (veil) provides symbolic problems for the French state, especially in the context of the growth of right-wing political parties like Le Pen's *Front Nationale* (Raissiguier, 1995). Strong civic republicanism perhaps carries more of an implication of monoculturalism than the haphazard and often implicit identities available to the people of the British islands.

The other great European state, Germany, is also characterised by anomalies, fuzzy boundaries and ambiguities (Forsythe, 1989). Before the unification of East and West, it was not even clear where 'Germany' was. Defining nationality in terms of *ius sanguinis* rather than *ius soli* resulted from a complex political and social history, especially as the history of German nation-ness and statehood proved to be so complex and bloody since 1871. Forsythe argues that the result has been a hierarchy of German-ness according to 'emic' (native) categories (prior to unification, but now only marginally less complex): (a) FRG citizens of German descent living in the Federal Republic, and *'aussiedler'* living in the FRG; (b) GDR citizens of German descent living in the GDR; (c) *Restdeutsche* living in land still claimed by some as Germany or in other areas of Eastern Europe; (d) *Auswanderer*: emigrant FRG citizens of German descent living in other Western countries (German speakers); (e) German speakers living in German-speaking foreign countries (e.g. Austria); (f) people of German descent living in foreign non-German speaking countries (e.g. the US), who may or may not speak German (Forsythe, 1989: 146).

It becomes plain, then, that while the relationship between ethnicity, nationality and citizenship in the UK is fuzzy, the situation in other countries is only marginally less complex. This suggests that we need more sensitive instruments with which to comprehend national identity. The literature on nationalism makes frequent allusion to Renan's famous dictum that the nation is a 'daily plebiscite', requiring the active commitment of people and their shared belief that it should continue. As was pointed out in the previous chapter, Renan's dictum was actually the anguished response of a liberal nationalist to the forced incorporation of eastern France by Germany in 1871. How, he asked, could people be ruled if they did not give their daily and active assent? The question of legitimacy continues to be a key question for states in the late twentieth century. Max Weber's dictum remains: the persistence of regimes is to be explained primarily in terms of people's belief in their legitimacy (Beetham, 1985: 256).

Personal nationalism

The tendency among students of nationalism and national identity is to focus on the 'national' rather than on the 'identity' part of the term. David Miller, for example, in his treatise *On Nationality* comments that 'to understand what we mean when we talk of someone having a national identity, we must first get clear about what nations are' (1995: 17). In other words, the weight of the question conventionally rests on the existence or otherwise of the nation, rather than on the mechanisms whereby individuals come to construct and mobilise national identity/ies.

Here we encounter once more the familiar issue in sociology, that of structure versus action. The tension is between accounts which focus on how, on the one hand, legal, political and cultural institutions lay down definitions for actors and accounts which argue on the other, that actors have more freedom to construct identities for themselves. In the last few years there has been a growing interest in 'personal' nationalism, whose starting point is Renan's dictum of the 'daily plebiscite', the everyday affirmation of national identity. Michael Billig, for example, has drawn attention to what he terms the 'banality' of nationalism so that 'the flags melt into the background as "our" particular world is experienced as *the* world' (1995: 50). The most obvious expression of this is the daily pledge to the flag which takes place in US schools. He comments:

> The ceremony is a ritual display of national unity. Children, in knowing that this is the way in which the school day starts, will take it for granted that other pupils, the length and breadth of the homeland, are also beginning their day similarly; and that their parents and grandparents, if schooled in the United States, did likewise; they might even suppose that all over the world the school day starts thus.
>
> (Billig, 1995: 50)

Billig's account is a useful antidote to the view that nationalism is a top-down phenomenon practised on a gullible public for political reasons. The everyday affirmation of national identity is an active process, reinforced by the banal symbolism of national identity, most obviously the national flag. Only where that

40

flag is seen as problematic, or where there is an alternative national emblem – as in Northern Ireland where the British and Irish flags are key icons implying competing national identities – does it fail to work its magic. Often, we cannot read off the meaning simply from the fact that different flags fly. For example, to Scottish Nationalists, flying the Saltire (St Andrew's cross) may signify a counter-nationalism to that of the British state, whereas to Unionists it implies that being Scottish and being British are complementary not competing identities.

The American writer Carlton Hayes noted the significance of the iconography of the flag and its accoutrements after 1945. He wrote:

> There are universal liturgical forms for 'saluting' the flag, for 'dipping' the flag, for 'lowering' the flag, and for 'hoisting' the flag. Men bare their heads when the flag passes by; and in praise of the flag poets write odes, and to it children sing hymns and pledge allegiance. In all solemn feasts and fasts of nationalism, the flag is in evidence, and with it that other sacred thing, the national anthem. An acute literary critic in his purely secular capacity might be tempted to cavil at phrases in 'Rule Britannia', in 'Deutschland über alles', or even in the 'Marseillaise'. He might object on literary grounds, to such a lame beginning as 'Oh say, can you see?'. But a national anthem is not a profane thing and does not admit of textual criticism. It is the *Te Deum* of the new dispensation; worshippers stand when it is intoned, the military 'at attention', and the male civilians with uncovered heads, all with external show of respect and veneration.
>
> (Hayes, 1960: 167)

We might expect that in the absence of mass war, such veneration has waned among the populations of Western states, but the taken-for-grantedness remains. Similarly, flags are not the only such icons expressing nationality. Benedict Anderson has pointed out that in the modern world we have grown very used to recognising the geographical silhouette of the country to which we belong. Indeed, it comes in the shape of badges, on national stamps, sports emblems and so on. The everydayness and implicitness of the emblem reinforces our identity with it, and we learn to recognise it from atlases, weather-maps etc. As Eley and Suny argue: 'for nationalism to do its work, ordinary people need to see themselves as the bearers of an identity centred elsewhere, imagine themselves as an abstract community' (1996: 22). It is the mundaneness and ubiquity which matter. Perhaps there is too much of a 'forced' quality in this statement, as if reinforcement comes by deliberate stealth, rather than by willing involvement in constructing a national identity, a guarantee, as it were, that we know who we are, both individually and collectively.

The point about the potency as well as the implicitness of the national flag is taken up by Anthony Cohen (1996) in his perceptive comments on 'personal' nationalism. He acknowledges that flags and other national symbols have the power to provide us with the means by which to think, but 'the assumption that under normal circumstances they can make us think in specifiable ways is mistaken. It privileges culture over thinking selves, instead of seeing it as the product of thinking selves' (ibid.: 167). Similarly, we can think of examples where the mobilisation of such symbols fails to work its magic, as in the case of Scotland's stone of destiny/Stone of Scone which was returned to Edinburgh on St Andrew's Day, 1996, at the behest of a Conservative Secretary of State seeking some political advantage. By all accounts, the ploy failed (A.P. Cohen, 1997), showing that there is nothing predictable or automatic about working the spell.

What we see in the working (and non-working) of such national myths is the operation of what Foucault referred to as the metaphysics of power, the creating of modern subjects through invisible practices. With regard to nationality, or 'nation-ness', these are the day-to-day interactions and practices which produce inherent and usually unarticulated feelings of belonging, of being 'at home' (Verdery, 1993). In other words, the 'nation' is an aspect of the political and symbolic order as well as a world of social interaction and feeling. In Anthony Cohen's phrase, the individual is represented as the nation writ small, and the nation as the individual writ large: 'Individuals "own" the nation; the nation conducts itself as a collective individual' (1994: 157). And again:

> It is to say 'I am Scottish', when Scottishness means everything that I am: I substantiate the otherwise vacuous national label in terms of my own experience, my reading of history, my perception of the landscape, and my reading of Scotland's literature and music, so that when I 'see' the nation, I am looking at myself.
>
> (A.P. Cohen, 1996: 805)

This is the personalisation of nation-ness, which makes it appear natural, inevitable and taken-for-granted, except in the case of the Stone of Scone, its 'glamour' does not work automatically. Neither is it reducible to a single dimension. We mentioned earlier that in Scotland a 'sense of tribe' (defining Scottishness in terms of blood, genealogy) is perhaps weaker than a 'sense of place' (in terms of residence, territory). Scotland's best-selling tabloid newspaper has run a campaign using car stickers proclaiming 'I am a real Scot from [place]' which speaks to this. 'Real-ness' is defined by residence in any town or city in the country. As the historian Christopher Smout has pointed out, it is enough to come from the town of Bathgate, for example, rather than to have a grandmother who came from Bathgate (Smout, 1994). By implication, best of all to have a granny who came from Bathgate, and to come from Bathgate yourself.

What we have here is a good example of what Bourdieu called 'habitus', a set of social arrangements which have been internalised. Commonly held dispositions make up socially defined structures, but these are also subjectively created in the sense that the individual who internalises them actively does so. Blowing one's nose, for example, is a highly individual act, but set within a taken-for-granted set of social procedures and etiquettes. 'Objectively regulated and regular without being in any way the product of obedience to rules, they can be collectively orchestrated without being the product of the organising action of the conductor' (Bourdieu, 1984: 72).

Conclusion

We are now in a position to examine how the repertoires of national identities come to be generated by the mobilisation of 'history'. This is the task of the next chapter. Identities are constructed within discourses or cultural representations which lay down how we define ourselves and the conditions under which we do so. However, as Hall has argued, identity is a point of 'suture', a meeting point between these discourses and practices which 'speak' to us, and the processes which actively involve us as 'subjects' (1996a: 5–6). Suturing, he says, should be thought of as an articulation between subjects and the cultural representations to produce identities which are 'as it were, the positions which the subject is obliged to take up while always "knowing" . . . that they are representations'. And so to history.

3

INVENTING THE PAST

History and nationalism

To have common glories in the past, a common will in the present;
to have accomplished great things together, to wish to do so again,
that is the essential condition for being a nation.

Ernest Renan's famous essay 'What is a Nation?' places 'history' at the centre of the nationalist project, but it is a history which requires careful interpretation. 'Getting history wrong' is the precondition of nationalist history because it requires not only collective remembering but collective forgetting. This 'forgetting', said Renan, 'I would go so far as to say historical error, is a crucial factor in the creation of a nation, which is why progress in historical studies often constitutes a danger for [the principle of] nationality' (1990: 11).

Traditions as inventions

The inventing of traditions, the title of a collection of essays edited by Hobsbawm and Ranger (1986), is nowadays treated with due suspicion, because we are better aware of the ways in which historical accounts are used as tools in the contemporary creation of political identities. We have grown used to the idea that history is not a product of the past, but a response to the requirements of the present. Indeed, we might say that all traditions are 'invented' insofar as they are constructed and mobilised for current political ends in some way or another. In this respect, there are no 'real' (as opposed to 'invented') traditions. The problem with this approach, however, is that it usually operates in a differential manner. The 'construction' of tradition is often a charge made against new or oppositional nationalisms rather than those of the 'centre' whose traditions are deemed matters of fact, because they are matters of power. In this chapter, we will examine examples of the mobilisation of history by nationalisms of the centre and the periphery, and suggest that all types have to be treated equally.

The conventional wisdom about inventing national traditions is that much of it occurred in Europe between the 1870s and the outbreak of the Great War in 1914. This, of course, was the period which saw the culmination of European national consciousness leading to its expression in 'world' warfare with its tragic consequences. In his useful review of 'mass-producing' traditions in this period, Eric Hobsbawm (1986) documents their role in state-building in the context of the extension of electoral democracy and the emergence of mass-politics. In d'Azeglio's famous phrase, 'We have made Italy; now we must make Italians' (Hobsbawm and Ranger, 1986: 267). This was a particular problem for that state because the cultural raw material (language, symbolism etc.) was especially weak and, we might argue with hindsight, never quite held together anyway, as the secessionary tendencies of the affluent north ('Padania') have made plain little over a century later.

However, established republics like France also indulged in nationalist reconstruction in this period. It is interesting that Bastille Day was invented in 1880 rather than 1789, and that the mass production of public monuments – 'statuomania' – reached its height in France as in other younger states in this period. Similarly, it was not until 1879 that *La Marseillaise* became the national anthem, and 14 July became the national feast in 1880. Why this should be so reflects the modernisation of European states at the end of the nineteenth century, faced with demands for democratic participation. In Eugene Weber's celebrated phrase, peasants had to be turned into Frenchmen (just as Italians had to be 'made'). Just why this was necessary so soon after a thoroughgoing revolution only a century before can be gauged from the startling fact that by the 1860s, fully a quarter of the French population did not speak the language. 'In short', says Weber, 'French was a foreign language for a substantial number of Frenchmen, including almost half the children who would reach adulthood in the last quarter of the century' (1977: 67). This was an issue in rural and southern parts of the country (where 'langue d'oc' rather than 'langue d'oil' had been the norm), but it is surprising in a state as recently formed and thoroughly revolutionised as France. Weber comments:

> There is a story told in a Peruvian novel about Indian peasants who thought that a war with Chile was being waged against a general of that name, and were nonplussed when told that Chile was one country and Peru another to which they belonged. To be sure, few French peasants could have been that uninformed, but one may still wonder what their image of their country was, how much they knew about the country to which they belonged.
>
> (Weber, 1977: 108)

In contrast, the concept of 'France' as '*une ensemble d'idées*' which Renan espoused about the same time in his famous essay was probably too elitist and rarefied for the peasantry whose world was much more local and personalised. The key institutions which 'made Frenchmen', according to Weber, were the village school system of the Third Republic, the fact that education became useful as a means of social mobility up and away from the countryside, and above all, the sequence of wars with Prussia/Germany which induced conscription. The French state also supplied the first modern maps of the country soon after the Franco-Prussian war, so that 'by 1881, few classrooms however small, appear to have lacked a map' (Weber 1977: 334), and the image of the national hexagon began to be both recognised and hegemonic. Weber comments that the famous geographical icon can be seen as a colonising symbol reflecting a complex of internal territories conquered, annexed and integrated into the political and administrative whole. Despite the revolution, the Catholic church remained dominant, and by the 1870s, 98 per cent of the population was considered Catholic, leading to the rhetorical question: '*Dieu, est-il français?*', especially because French as opposed to patois was the language for addressing God and the gentry.

The idea of 'France' which began as an elite concept was extended by a process akin to colonisation through communication (roads, railways and above all by the newspapers – '*le papier qui parle*') so that by the end of the nineteenth century popular and elite culture had come together after a break of two centuries. Three major cultural innovations had helped to bring this about (Hobsbawm, 1986): education – the development of the secular equivalent of the church, sometimes both competing with and complementing it; the invention of public ceremonies such as Bastille Day; and the mass production of public monuments. Of these, none was more powerful in its iconography than Jeanne d'Arc on the one hand, and 'Marianne' on the other.

National iconography

In many respects, these two female icons were in competition with each other. On the one hand, Jeanne d'Arc was a fairly shadowy and episodic figure before the Revolution, being in turn a serving girl and a serving maid, but neither a symbol nor a saint until so elevated by the Catholic church in the 1870s and subsequently canonised in the 1920s (Gadoffre, 1951). She came to represent the 'victor-virgin', as well as 'mother-earth'. On the other hand, Marianne began as a generic name for a host of feminine images, but is most strongly associated with republicanism, with two forms: in peacetime, as a full-breasted matron crowned with ears of corn, and in wartime as the virgin warrior, a proud but helmeted figure. The appeal to revolutionaries lay in the association with Greco-Roman antiquity, and most obviously was borrowed from the figure of Liberty on Roman coins. The name 'Marianne' seems to have been borrowed from a late eighteenth-century novel by Marivaux, and became an image not of France as such but of its republican regime: 'The change in sex of the national image on the fall of the monarchy represents the assertion of virility of an adult people which has cast off the paternal authority of the monarch, and regards the state no longer as a father to be obeyed, but as a spouse to be adored' (Gadoffre, 1951: 583).

The ways in which nations and regimes come to be personified thus are complex, especially as the iconography operates for opponents as well as supporters, albeit in different ways. Marianne, for example, was given a slightly lewd connotation, especially for monarchists, which was not difficult given that in the original novel she was depicted as a woman of easy virtue. Symbols can be inverted by opponents into hostile stereotypes. Thus, 'John Bull, for Germany becomes a caddish, insolent ogre; Uncle Sam, for Europe, a desiccated, heartless Shylock; and the German Michel for France, a sly double-crossing fool; in the same way that Marianne is all too easily transformed into a flighty harum-scarum' (ibid.: 584). As the popular press developed, and with it political cartoons, the personification of nations, both supportive and hostile, reinforced national self-identity as Hobsbawm points out:

> The point about the 'Deutsche Michel' is that his image stressed both the innocence and simple-mindedness so readily exploited by cunning foreigners, and the physical strength he could mobilise to frustrate their knavish tricks and conquests when finally roused. 'Michel' seems to have been essentially an anti-foreign image.
>
> (Hobsbawm, 1986: 276)

The promotion of 'national' figures should not be seen as a means of communicating with illiterate peoples, for they multiplied at the point at which mass education took off. The main purpose of schooling of this sort was to imbue pupils with the new patriotism rather than simply to teach them new technical skills such as reading, writing and counting. This can be seen in the mobilisation of 'national' history and geography, and the 'national' curriculum (a concern of a late twentieth-century Conservative government rather than a late nineteenth-century one).

The social construction of history can often be seen in cases where there are competing accounts on offer or changes over time. For example, as Robert Anderson (1995) shows, the curriculum for teaching (especially history) in Scottish schools in the late nineteenth century reflects these shifts rather well. The 1873 Code drawn up by (as it was known then) the Scotch Education Department (SED) had a greater emphasis on Scottish (over British) history than the 1886 Code which abandoned Scottish and local emphases. The political aims of at least one Schools Inspector were clear: 'one must question the value of a school history that lands a child in the midst of loose laws and looser passions, and unquestionably helps . . . to maintain sentimental Scotch antipathy to England' (Anderson, 1995: 214). However, in the 1880s there was resistance to the use of the term 'English' rather than 'British' in history textbooks, and by 1907 the SED was stressing that Scottish history was central to the curriculum, with an emphasis on Scotland's contribution to empire. The general message was that Scotland and England, once historic enemies, now formed the basis for a world empire (ibid.: 219–20).

In like manner, the icons of history are redrawn according to the political and cultural needs of the day. For example, William Wallace, that icon of Scottish national identity, was resurrected in the 1990s by Hollywood and turned into *Braveheart*. In many ways the survival of mere fragments of history is the boon to heritage makers, because it allows more easily the re-presentation of national myth. Graeme Morton shows how Wallace, despite his execution by the English state in 1305, could be refocused in the nineteenth century as the fusion of nationalism and unionism. 'During the age of nationalism', he argues, 'William Wallace secured his position as Scotland's most efficacious patriot, fulfilling the agenda of friends and foes of the Union' (Morton, 1998a). In like manner, other national figures like Jeanne d'Arc, John Bull, William Tell, Uncle Sam, Marianne, Michel and so on were based on primordial images common to most civilisations which were, as we have seen, imbued with ambivalent emotional significance. These sat alongside more abstract symbols such as 'Liberty', 'Britannia', 'Germania' and so on.

These icons were not narrowly defined in political terms either. As Taylor has pointed out: 'If John Bull symbolised anything in the early twentieth century it was the national economy, and not the British empire' (M. Taylor, 1992: 94), and its politicisation had more to do with its successful capture by the Conservative Party as defenders of manufacturing industry rather than the empire. The icon John Bull dated from 1712 in pamphlet form and in print from the 1760s when it took on an anti-Scottish character similar to John Wilkes' critique in the *North Briton* that Scots had undue influence in the British state. Nevertheless, no single political or social group ever had a monopoly over the John Bull icon because the language of patriotism was available to a wide set of interests throughout the eighteenth and nineteenth centuries, and it was to be found in critiques of taxation, constitutional liberties, the threat of foreign invasion, Catholic emancipation, Ireland, Europe (why Eurosceptics on the political Right do not mobilise it in the 1990s might have something to do with its rural-yeoman imagery).

The extension of the state into all corners of social life was typified by the simple postage stamp which became an implicit yet powerful icon of the nation, most obviously in the issue of historic stamps to celebrate jubilees and national occasions. In the case of the British state, it was not even thought necessary to put the name on the stamp, simply the head of the monarch, thereby reinforcing the sense of '*l'état, c'est moi*' quality of Crown identity where people were defined as subjects rather than citizens. Postage stamps, along with coins and bank notes, as well as what Billig has called 'routine flags' served to deliver the 'banal' nationalism which the state required (Billig, 1995). The supreme trick is to set up as the implicit national standard by a technique of non-naming. Thus, the British stamps do not mention the name of the state (being the first country to issue stamps is an obvious advantage); the English Football Association is 'the' FA, the English Rugby Football Union is simply RFU and so on. Other nationalisms were forced to be explicit about their naming by prefixing the national adjective ('Scottish', 'Irish', 'Welsh'), but the implicit standard was English which even denied its nationalism at all. (The parallels with implicit and explicit gendering are obvious.)

Where identities were or became problematic, these could not be taken for granted, as in the iconography of nationhood in Scotland which has jealously guarded its bank notes and its national flag(s) from the taken-for-granted supremacy of the Anglo-British state, which has in any event allowed its state flag to become a symbol of English nationalism. In like vein, sporting occasions came to take on added political and cultural value from the late nineteenth century as the nation was 'represented' in competition short of war. Thus the familiar social world, its dispositions, practices and routines, became habitualised and implicit, but carrying powerful messages about who 'we' are and where and who we had come from. Billig has captured this implicitness in his comment that 'the nation is flagged, but the flagging itself is forgotten as the nation is mindlessly remembered' (1995: 143–4). The use of terms like 'we' and 'us' and 'around the country' acknowledge the sense of place. At the same time, the world is shrunk. The US has its 'world series' in baseball (and Scotland its 'world pipe band championship') so shrinking the world to the concerns of place and people.

Mobilising history

The weight of research has been on the ways in which states mobilised national iconography in the nineteenth century with a view to strengthening political legitimacy at a time when extending the franchise was both necessary and risky for the *status quo*. Writers like Hobsbawm have no difficulty with such an interpretation, but tend to view similar uses by nationalists in the late twentieth century as inappropriate to the conditions of the times. Before we assess whether they are right or not, we ought to give some instances of the ways in which 'history' continues to be mobilised by nationalists today. Two might suffice, taken from different points in the West.

In its appeal to the voters of Quebec (slogan: '*Je me souviens*') in the referendum in 1995 which it lost narrowly, the Parti Quebecois government mobilised the past as the ally of the present as follows:

> The time has come to reap the fields of history. The time has come at last to harvest what has been sown for us by four hundred years of men and women and courage, rooted in the soil and now returned to it.
>
> The time has come for us, tomorrow's ancestors, to make ready for our descendants harvests that are worthy of the labours of the past. May our toil be worthy of them, may they gather us together at last.
>
> (Bill 1, An Act respecting the future of Quebec, preamble,
> Declaration of Sovereignty, 1995)

The key descriptor in this passage is 'tomorrow's ancestors' which encapsulates the seamless quality of the past, present and future, the continuity and coherence of the people of Quebec moving, in Benedict Anderson's phrase, 'up and down history' (1996a: 26). The images are those of sowing and reaping in the 'fields of history', of 'harvests', of 'soil', of 'toil', of 'labours of the past' which cast a duty on the present incumbents and descendants of the early settlers four hundred years ago. There can be little doubt what the present population was expected to do, although insufficient numbers did this duty to have Bill 1 pass.

The other example is taken from the Constitution of the Republic of Croatia which came into being in the early 1990s amid the ruins of the former Yugoslavia. The opening section – historical foundations – is reproduced in full here as it captures Anderson's notion of the nation 'moving calendrically' through time. The time sequences are highlighted because they suggest a seamless continuity, even at those historical conjunctures which would seem to offer embarrassment, such as the fascist regime of the 1940s:

> The millennial national identity of the Croatian nation and the continuity of its statehood, confirmed by the course of its entire historical experience in various statal forms and by the perpetuation and growth of one's own state, based on the Croatian nation's historical right to full sovereignty, manifested itself:
>
> * in the formation of Croatian principalities in the seventh century;
> * in the independent mediaeval state of Croatia founded in the ninth century;
> * in the Kingdom of Croats established in the tenth century;
> * in the preservation of the subjectivity of the Croatian state in the Croatian–Hungarian personal union;
> * in the autonomous and sovereign decision of the Croatian Sabor of 1527 to elect a king from the Habsburg dynasty;
> * in the conclusions of the Croatian Sabor of 1848 regarding the integrity of the Triune Kingdom of Croatia under the power of the Ban, on the basis of the historical statal and natural right of the Croatian nation;
> * in the Croato-Hungarian Compromise of 1868 regulating the relations between the Kingdom of Dalmatia, Croatia and Slavonia and the Kingdom of Hungary, on the basis of the legal traditions of both states and the Pragmatic Sanction of 1712;
> * in the decision of the Croatian Sabor of October 29, 1918, to dissolve state relations between Croatia and Austro-Hungary and the simultaneous affiliation of independent Croatia, invoking its historical and natural right as a nation, with the State of the Slovenes, Croats and Serbs, proclaimed on the theretofore territory of the Habsburg Monarchy;
> * in the fact that the Croatian Sabor never sanctioned the decision of the national Council of the State of Slovenes, Croats and Serbs to unite with Serbia and Montenegro in the Kingdom of Serbs, Croats and Slovenes (December 1, 1918), subsequently (October 3, 1929) proclaimed the Kingdom of Yugoslavia;
> * in the establishment of the Banovina of Croatia in 1939 by which Croatian state identity was restored in the Kingdom of Yugoslavia;
> * in laying the foundations of state sovereignty during the Second World War, through the decisions of the Antifascists Council of the

National Liberation of Croatia (1943), as counter to the proclamation of the Independent State of Croatia (1941), and subsequently in
the Constitution of the People's Republic of Croatia (1947), and
several later constitutions of the Socialist Republic of Croatia
(1963–1990). At the historic turn-point marked by the rejection of
the communist system and changes in the international order in
Europe, the Croatian nation reaffirmed at the first democratic elections (1990) by its freely expressed will its millennial statehood and
resolution to establish the Republic of Croatia as a sovereign state.

Constitution of the Republic of Croatia

We can see from this presentation of 'historical facts' that Croatia has awarded
itself calendrical status, moving down through history in a linear way towards its
self-determined destiny. The time-points are as sign-posts on the way: the seventh
century – the ninth century – the tenth century – 1527 – 1712 – 1848 – 1868 –
1918 – 1929 – 1939 – 1943 – 1947 – 1963 – 1990. Where episodes of history are
potentially embarrassing such as the fascist period, an alternative and politically
acceptable medium – the [legitimate] Antifascists Council of the National
Liberation of Croatia (1943) – is juxtaposed with the [illegitimate] fascist
Independent State of Croatia (1941).

What we have here is an up-to-date example of what virtually all states attempt,
namely, the capturing of history in the national interest. In Homi Bhabha's useful
phrase, nations are like 'narratives' which tell themselves and others stories about
who they are and where they have come from. History and the nation are insepa-
rable. To recapitulate Anderson's description: 'the idea of a sociological organism
moving calendrically through homogeneous empty time is a precise analogue of
the idea of the nation which is also conceived as a social community moving
steadily down (or up) history' (Anderson, 1996a: 26).

The point about this mobilisation of history is that it is an exercise in legitimation; it is not to be taken as a history lesson in the sense that it is an accurate
account of the past (although its authors clearly intend this to be the case). We
might characterise it as 'myth-history' in the sense that it sets out to celebrate identity and associated values, and to describe and explain the world in which such
identity and values are experienced. No amount of (or at least not much) cold
water can be poured over the 'facts' as presented in an attempt to wash them away
with an accurate history. Just as there is no such thing as 'real' traditions (as
opposed to invented ones) – all are invented, constructed, in Anderson's word,
imagined – so tradition is an appeal to the present, not the past. Karl Marx recognised this in his celebrated comment in the 'Eighteenth Brumaire':

> and just as when they seemed engaged in revolutionising themselves and
> things, in creating something that has never existed, precisely in such
> periods of revolutionary crisis, they anxiously conjure up the spirits of the
> past to their service and borrow from them names, battle cries and

costumes in order to present the new scene of world history in this time-honoured disguise and borrowed language

(Marx, 1959: 320)

The point Marx was making here is that inventing traditions is most often done precisely at the moment when change is being fostered, at the point at which it is necessary to mobilise the past as justification for going forward in a new direction. To present the future as a radical break with the past is difficult and dangerous, and while revolutionary regimes sometimes succeed in so doing, they frequently have to call up national, historic ghosts when it is necessary. After all, Stalin opted to mobilise a 'patriotic' war with all its historic richness against Hitler's regime in 1940. Less dramatically, the Scottish National Party, which steadfastly eschewed linking itself to an 'older' Scotland, sought to make political capital out of the Oscar-winning movie *Braveheart* which bore only a passing resemblance to historical events.

Much depends on how history connects with the political and cultural context. For example, the dominant style of historical scholarship in Japan has been '*Kokkahattenshi*', the style of history which emphasises the development of the state (Irumada, 1997). This style stressed the process of nation-building and helped to legitimate the rule of central government, and the expansion of national territories. Such a history downplayed the cultural and ethnic diversity of the country, and implied the peaceful incorporation of the northern territories of Tohoku and Hokkaido into the state system. Only in recent years, and especially following the collapse of communism, has there been a revival of 'regional' history (*Chiikishi*).

Narrating the nation

All in all, the 'past' is a powerful source of legitimacy for those who would change the present for a new future. Stuart Hall (1996b) has pointed to the significance of 'discursive strategies' in the telling of national cultures. The 'narrative' of the nation is told and retold through national histories, literatures, the media and popular culture, which together provide a set of stories, images, landscapes, scenarios, historical events, national symbols and rituals. Through these stories national identity is presented as primordial, essential, unified and continuous. People of the late twentieth century are linked in a linear fashion with those of the distant past, even those – like fourteenth-century peasants in the case of the Hollywood movie *Braveheart* – with whom they manifestly would have little in common. To borrow the words of the English novelist L.P. Hartley, the past is a foreign country. The national 'story' usually contains a foundation myth, a story which locates the origin of the nation in mythic time, and which provides an alternative history or counter-narrative predating ruptures or dispossessions. Becoming 'a nation again' is to evoke a future imaginable throughout the past. This nation is thought of as containing a pure, original people or folk.

Anthony Smith tries to capture this through his concept of 'ethnie' in which the myth of a common ancestry and shared historical memories are key elements. 'The sense of "whence we came" is central to the definition of "who we are"' (Smith 1991: 22). Similarly, actual history is often forgotten in favour of a foundational legend. Hence, those involved in the nineteenth-century liberation struggle in Greece claimed their legend of antiquity, as the founders of democracy who could not possibly be denied what they themselves had bequeathed to the rest of the world (Herzfeld, 1992). In like manner, claiming to be 'God's chosen people' is a common enough feature of many ethnic/national groups for all of whom it cannot be true (unless more than one God is imagined or s/he is promiscuous with favours). Hence, Jews, Muslims and denominations of Christians from Poles (Catholic) to Scots (Presbyterian) to English (Protestant) are able to identify themselves in this favourable light, especially *vis-à-vis* 'Godless' nations who may have superior force but not God on their side.

None of this is, of course, enough without a priesthood, religious or secular, which is able to read the appropriate runes, and to pronounce on the uniqueness of the nation. The intelligentsia provide the successors to the ecclesiastical priesthood. In Smith's words: 'Instead of being merely a chosen vessel of religious salvation and a passive recipient of divine ordinance, the "people" now become the source of salvation and the saints and sages of old become manifestations of the people's national genius' (Smith, 1991: 64). The role of the intelligentsia is to furnish 'maps' of the community, its history, destiny and place, as well as to furnish 'moralities' to inspire the public virtues expressing the national character.

The means of so doing was aided by the shift away from Latin to vernacular languages. We saw in the last chapter that English national identity was largely constructed by means of 'the book', linking Protestantism and the means of its dissemination through English (Greenfeld, 1992). Benedict Anderson (1983 and 1996a) shows how the development of 'print-languages' laid the basis for national consciousness in three ways: it created unified fields of communication and exchange which reached beyond and below the elite; print-capitalism gave a new fixity to language, manifested via official dictionaries, grammars and etymologies; and print-capitalism created languages of power such as 'standard English', and 'HochDeutsch' which were elevated to new politico-cultural eminence. This association of linguistic distinctiveness with national culture became so strong that language was often taken as the root, the expression of such culture, even when (as in the case of the Quebecois) that language 'belongs' to another people. Similarly, where the vernacular language was absent (as in the case of the Scots, give or take debates about versions of 'English'), many scholars deemed this a considerable drawback for national self-determination (Anderson, 1996a: 90). Be that as it may, in Anderson's words: 'the convergence of capitalism and print technology on the fatal diversity of human language created the possibility of a new form of an imagined community, which in its basic morphology set the stage for the modern nation' (ibid.: 46).

The 'capture' of history took its obvious expression in the founding of national museums in which the nation's 'heritage' could be shown to best advantage. The tale could best be told by constructing a narrative involving a golden age, a period in history when the nation was 'itself', and thence could be found again. The late nineteenth century was an important period for (re)constructing the national legends. In Ireland, for example, 'the vision of an ethnic golden age told modern Irish men and women what was "authentically theirs", and how to be "themselves" once again in a free Ireland' (Smith, 1991: 67). This was especially important in colonial situations in which people were culturally and ethnically treated as inferior. Finding one's culture was a key part of the national endeavour, not an optional extra (see Fanon, 1967). Anderson argues that the colonial rulers of Southeast Asia at first showed little interest in the monuments of previous civilisations in the conquered lands, but that they came to see the ideological benefit of being able to show, in architecture, that the original builders of these monuments were superior to the colonial natives they encountered themselves. In other words, the message went: 'Our very presence shows that you have always been, or have become, incapable of either greatness or self-rule' (1996a: 181). Further, monumental archaeology linked with tourism allowed the state to appear as the guardian of 'tradition', especially as these were depicted as bereft of people so that they were 'repositioned as regalia for a secular colonial state' (ibid.: 182). When post-colonial states inherited this kind of political museumising, they were able to use it to advantage to claim for themselves a lineage of heritage which legitimised their own rule. Thus, in Mexico City there is only one statue of Cortes, and that was erected in the 1970s in an unprominent place by a desperate regime (Anderson, 1996a: 199). More spectacularly, the national Museum of Anthropology in Mexico City is virtually a claim for the lineage of the Aztec empire with no mention whatsoever made of the Spanish influence. This is rewriting history with a vengeance.

Where culture was missing, or at best embryonic, it had to be 'made'. The Finns, for example, embraced the ballads and poems of the Kalevala, based as these were on Karelia, as their land of heroes, which was also part of the frontier of the nation in geo-political and cultural terms. If the region was the fount of the people's culture as well as a frontier zone, it had to be fought for lest the culture disappear. Nor was Finland unique. As Neal Ascherson pointed out:

> We talk easily about the forging of a nation, but forgery has played a very real part in the foundation or revival of many nations. In Scotland, we should know that better than most. Ossian was a forgery, but the emotions about nations and history roused by James Macpherson's pastiche of genuine Gaelic myth cycles was real enough. Finland's national epic, the Kalevala, emerged rather later, but doesn't bear close inspection either.
>
> (Ascherson, 1988: 61)

What the quest for a national culture did was to generate a search for, and a gathering together of, ethno-history. This took the form of setting up national galleries, museums and academies to capture and celebrate the nation. 'National' art was cultivated in the form of painting, sculpture, architecture, music and so on. If national art did not exist, then it was the role of artists to invent it, or at least discover or recover it from the fragments of the people's culture (hence the interest in folk song and folk art). Many artists became in turn synonymous with national culture, as Smith points out – examples being Chopin, Liszt, Dvorak, Bartok, Elgar, Verdi, Wagner, Grieg, and Sibelius. He comments:

> It is the intellectuals – poets, musicians, painters, sculptors, novelists, historians and archeologists, playwrights, philologists, anthropologists and folklorists – who have proposed and elaborated the concepts and language of the nation and nationalism, and have, through their musings and research, given voice to wider aspirations that they have conveyed in appropriate images, myths and symbols.
>
> (Smith, 1991: 93)

Hence, there is a strong, but by no means inevitable, association of a cultural renaissance with political developments. In those countries, like Scotland, where the association was more complex, many argued that its national culture was 'deformed' and that this itself led to the failure to pursue the political goal of independence (Beveridge and Turnbull, 1989). Others argued that in this regard Scotland was a deviant case (thereby reinforcing the dominant thesis, albeit obliquely), an exception which proved the general rule. Having said that, the cultural renaissances of the 1930s and the 1970s have both been linked to a political upsurge in nationalism, so that Scottish exceptionalism need no longer apply.

Placing the nation

If there was a resurgence of interest in time (history, connecting the past-present-future), then a corresponding enthusiasm grew for mapping the nation, discovering its place. We are familiar enough with territorial disputes over 'national' land, where the significance of the 'soil' is sacred. The Serbian legend that the soil of Serbia is that on which any Serbian blood has been spilled is merely an exaggerated version of this. Benedict Anderson's comments about mapping colonial territory also have lessons for 'home'. He points out that the map is to space what the clock is to time – a form of representation laden with power implications. We have naturalised these devices so that maps and clocks *are* place and time rather than their representation. Only in cases where different cultures dispute the meaning and hence the use of land does it become contentious, as in the clash between the Inuit and Whites in Northern Canada, so that the two meanings simply cannot coexist so fundamental are their contradictions (Brody, 1988). In these instances, the powerful win out.

Maps depict 'property spaces' or sovereignties in which the power order is implicit but nevertheless clear. For example, as the geographer Peter Taylor (1993) has pointed out, the language used to describe England is as follows: the core is the 'Home Counties', and the peripheries are 'the North', the 'West Country', the 'Midlands' (not the 'centre' of power, of course), and so on. This power map correlates clearly with the distribution of royal establishments, so that few exist on the periphery. Power is implicitly centred by such devices.

Anderson comments on the mental power of the map as logo, as a pure sign of the country in its outline. 'In its shape, the map entered an infinitely reproducible series, available for transfer to posters, official seals, letterheads, magazines and textbook covers, table cloths and hotel walls. Instantly recognisable, everywhere visible, the logo-map penetrated deep into the popular imagination, forming a powerful emblem for the anti-colonial nationalism being born' (1996a: 175). While Anderson gives the examples of the Third World, there are some anomalies which are worth thinking about. We have little trouble 'imagining' France, Italy, Spain (though usually incorrectly equating it with the Iberian peninsula), and Germany has had to be redrawn after unification between East and West. 'Britain' is imaginable only in a fuzzy way – does it include Northern Ireland or not (usually not), whereas 'Ireland' is the island rather than the territory of the Republic. 'Scotland' is a familiar logo representing as it does a northern peninsula, but 'England' is largely conspicuous by its representational absence except in its incorrect manifestation as the British island (an error deliberately compounded by Shakespeare with his comment about it being set in a silver sea: he was reinforcing the point of *English* ownership of this island). It is unlikely that many of its current nationals would easily recognise England from its strict geographical outline alone.

Representing the nation is as much a question of geography as it is of history. The historian Simon Schama (1996) argues that national identity would lose much of its 'ferocious enchantment' without the mystique of a particular landscape tradition: 'its topography mapped, elaborated, and enriched as a homeland' (1996: 15). This process may involve taking liberties with landscape. Schama reminds us that the engravings by the eighteenth-century artist Paul Sandby of a view in Strathtay in Scotland showed a marked increase in the elevation of the mountains between 1747 and 1780 to conform with expectations of what mountains should be like.

Imagining the nation implies that it has a picture, and Schama argues that landscapes are culture before they are nature, that they are constructs of the imagination projected onto wood and water and rock. German culture was seen as rooted in its native soil, and such a vision drove Herder, the romantic nationalist, to view the essence of the nation as organically rooted in the topography, customs and communities of the local native tradition (ibid.: 102). Germania – forest – contrasted with Roma – city, with the forests the home of *Gemeinschaft*. Indeed, as a result, forestry became a serious academic and scientific discipline, helping to define *Deutschtum* – Germanness. This obsession with the forest patently influenced German romantic nationalism, but also those on the Left like Walter Benjamin. They had shared contempt for bourgeois urban materialism (ibid.: 117). '*Germanentum*', the idea of a biologically pure race, meant that German racial and national distinctiveness were attributed to its woodland heritage.

The English, says Schama, are not immune from this phenomenon. The mythic memory of 'greenwood freedom' was prime material for nineteenth-century novels, including Walter Scott's *Ivanhoe* in which Anglo-Saxon rural liberties were contrasted with Norman tyranny. The woodland was deemed the locale of liberty, despite the fact that by 1066, only 15 per cent of England was wooded. Nevertheless, 'The forest as the opposite of court, town and village – the sylvan remnant of arcady, or what Shakespeare called the "golden world" – was an idea that would lodge tenaciously in the poetic and pious imagination' (ibid.: 142). Into or out of this world came figures like Robin Hood, 'an elegy for a world of liberty and justice that had never existed' (ibid.: 149). The popularisation of these tales came precisely at the time (in the late sixteenth century) when the woodlands were being pressed into service for ship-building. These were being cut down as the governments played the panegyric for the greenwood, and as the royal forests were being treated as early industrial resources. The language of Hearts of Oak was used to connect both trees and ships.

What is interesting about this English narrative is that it runs across what MacDougall (1982) calls the 'racial myth' of English history. Celebrating the freedom of Anglo-Saxon England *vis-à-vis* Norman despotism and order is an old and continuing motif. He argues that the myth arose in the sixteenth century in response to complex religious and political needs, and matured over the next three centuries in step with England's imperial status. The myth incorporated a Teutonic element, and had four postulates: that German peoples as a result of unmixed origins and their universal civilising mission were inherently superior to others; that the English were mainly of German origin, and their history begins with the landings of Hengist and Horsa in Kent in AD 449; that the qualities of English political and religious institutions, the freest in the world, derived from its Germanic forebears; and finally, that the English, more than other Germanic peoples, represented the traditional genius of their ancestors, and so have a special burden of leadership in the world community.

The Anglo-Saxon myth still has its uses. The Eurosceptic Conservative MP, Richard Body, when asked in 1995 to define Englishness for the political magazine *New Statesman and Society*, replied:

> Surely Englishness is grounded on Anglo-Saxon values. Before the Normans came to conquer and corrupt, England was far more demo-cratic than today; everyone's voice was heard in a society of plain-living and plain-speaking, where extremes of wealth and poverty were not permitted, and where personal freedom abounded, blended with a sense of community.
>
> The Anglo-Saxons were libertarian, and believed in vigorous freedom of speech, which led to truth in a trial by jury, as much as in the Witan. The Englishness mocked in *NSS* [*New Statesman and Society*] belongs to the Normans. Snobbish, conformist, pageant-adoring and hard of heart, the

Normans introduced a contrast, which has given England two distinct streams that have mingled uneasily.

(*New Statesman and Society*, 24 February 1995: 39)

This caricaturing of England into Norman and Anglo-Saxon owes little to history and more to ideology. It is an enduring myth which celebrates the indigenous values of liberty and democracy, with alien ones of order, regulation and conformity. It has its own counterpart in a similar but inverted caricature in Scotland between the 'Celt' and the 'Anglo-Saxon', but this time the latter is the 'other'. We might set up these antinomies as follows:

CELT	ANGLO-SAXON
feminine	masculine
community	society
feeling	reason
nature	culture
left	right

What we are dealing with here are not simple caricatures but antinomies of *Gemeinschaft* and *Gesellschaft* familiar to sociologists. The former symbolised an organically bonded community, and the latter a mechanistically organised society. The purpose of this antinomy is not to describe actual societies but to locate its moral virtue in the personal, the immediate, the social. Mobilising the 'Celtic' against the alien has been done by the Irish and the Scots, and in the 1990s provides a new identity template for East Europeans struggling in a world dominated by impersonal forces of economic and political power (Chapman, 1992).

What is surprising about Richard Body's comments in *New Statesman and Society* is that they come from an Englishman – in general, large and powerful nations do not need to mobilise in this way. His views plainly are driven by feelings of marginalisation and alienation from centres of power, in this instance the European Union, and implicitly, that which is French/Norman. The powerful do not usually need to define the 'other', and as a consequence there is very little on 'English' nationalism as such. As Bernard Crick observes: 'Look under "nationalism" in the subject catalogue of any great library: under sub-headings you will find, obviously, Italian, French, German, Polish nationalism and so on, certainly Irish and Scottish, possibly Welsh; but under 'English' either very few books or none' (1995: 171). Being English is rarely articulated, merely assumed. The same issue of *New Statesman and Society* which carried the comment by Richard Body MP was devoted to an examination of 'Englishness' (despite Body's view that the terms of reference were 'Norman'). G.K. Chesterton's comment: 'Smile at us, pay us; but do not quite forget; For we are the people of England, that have never spoken yet' is enigmatic to the point of invisibility. (At the 1997 general election, the independent MP, journalist Martin Bell, found it an appropriate epitaph for his victory in the constituency of Tatton over his Conservative opponent Neil Hamilton.) The comment by the popular actress Barbara Windsor: 'I always laugh when Scottish people and Irish people want to be different. We're all British, we're all the same', is plain confused; and Tony Benn's terse 'I don't believe in Englishness; I'm a socialist', sweeps away national identity as politically unimportant and misleading. Bernard Crick (1993) has made the observation that 'Englishness' has, since the 1707 Treaty of Union which created the United Kingdom, presented political problems to the state that Scottish, Welsh and Irish nationalism did not (at least to the same degree). The presence of so many English nationals asserting their Englishness (over their Britishness) would have called into question the foundations of the state itself. As a consequence, says Crick, Englishness went underground, only to re-emerge when the assertion of 'Celtic' forms of nationalism and the perceived threat to 'national' sovereignty from Europe called it up.

We can see then that nationalisms ebb and flow, that explicit forms tend to be oppositional, and that powerful nationalism – frequently calling itself 'patriotism' – is usually implicit. How better to handle counter-nationalisms than by denying them a powerful 'other' against which to measure themselves? History is a vital ingredient in constructing the nation. The Conservative thinker Roger Scruton comments: 'People united by language, association and territory triumph and suffer together. An historical narrative is manifest in the very associations which serve to combine them, and the memory of it is attached to the landscapes, the towns, the institutions and the climate by which they are surrounded' (Scruton, 1990: 71). In these terms, both powerful and subordinate nations use history to their advantage. Scruton's own account of England focuses its 'authoritarian individualism', its mix of strong if implicit nationalism and personal liberties. The assertion of this in recent years relates to its perceived erosion by threats to the British Union from without and within.

Living and dying histories

This brings us to an important point in the argument. All nations have 'histories' – otherwise they would not exist as 'imagined communities'; they would, in Gellner's phrase, be nations without navels. But history often does not have a future; it can be 'over'. In other words, we can find instances of 'dead' history which does not connect with present and future tenses, which is no longer deemed relevant. Similarly, history can be reconnected to the concerns of the present and future, and be made to 'live' again. This depends vitally on the use to which it can be put.

To exemplify this, let us examine the changing fortunes of Scottish and British 'history'. In the first case, it was deemed to have 'ended' in 1707, only to be reactivated in the second half of the twentieth century. In the case of Britain, the vitality of this 'forged' nation (as Colley describes it) seems to have ebbed away as a project for the future. The two processes are clearly connected.

Scotland has no shortage of history; indeed, it can be argued that it has too much. By this I mean that for much of the past three hundred years Scotland was deemed to be 'over'. Its identity lay firmly in the past, obviously before the Treaty of Union of 1707 when it was an independent state. Thereafter, its elites came to believe that the future belonged to the political entity of 'Britain', whereas the past was Scottish (Kidd, 1993). This is best typified by the comment usually attributed to Walter Scott that the 'heart' was Scottish, but the 'head' British. In other words, while one could be culturally a Scot, politically progressive forces had to be British, for to be British was to be enlightened, rational and forward-looking. Construing identity as dual and complementary became the order of the day.

A dominant expression of this in the mid-nineteenth century was what has been called 'unionist-nationalism', the fusion of a Scottish past with a British future. Graeme Morton (1994) has argued that, in the mid-nineteenth century, a view prevailed which held that only because Scotland won and retained her independence in 1314 was she able to enter the Union of 1707 as an equal partner with England in the British state. The National Association for the Vindication of Scottish Rights, for example, which was founded in 1853, expressed a sense of patriotism which allowed it to proclaim admiration for its partner, England. Similarly, the erection of the monument in Edinburgh to Walter Scott which was begun in 1833 stresses the Scottish contribution to English heritage. And perhaps more surprisingly (given Scott's political Toryism), those who raised funds for the erection of monuments to the two prime Scottish patriots, William Wallace and Robert the Bruce, did so by stressing their contribution to the Union. The Earl of Elgin, who claimed descent from Bruce, took the chair at the inauguration in 1856 of the movement to build the Wallace monument, and spoke in the following terms:

> if the Scottish people have been able to form an intimate union and association with a people more wealthy and more numerous than themselves, without sacrificing one jot of their neutral independence and liberty – these great results are due to the glorious struggle which was commenced on the plain of Stirling and consummated on that of Bannockburn. . . . And, gentlemen, if time permitted, I would even undertake to show that it is the successful struggle carried on under Bruce and Wallace that it is only the Union between Scotland and England has not only been honourable to the former but profitable to the latter . . . [With reference to the troubles in America and Ireland] I believe, therefore, that if the whole truth were to be told in this matter, we might show that England owes to Wallace and Bruce a debt of obligation only second to that which is due to them by Scotland.
>
> (Morton, 1994: 215)

What we have here is a nice instance of how history can be mobilised for political purposes quite different from what we would expect today, for in the late twentieth century Wallace and Bruce are icons of independence, not union (see, for example, the genre of heroic movies on the subjects). There is another twist to the Wallace/Bruce representation which speaks to the present, an embryonic class conflict, with Wallace the commoner and Bruce the aristocrat. The late Marinell Ash (1980) gave an interesting account of this construction, pointing out that popular histories often treated Wallace as the plain-speaking forerunner of democracy and Bruce as the devious aristocrat, a piece of myth-history employed by the makers of the Hollywood movie *Braveheart* to give it added connection to current political concerns.

Playing the game of history is a fairly common pursuit in Scotland. Much of it gets written as a version of Scotland versus England, when even a cursory review of events and personages like Culloden, Glencoe, Mary Queen of Scots and so on indicates that life was much more complicated than that.

Nevertheless, historical events and processes can be threaded together in such a way as to present a continuous narrative. Pictish resistance to the Romans (and Saxons) reinforces the warlike reputation of the Scots, and allows film-makers to present the thirteenth-century lowlander William Wallace as a third-century Pict. The Celts in general provide an important myth of origin, and an alternative set of values to southern Anglo-Saxons. The capture of St Andrew as Scotland's national saint owes more to the politics of ecclesiastical claims of the English diocese of York than to any actual connection between St Peter's brother, Andrew, and the northern kingdom. Claiming from the Pope, Peter's successor, such high-level protection helped to see off the southern claim. It helped too that an apparition of St Andrew could be claimed by the Pictish king Hungus prior to his battle with the Anglian Athelstane in AD 345. Having recourse to the papacy in the fourteenth century by means of the self-styled Declaration of Arbroath helped to consolidate independence fought for at Bannockburn in 1314, even though the document came to prominence only at the end of the seventeenth century in a bid to stave off impending Union with England. Establishing legitimacy through history, this time as lineage, was the purpose of the deWit portraits of the early monarchs of Scotland in an attempt in the 1680s to shore up the regal claims of the late Stewart kings, Charles I and II (Bruce and Yearley, 1989).

What is interesting about such snippets of legend is not that they were unique to Scotland, but that they could be mobilised when current political events demanded it. Plainly, they were of little use in the early eighteenth century in preventing the Treaty of Union, but had their own validation of that event in proving that Scotland was a historic nation entering a formal treaty with its large, southern neighbour. As such, however, Scotland was 'over' by this time, and its history was deposited in the past. The future was British.

Linda Colley (1992) has shown convincingly how the new state of Britain was 'forged', both in the sense of being hammered together out of two distinct states in 1707, and also in the sense that it was fabricated somewhat artificially (in the sense of 'forgery'). War with France and the celebration of Protestant liberty helped to reinforce this new-found sense of unity, and the new state of 'Britain' could also mobilise its ancient qualities of tribal Britannia, thus incorporating Wales (Williams, 1980). A shared sense of being a Protestant 'chosen people' threatened by authoritarian Catholic states like France reinforced this new sense of political identity. Progressive opinion, which included Enlightenment thinkers, was happy to acknowledge this pan-British future as the fount of liberalism and rationalism.

What is now evident, however, is that in the late twentieth century this sense of 'Britain' has been eroded. It has largely become a matter of sentiment not reason, of the past not the future, at least to many inhabitants of these islands. The absence of war for over half a century means that connecting military events back into the past is no longer appropriate, although the small war in the Falkland Islands in the early 1980s achieved short-term political success for Mrs Thatcher, at least in England. Treating 'Britain' as 'England' shows continuity over a thousand years, but imperial decline and Celtic alienation from this interpretation of history show up its limitations as a state-national myth. At the same time, nationalists on the periphery take on the task of showing that British history is 'over', painting it as a brief interlude in the long journey of the national (Scottish, Irish, Welsh, even English) entities in these islands. Just as Scottish history, in 1707, was 'dead' history, over and done with, so it seems that in the late twentieth century 'British' (as opposed to English) history now seems 'over'. The connections no longer work, or if they do, it is through the national histories rather than a single state history.

We have taken the examples of Scottish and British histories to make the point that it is how history is used that matters rather than the availability of the raw historical materials. 'History' may often be dormant – concerned with the past – while it can also be 'charged' with connecting the past-present-future in a national narrative. When and why this happens depends on the political and cultural circumstances of the day. Nations can be imagined and constructed with relatively little historical straw. The Danish historian Ufe Østergård (1992) has shown how in the second half of the nineteenth century a new conception of Denmark and the Danes was shaped out of fragments of peasant experiences by Nikolaj Grundtvig in particular. His notion of 'Danishness' based on moderation and a democratic spirit as its basic virtues, linked back to the early Sagas and the Anglo-Saxon poem *Beowulf*, and out of these he fashioned a single Danish synthesis of land, country, God and people. By the twentieth century, communitarian peasant traditions of solidarity were transmitted from pre-modern village society to social democracy with attractions for a new working class. The ideology of 'everyone in the same boat' served as a class ideology for a variety of political movements, and helped to form the characterisation of Danish culture as being based on the three 'graces': *Hygge* (cosiness), *Tryghed* (security) and *Trivsel* (well-being).

Conclusion

Let us return to Renan's famous remark that nationalism involves 'getting history wrong'. He said this, not because nationalists were by and large bad historians in a technical sense, but because history was and is the central resource. There is an interesting comment by Benedict Anderson in the later editions of *Imagined Communities* (1996a) which seeks to correct an earlier comment on Renan's 'need for forgetting'. The original comment by Renan was 'tous citoyen français *doit avoir oublié* la Saint-Barthelemy, les massacres du Midi au XIIIe siècle'. Anderson accuses himself of 'peremptory syntax' in the 1983 edition by reminding himself that Renan did not say '*doit oublier*' but '*doit avoir oublié*' ('obliged to have forgotten'). That is, says Anderson, 'in effect, Renan's readers were being told to "have already forgotten" what Renan's own words assumed they naturally remembered!' (1996a: 200). In other words, the state is reminding every French person of a series of antique slaughters which had become 'family history'. 'Having to "have already forgotten" tragedies of which one needs unceasingly to be "reminded" turns out to be a characteristic device in the later construction of national genealogies' (ibid.: 201), a new form of consciousness unique to modern times.

The nation's narrative, to borrow Bhabha's phrase, involves actively forgetting as well as actively remembering. The people are not simply historical objects or events, passive parts of the body politic, but also subjects of 'a process of significa- tion that must erase any prior or original presence of the nation-people to demonstrate the prodigious, living principle of the people as that continual process by which the national life is redeemed and signified as a repeating and reproduc- tive process' (Bhabha, 1990: 297). History is not the dead weight of the past on the present, but the very means whereby identity is shaped in an active and ongoing fashioning.

4

'DEVILS AT HIS BACK'

Nationalism and Ernest Gellner

In his obituary of Ernest Gellner, John Hall commented that he wrote 'with devils at his back' (1996: v). Hall continued: 'his theory of nationalism contained a tension between dislike of its potential for political exclusion and realisation that the nation-state remained the receptacle most likely to advance citizenship' (ibid.). Gellner's theory of nationalism has undoubtedly been central to how we have come to understand the phenomenon in the last thirty years. His views have been the template for supporters and opponents alike.

Why devote a chapter to the works of one person? Put simply, the modern study of nationalism began with Ernest Gellner in the mid-1960s. Some may object that it began much sooner than that. After all, what of the work of Kuhn, Cobban, Hayes, Deutsch and others who did much to shape our modern understandings of nationalism in the early and middle years of this century? Important though their contribution was, none had the impact on modern scholarship and debate which Gellner's work has had. An analysis of citations in studies of nationalism would probably reveal that his writings are more often referred to than those of anyone else. This may seem odd to some because there is also a view that he formed his key ideas and theories in his early work on nationalism and did not deviate much from them in the course of the next thirty years. In other words, they claim, Gellner said it all in his 1964 essay in *Thought and Change,* and simply defended his position with customary vigour and stubbornness. There is of course some truth in this, and the collection of his essays entitled *Nationalism* published posthumously in 1997 lends support to this view. However, Ernest Gellner was too rich a thinker to be bound by this one small volume. His challenges to orthodoxy and his readiness to tilt at most available windmills established him as the key thinker on nationalism of the twentieth century. That is why the 'line' of this book which is concerned with forms and expressions of nationalism is broken in this central chapter by an examination of Gellner's work in this area. If there is one idea which he held to through thick and thin it was that nationalism is not some historical legacy which needs to be swept away with the detritus of the past. Rather, the condition of nationalism is central to modern society. People in contemporary societies are nationalists because they have to be.

Tensions and contradictions were the stuff of both his theories and his life. How these were connected is best summed up by his comment that it was the experience of living on the edge of so many nationalisms without properly belonging to any, without accepting their expression, which impelled him to think about nationalism (1996d). His parents came from the borderlands of Bohemia, speaking German and without considering themselves Czech, and he grew up in a Czech-Jewish household in the 1920s and 1930s in which, in his own words: 'I was somehow instructed to consider myself Czech' (ibid.: 41). He himself had no religious feelings, but retained ethnic ones, which he expressed as: 'I have a feeling of obligation to Auschwitz, not to Jerusalem' (ibid.: 42). His family went to England in the 1930s and he was taught thereafter in the English educational system.

His intellectual perspectives were explicitly shaped by where he was brought up. He commented: 'If you come from the Habsburg area you have a particular sensitivity to the tension between the positivist universalism [. . . represented by Mach, Popper, Hayek, von Mises and so on] and the organicist romanticism of the nationalists [such as Herder]' (ibid.: 43). Gellner was not a nationalist, but understood where it was coming from. He refused the conventional wisdom that it derived from atavistic, ethnicist instincts, and saw it as a fundamental and modern phenomenon. His early work (most notably *Words and Things*, 1959) showed him to be deeply hostile to linguistic philosophy, and throughout his life he rejected the philosophy of relativism, arguing that all cultures were certainly not equal.

He was a strong supporter of 'civil society', arguing that in both the Marxist and Muslim worlds the state was too strong and civil society too weak. An opponent of communism, he argued that civil society provided institutions and associations strong enough to balance the state and to prevent the monopolisation of power and tyranny. A liberal, Gellner rejected the absolutisation of the market ushered in by the New Right from the 1970s, and reinforced by the fall of communism after 1989. He dismissed over-reliance on the market mechanism as 'bad philosophical anthropology' (humans do not seek fulfilment in the accumulation of things). He attacked laissez-faire theories as based on the 'absurdity of man as the aim-pursuing animal' (1996e: 628), as being ecologically disastrous (the power of modern technology is too great to be left to its own devices), and historically inappropriate (the real culture of low-tech laissez faire existed in the late eighteenth century at the time of Adam Smith). His opposition to communism was matched with regret at its passing. It had represented a rival civilisation, one which stood for something different. He commented: 'I would have preferred a gradual ideological and institutional transition – one which would preserve the idiom and ritual of the past' (1996b: 35).

Gellner's great intellectual and personal strengths derived from this maintenance of contradictions: he was a Jew who was not a Zionist; a Czech who was shaped by German culture; a liberal who decried market forces and who regretted the passing of communism; a scholar who was equally at home in the disciplines of philosophy, social anthropology and sociology; a cosmopolitan who understood nationalism; a student of nationalism who saw it as neither necessary nor contingent. To him, nationalism is 'a phenomenon of *Gesellschaft* using the idiom of *Gemeinschaft*: a mobile anonymous society, simulating a closed community' (Gellner, 1995).

In this chapter, we will examine Gellner's account of nationalism starting with its earliest formulations, and charting how his approach and interests developed over thirty years of published work. It is interesting how other writers on nationalism have found his work unavoidable, yet all too often prone to misunderstanding given its subtleties. For example, as we saw in the previous chapter in his encounter with Anthony Smith, Gellner was often characterised as a modernist, as a writer whose sole interest lay in explaining the emergence of nationalism out of industrialism. Yet, his later work on nationalism in post-communist Eastern Europe is in a direct line of descent. Gellner's famous aphorism – 'Nationalism is not the awakening of nations to self-consciousness; it invents nations where they do not exist' (1964: 168) – is usually taken as support for the 'invention' of nationalism thesis, but few recall the rider which follows it to the effect that this cannot be done without the prior existence of 'culturally distinctive marks'. In large part, such misunderstandings derived from Gellner's delight in adopting positions contrary to conventional wisdoms in order to see where they would lead intellectually. Interpreting his work is fraught with danger because of his penchant for seeking out the counter-case, the alternative hypothesis.

The Gellner aphorism about nations and nationalism is to be found in his early comments in *Thought and Change* published in 1964. His essay on nationalism in that volume laid out the original formulation which was embellished in his later work in the 1990s when he was stimulated to make sense of nationalism once more following the fall of communism. In between, he was fond of saying that he had nothing more to say on the subject beyond what he had written up to 1983 when *Nations and Nationalism* was published. The refinement of his theory, as he put it (Gellner, 1996a: 111), took the form of postulating five stages on the path from a world of non-ethnic empires to one of homogeneous nation states. His later interest in Eastern and Central Europe coincided with the publication by Miroslav Hroch, a fellow Czech, of his book *The Social Preconditions of National Revival in Europe* in 1985. While Eric Hobsbawm is usually credited with its becoming available in English, it seems to be much closer to Gellner's approach to nationalism than Hobsbawm's own pessimistic account.

Hroch's attempt to periodise nationalist movements according to their connection with material conditions was not accepted by Gellner who found it too willing to take nations for granted; we will examine Hroch's thesis in detail later in this chapter. It is, however, worth pointing out that Hroch's typology coupled with the political events after 1989 brought Gellner back to a re-examination of nationalism in the later stages of his life. Looking at his work on nationalism, we would conclude that Gellner was primarily interested in the classical problem of 'transition', how and why nationalism in its modern form emerged in the context of industrialism. His later work on time-zones in Europe in which he identifies four – from the westernmost on the Atlantic seaboard to the territories of the old Tsarist empire – is able to absorb this interest in post-communist nationalism. It is noticeable, however, that despite his expertise in Islam, he never wrote at length about 'Third World' nationalism, nor did he express much interest in nationalist and regionalist movements in Western Europe, preferring as we shall see, to explain these in terms of contingencies rather than as defining necessities.

National as modern

Gellner's writing on nationalism between 1964 when *Thought and Change* was published, and 1983 when *Nations and Nationalism* appeared, provides the base of his approach. In essence, he rejected the fashionable notion that nationalism was a throw-back to a more atavistic age. Both liberalism and Marxism had predicted its decline as a consequence of free trade on the one hand, and class struggle on the other. Both, Gellner thought, overstated the power of reason, and both typified nationalism as representing dark, atavistic forces (what he called the 'dark gods' theory of nationalism). He commented in suitably combative style: 'Those who oppose nationalism hope that Reason will prevail, aided perhaps by Student Exchange Schemes, the British Council, foreign holidays, re-written history books and au pair girls' (1964: 149).

Above all, the central mistake of both friends and enemies of nationalism was to see it as 'natural'. This doctrine of nationalism has three components: it assumes that 'nationality' is a central human condition; that people have a psychological need to live with those like themselves; and that this is an ethical good. Gellner rejected this thesis, and argued that there is nothing 'natural' about nationalism, but that nevertheless there are powerful economic and social conditions which do make it irresistible in the modern age. This is the stance which is most associated with Gellner, and which causes critics to argue that he is a modernist. However, Gellner is also critical of the counter-stance that nationalism is merely contingent – a position associated with Elie Kedourie – and while he accepts that this is logically so (it does not spring from a universal root), it does not imply that it is sociologically contingent, and possesses no such roots in our own time.

The key to understanding nationalism lies in the relationship between culture and structure, and especially the inverse relationship between the two. On the one hand, in a highly structured (primitive) society, there is no incompatibility between culture and structure, one reinforcing the other. In Gellner's words: 'In simple societies culture is important, but its importance resides in the fact that it reinforces structure – the style of being and expression symbolises, underlines the substance, the effective role, activities, relationships.' On the other hand, in modern societies, 'culture does not so much underline structure: rather, it replaces it' (1964: 155). What Gellner meant by this was that in modern society our citizenship is something we carry actively and directly: it is not laid down for us by prior membership of a group.

> If a man is not firmly set in a social niche, whose relationship as it were endows him with his identity, he is obliged to carry his identity with him, in his whole style of conduct and expression: in other words, his 'culture' becomes his identity. And the classification of men by 'culture' is of

course the classification by 'nationality'. It is for this reason that it now
seems inherent, in the very nature of things, that to be human means to
have some nationality.

(Gellner, 1964: 157)

This assumption of nationality in modern society is not the result of sentiment or
historical folk-memory, but is an essential part of the modern condition. Being
national is the modern condition, and the natural form of political loyalty. Every
person is a clerk because there is an assumption of universal literacy, and clerks are
not horizontally mobile because they cannot move from one language-zone to
another very easily. The condition of language in which he/she is reared and operates is commonly the vernacular, the language of home, school and state, which in
turn reinforces nationalist tendencies. Modern loyalties correspond in large part
with political units defined by language which is the dominant mode of instruction
and expression in the education system. In other words, the state is, in these terms,
a cultural system, but one in which the population actively attests to its nationality.
This is a key point in Gellner's argument, as it allowed him to argue that nationalism does not derive from atavistic and sentimental attachment, but is made and
mobilised by the conditions of modernity themselves. That is why Gellner had no
truck with either pro- or anti-nationalists who wish to essentialise nationality, and
why he is frequently associated with a modernist position which sees nationalism as
a form of secular religion for the modern state.

Nationalism and industrialism

The second and related aspect of Gellner's theory of nationalism concerns the
relationship between nationalism and industrialism. In his 1964 essay he
connected industrialisation and modernisation as these proceed in an uneven
manner, as 'uneven development'. The metaphor is of territories being hit by a
tidal wave of economic and social change which turns the established orders on
their head, but in a successive rather than a simultaneous way. Hence, he argued
that 'nationalism is a phenomenon connected not so much with industrialisation
or modernisation as such, but with its uneven diffusion' (1964: 166). In sociological
terms, the social stratification system which results is unhallowed by custom, is not
well protected by various social mechanisms, and is 'remediable' by national secession. As a result, nationalism becomes a natural phenomenon, flowing from one
territory to another. Waves of industrialisation and modernisation spread out,
disrupting older political units, either small tribal ones or loose imperial ones.
Where cleavages coincide with cultural differences, then political and social
conflict emerges more easily.

In this regard, Gellner's is a materialist theory of nationalism, deriving from the
view that waves of economic and social changes disrupt political territories. He
was, however, critical of Marxist accounts which in his view make not one but two
(linked) classical errors: the expectation of the continuing and increasing misery of

the proletariat, and the underestimation of nationalism. In fact, the lot of workers improves and they come to make common cause with new recruits to industrial misery, while it is not possible to foster solidarity between societies at different stages of industrialisation.

Gellner's developing interest in nationalism next appeared in 1973 in his essay *Scale and Nation*. He was interested in the scale of social and political units, and how it was that a sense of loyalty and identification was generated by modern political units, especially as modern states are generally larger than traditional units such as tribes and villages, and sentiment can be independent of the objective existence of the political unit in question. 'In other words', said Gellner, 'nationalism is not an ex post facto ratifier of actual political might, but possesses a kind of independent criterion of legitimacy of its own' (1973: 2).

The key feature of modern societies is their twin directions of seeming opposites: greater differentiation, and greater standardisation. The link is that modern industrial societies have an elaborate division of labour, yet rapid change and high rates of social mobility. Because change is the characteristic feature of such societies, people have to be ready for change, and the main agency for sensitising people to this is the education system which becomes the central institution in society. He comments:

> Modern societies possess a very homogeneous educational system which provides a basically common generic training for the whole population, or for as much of it as possible, and on the basis of which a much more specialised and extraordinarily diversified system of occupations is erected, as a kind of second stage.
>
> (Gellner, 1973: 7)

The key function of education is not to give specific training but a generic one (Gellner likens it to an army's 'basic training'), and as a result, education becomes 'a universal condition of citizenship' (ibid.: 8). Thus, modern society is both more homogeneous (everyone gets the same basic training), and yet more diversified (the complex division of labour).

On this sociological base, Gellner builds a theory of nationalism, which can be summed up by his reiteration that 'every man is a clerc' (ibid.: 10). This results from the mobile diversification required of the complex division of labour; a shared common minimal culture (including literacy and numeracy); and the agency of an elaborate education system. The range within which mobility is feasible is the range of culture and language, reflected in the common educational system. These culturally imposed limits of mobility generate in turn the limits of loyalty, and thus the 'nation' begins to operate. As Gellner points out: 'nationalism is basically a movement which conceives the natural object of human loyalty to be a fairly large anonymous unit defined by shared language and culture' (ibid.: 11).

The next important stage in his explanation is his argument that modern societies which undergo rapid rates of social change do not tolerate deep and permanent inequalities the way traditional societies do. Shameless ascriptive rank does not work under the conditions of rapid change. Caste, estate or rank tends to be eroded and replaced by fluid, loose classes. Hence, the cultural differences which reflected status differences tend to become blurred, and melt into each other, or if they exist, they are 'gradual and non-extreme, and it is generally possible to "pass"' (ibid.: 12). In other words, 'under modern conditions, it is precisely the economically imposed mobility which makes rigidly ascribed status, frozen by deeply ingrained cultural traits, unacceptable' (ibid.: 13).

To the objection that the poorer parts of the world do not generate nationalism (Kedourie's point), Gellner argues that it is poverty in conjunction with mobility which generates discontent. In like manner, it is rarely the poor who form the base of nationalist movements, but the relatively economically privileged who suffer relative political under-privilege who are most susceptible to nationalism. In other words, it is relative and perceived deprivation, especially resulting from dislocation between economic and political power which matters, because under modern conditions economic privilege and political under-privilege are usually intolerable. Gellner is making the point that nationalism operates to bolster the state via its acculturation by way of education, but also provides the raw materials for mobilising those who feel aggrieved at their unequal treatment, and who set up a counter-nationalism where territory matters.

By 1981, in an essay entitled 'Nationalism' in the journal *Theory and Society*, Gellner was beginning to formalise his theory into a series of salient and conspicuous traits of modern or modernising societies.

- Modern society is politically centralised: the centralisation of industrial society is not optional, but more complete and pervasive than agrarian societies.
- Modern society is economically specialised to a very high degree, especially in its productive activities.
- Industrial society is occupationally mobile: 'a society with an inherently unstable technology, and one habituated to continuous economic improvement . . . is doomed to the continuous emergence of new specialisms' (1981: 756).
- Specialisms require a high technical level and prolonged genuine training, especially through formal education: 'It is not the mother tongue that matters, but the language of the *école maternelle*' (ibid.: 757).
- Industrial society requires intra-generational, not merely inter-generational mobility.
- The political ideology of modern societies is not fixed, and can run from mild to extreme socialism.
- Neither tribalism nor quietism-on-principle is an available option in modern society: striving for participation is one of the general conditions of economic and political life.

Why, however, is this characterisation of society one which depends on nationalism? In strong centralised states, Gellner argues, there is considerable cultural homogeneity resulting from maintaining a complex infrastructure of education in the context of high levels of social and geographical mobility. In short, we have the modern national state.

- Modern society has an inherent tendency towards a fair measure of equality in style of life. What Gellner means here is not de facto equality – which such societies can cope well enough with – but the endemic and culturally conspicuous inequalities of status rather than class. The latter become impossible to maintain in mobile circumstances which generate gradations of wealth which do not map readily onto cultural fissures. Where they do, then ethnicity becomes the key to social conflict, rather than social class.
- As a consequence of its technological, productive base, modern society is homogeneous, literate, technically skilful and occupationally mobile. The mobility, skill and literacy are all part or precondition of its high level of consumption and its expectation of continuous improvement. . . . The homogeneity is in turn a consequence of these traits. People must be ready to occupy new slots; to communicate effectively with people whom they have not encountered before; and to subject themselves to 'universalistics' or 'objective' tests, examination, with respect to roles or positions they wish to occupy. The homogeneity presupposes a shared medium of communication and literacy. These pools of homogeneous liquid, so to speak, within which fish of the same kind can move without cultural net or hindrance, are of course precisely what the ideal of nationalism requires.

(1981: 766–7)

The point he is making here is not that nationalism requires homogeneity, but that the objective need for homogeneity manifests itself as nationalism. That is why modern social democratic or welfare state nationalism fits the model, even though it is rarely thought of as such. The assumption of egalitarianism and nationalism go together, not because resources are equally distributed, but because they do not run along cultural or ethnic fault-lines, and where they do, there is considerable trouble. Nationalism arises when lines of economic and political inequality run alongside those of culture, where 'a line of fission can seize upon some deep, ineradicable . . . diacritical signs, which confirm, exacerbate and ultimately confirm and engrain the boundary' (ibid.: 769).

We can see here that nationalism has two faces: a powerful one and a subordinate one. For the former, nationalism is the state religion in secular form, the cultural means for cementing the homogeneity of the society around its educational and technical requirements. For the latter, where economic inequalities fall along the cultural or ethnic fault-lines, nationalism becomes the potent expression of the blockages in the flows across boundaries. Whatever form it takes, nationalism is the *sine qua non* of modern societies, not its historic residue. Nationalism emerges in situations where the modern state is taken for granted.

Nations and nationalism

Gellner's *Nations and Nationalism* published in 1983 represents the most comprehensive statement of his theory in its first phase. Nationalism, he says, is primarily a political principle which holds that the state (political) and the culture (national) should be congruent. In essence, nationalism is a theory of political legitimacy requiring that ethnic and state boundaries should coincide. His focus is on rational society, and hence industrialism, rather than on capitalism as such which he sees as its sub-set. The key feature of industrial society is that it is the only society ever to live by and rely on sustained and perpetual growth (1983: 22). It is the first society ever to adopt the concept of 'progress', and its way of social control is by means of material enhancement, by keeping the system fluid in terms of such rewards, although it enters crisis when it is unable to sustain an adequate flow. High mobility and an open social order provide the conditions in which nationalism, because of its egalitarianism, prospers. Mobility requires egalitarianism, rather than the other way round. Gellner observed:

> A society which is destined to a permanent game of musical chairs cannot erect deep barriers of rank, caste or estate, between various sets of chairs which it possesses. That would hamper the mobility, and, given the mobility, would indeed lead to intolerable tensions. Men can tolerate terrible inequalities, if they are stable and hallowed by custom. But in a hectically mobile society, custom has no time to hallow anything. A rolling stone gathers no aura, and a mobile population does not allow any aura to attach to its stratification. Stratification and inequality do exist, and sometimes in extreme form; nevertheless, they have a muted and discrete quality, attenuated by a kind of gradualness of the distinctions of wealth and standing, a lack of social distance and a convergence of lifestyles, a kind of statistical or probabilistic quality of the differences (as opposed to the rigid, absolutised, chasm-like differences typical of agrarian society), and by the illusion or reality of social mobility.
>
> (ibid.: 25)

The key motor in all this is education which furnishes a generic training, and shapes society like an army in terms of its integrated and fine-tuned organisational features. However, the key difference in terms of social order is that modern society is largely self-regulating. At its centre is the professor, not the executioner; the doctorate rather than the guillotine is the emblem of state power. 'The monopoly of legitimate education is now more important, more central than is the monopoly of legitimate violence' (ibid.: 34). Hence, nationalism grows in the medium of this rational, egalitarian ethos.

What Gellner is referring to here is not an explicit set of values and beliefs about everyone being equal, but an implicit balancing mechanism which sustains broad equality of status. Egalitarianism becomes a kind of null hypothesis. In his words, industrial societies are characterised by 'social entropy', whereby the rapid flows of goods and rewards across positions maintain a broad equilibrium as the null hypothesis. On the other hand, entropy-resistance – trying to hold on to rewards on the basis of status or rank rather than ability – creates fissures which quickly become set, and in turn generate an ethnic division of labour. Gellner gives the instance of a hypothetical case of a pigmentationally blue sub-population. If such a population were concentrated at the bottom of society, then its easy identifiability coupled with this concentration leads to both a prejudice against blues, and a reaction by blues themselves against discrimination. Their colour comes to be associated with certain social practices and economic conditions. If the blues are also associated with a territory which they can claim to be the home of the blues, then a counter-nationalism can be mobilised. Thus, counter-entropy generates a considerable threat to the stability and smooth running of a society, much more than, say, economic inequalities which are randomly distributed through the population, and which do not come to be associated with a particular ethnic formation. In other words, it is the association of economic (and political) inequalities with ethnicity which is threatening to society, not social inequality *per se*. Cultural fissures of this sort go against the entropic flow, and are not easily tolerated, especially when they become frozen, aggravated, visible and offensive.

In these respects, the cultural and social markers of ethnicity become crucial. They operate as the delimiters of social identity, the parameters around which social discontent forms. Such delimiters as language, religion and culture are not in themselves the causes of ethnic feeling or nationalism, but are the raw materials around which social protest and political movements coalesce. In *Nations and Nationalism*, Gellner uses the prescient example of Yugoslavia where the ex-Muslim population of Bosnia secured the right to describe themselves as 'Muslim' for nationality purposes in the census. Such a label was not being used to describe their religion, nor to express solidarity with others who were Muslim (such as the Albanians of Kosovo); they were using the epithet to distinguish themselves from Serbs and Croats, in whose case the 'religious' identities of Orthodox and Catholic marked them out for themselves and for others in the Yugoslavian state. In this regard, being Bosnian came to mean being Muslim, however attenuated the religious identity, because it was a cultural marker of difference of a group whose political leverage in a problematic state was tenuous, as events a decade later were to show. Being an 'ex'-Muslim was enough because it did the job of cultural marker in the context of political competition. In this example, Gellner was making the important point that an identity transition was taking place from faith to culture to ethnicity and eventually to state (1983: 72).

While Gellner used examples such as this to good effect, his prime purpose was to identify the key characteristics of nationalism in theoretical form. In his essay on 'Nationalism' in *Theory and Society* (1981) he began to sketch out the main parameters, which he developed further in his 1983 book. He identified three such boundaries:

- whether or not people had access to education – which conferred the cultural franchise
- boundaries between cultures: as defined by participants themselves, such as language or religion
- the rough boundary between power-holders and the rest – usually in political terms.

Using these parameters, we have eight possible cases, only three of which generate nationalism. These are: where power-holders have access to high culture and also possess educational skills, while the powerless are education-deprived, but sharing a folk culture or cultures which has or have the potential of rivalling high culture of the elite. Gellner labels this the classical Habsburg (and points east and south) form of nationalism. The second type of nationalism is generated in conditions where there are differences between power-holders and those without it, and these differences correlate with cultural ones, but, as regards education, there are no significant differences between the relevant populations. Gellner labels this West European classical nationalism of the liberal variety, and in historical terms it corresponds with the unification nationalisms of Italy and Germany in the nineteenth century. In both countries there was little cultural inferiority, and rates of literacy and standards of education between holders and non-holders of power were about equal. Nationalism's task was to correct the inequality of political power by creating a political roof over the culture and civil society for its protection.

This 'unificatory' kind of nationalism Gellner contrasts with the first 'Eastern' type, and matches these with Plamenatz's distinction (1976) between 'Western' and 'Eastern' forms of nationalism, the first being benign and progressive, and the second malign and reactionary, a distinction which has become fixed in the literature as 'territorial' versus 'civic'. Gellner is only mildly critical of Plamenatz's distinction, arguing on the one hand that he does not make it clear whether the very unbenign Western forms of nationalism in the twentieth century are to be treated as merely an unfortunate aberration from the model, and on the other, that Plamenatz's account misses a third form of nationalism, that of the 'diaspora'. This form emerges where political power is held by one group, and educational resources by another, usually a more progressive culture than the former. This type is more common in traditional societies where, for example, traders are kept away from the levers of political power by its rulers. Gellner gives the examples of Jews – most obviously in the state form of Israel – the Greeks, Armenians, Chinese or Ibos in Nigeria.

The other five cases which the model generates are irrelevant to nationalism because, while political power and access to education are both operating, there are no cultural differences on to which these can be mapped. Hence, nationalism emerges where cultural differences operate in the context of power and education. In the rest of his work, it is plain that Gellner was primarily interested in the first two types of nationalism – Habsburg nationalism, and unificatory nationalism – rather than the third, for it seems that despite his anthropological work in North Africa, he was not particularly intrigued by 'Third World' nationalism, except insofar as it corresponded to the 'diaspora' variety which constituted his third model. As we shall see later in this chapter, he was to return to his European roots in the late 1980s and 1990s to develop his wave account of nationalism.

It is also clear that nationalist ideology and nationalist movements were of little interest to him either. He saw these as inherently prone to false consciousness and myth-making which invert reality. They claim to defend folk culture while systematically dismantling it in favour of anonymous, industrial society. 'It seems to me,' he said, 'that, generally speaking, we shall not learn too much about nationalism from the study of its own prophets' (1983: 125). Similarly, he counselled against following the strictures of anti-nationalists such as Kedourie who treats nationalism as a contingent, avoidable aberration. It is inscribed not in a doctrine, a set of self-evident beliefs, but in a set of social conditions for our time. This, of course, reinforces Gellner's account as a materialist one, for he is seeking the economic-social-political conditions which bring it, and the modern state, into existence. As we shall see later in this chapter, there is irony in the fact that someone like Miroslav Hroch, trained in the Marxist tradition, gives more weight to the nature and organisation of nationalist movements than the non-Marxist Gellner.

In essence, Gellner's theory of nationalism rests on the view that modern society – as industrial society – generates precisely the conditions within which it flourishes. It requires an unprecedented division of labour, which is premised on the need for people to be able and willing to move from one occupational position to another, across generations but also in one's own lifetime. To do this, 'they need a shared culture, and a literate sophisticated high culture at that. It obliges them to be able to communicate contextlessly and with precision with all comers, in face-to-face ephemeral contacts, but also through abstract means of communication' (1983: 141). High literate culture requires to be defended and promoted by the state, because only it is able to deploy the resources and establish and maintain the education system. The state is therefore coterminous with civil society. Because industrial high culture is no longer sustained by a church and expressed through a faith, it has to be sustained as a culture in a deliberate and explicit manner, and that, Gellner argues, is the function of nationalism. In modern society, 'one's prime loyalty is to the medium of our literacy, and to its political protector [the state]. The equal access of believers to God eventually became access of unbelievers to education and culture' (ibid.: 142).

If Gellner was primarily interested in the conditions under which nationalism emerged as the ideological handmaiden of the state in the West, we might ask what he had to say about the revival of nationalism and regionalism in that part of the world in the late twentieth century. The answer is – very little. We have already pointed to two aspects of nationalism which interested him: state nationalism

whereby it became the almost automatic outcome of the process of state formation or 'nation-building'; and oppositional nationalism which sought to destroy
archaic political and economic structures in the form of tribal or imperial entities.
As regards the latter, however, there is a once-and-for-all quality to Gellner's
approach, as if once the transition to modernity has been reached, nationalism
simply takes on its purpose of protecting state culture. This aspect of his work has
generated criticism both for his assumption that nationalism is 'over', and on the
grounds that he is too vague on what the precise mechanisms of change are: are
these industrialisation, modernisation, state-formation or what?

Does Scotland fit?

There is a nice example of his lack of interest in nationalism in the late twentieth-
century West – what has been called 'neo-nationalism', which we shall examine in
chapter 7 – in Gellner's review essay on Tom Nairn's *The Break-Up of Britain*, which
was published in 1977. Nairn's book has become a key text in understanding neo-
nationalism, and Gellner's reaction is interesting and revealing.

What intrigued Gellner was Nairn's comment that nationalism represents
Marxism's greatest failure. Gellner found Nairn's approach complex, even
tortured, the result of his own distancing from Marxism, although also an unwill-
ingness to give it up completely. In Gellner's view, Nairn is correct to stand on its
head Marx's view that class struggle is the motor of change and nationalism
merely epiphenomenal of it. He cited with approval Nairn's comment that:

> As capitalism spread, and smashed the ancient social formations
> surrounding it, they always tended to fall apart along the fault-lines
> contained inside them. It is a matter of elementary truth that these lines
> were always ones of nationality (although in certain well-known cases
> deeply established religious divisions could perform the same function).
> They were never ones of class.
>
> (Gellner, 1978: 106–7)

He was at pains to point out that in like manner Nairn does not propose to replace
class with nation, and neither does Gellner, reinforcing his well-known aphorism
that nationalism creates nations, not the other way round. He returned to his view
that it is uneven economic development which is the key to understanding nationalism. His own theory argued that nations crystallise as a consequence of
inequality, which in modern conditions cannot be tolerated any more, and the
significance of politicised culture – 'nationality' – is very great. He was drawn to
Nairn's account because of the puzzles which arise over the relation between class
and nation. Gellner commented: 'The "classes" that really matter are those which
are produced by uneven development; and they attain "consciousness" through
ethnicity. If "ethnic" differentials are lacking, they fail to reach "consciousness"'
(1978: 109).

How, then, does *The Break-Up of Britain* fit in? Gellner confessed to be much more intrigued by what he takes to be Nairn's central theoretical concern, the relationship between class and nation, Marxism and nationalism. He found that the 'Ulster' conflict, where life chances fall along the ethnic divide, was a clear case for the theory, but that Scotland was more puzzling. Its failure to develop full-blown nationalism in the nineteenth century presents difficulties, but as for the late twentieth-century 'second-round' version, then his own 'feeble' suggestion is that it is merely contingent and instrumental.

> In an era of economic centralisation, when a large proportion of resources is inevitably controlled by the state, any segment or region of society lucky enough to be endowed with the means for clear self-identification has good cause to constitute itself into a pressure group. Oil provided the Scots with the incentive, and the tartanry, which Nairn despises, with the easily intelligible and accessible symbolic means.
>
> (Gellner, 1978: 110)

We might, then, conclude that nationalism in Scotland had little to contribute to Gellner's theory of nationalism beyond the exploitation of unforeseen resources, and the mobilisation of cultural iconography. As I shall argue in chapter 7, new forms of nationalism – what I will call autonomism and neo-nationalism – presage the decline of the rounded, all-powerful modern state which Gellner made the central focus of his theory. Perhaps it is little wonder that he was unwilling to give too much credence to such forms of nationalism which undermined his approach in such a fundamental way.

Gellner's later theory of nationalism

After the publication of *Nations and Nationalism*, Gellner took the view that this book was his last word on nationalism. However, in the 1990s he returned to the subject, and wrote two important collections of essays, *Conditions of Liberty*, and *Encounter with Nationalism*, both published in 1994. His general approach was recognisably similar to his earlier one, although the language was slightly different. In *Conditions of Liberty*, he spoke of 'modular man', self-assembled like furniture, equal in culture as well as in the basic social status. Modularity makes civil society possible, but also makes it nationalist: 'He is not a nationalist out of atavism (quite the reverse), but rather from a perfectly sound though seldom lucid and conscious appreciation of his own true interests' (1994b: 107).

So far, so familiar. However, his later work develops an earlier argument, out of Plamenatz, that Eastern and Western nationalism developed differently, the 'ethnic' and the 'liberal'. The latter took the form of '*landespatriotismus*', while the former, based mainly in Central and Eastern Europe, drew on peasant cultures to a greater extent. This distinction grew into his model of 'time-zones' of Europe in which he described the temporal and typological forms of nationalism, starting with those on the Atlantic sea-coast. Such states were formed around the strong dynastic states in which there had been early standardisation of language and dialect. These cultural-linguistic regions were the Spanish, French, English and Portuguese states fashioned around the interests of a strong central monarchy. They were the earliest and the easiest to fashion in the modern age, as they did not require the redrawing of boundaries nor the need to rework ethnographic nationalism out of peasant cultures. The obvious geographical exception was Ireland, whose nationalist project was much more similar to those in zone III, in the 'East'.

The second zone is represented by the process of unificatory state-building associated with Italy and Germany, which case Gellner had identified in his 1981 typology of nationalism. Zone II roughly approximated to the territory of the old Holy Roman Empire, an area of political fragmentation but one well equipped with a pre-existing codified high culture. There was, then, no need for culture-building, merely state-building in order to provide a single and shared political roof. Gellner comments: 'the cultural bride was all ready and tarted up at the altar, only the political groom had to be found and his claims made good' (1994b: 114–15).

Zone III was to be found further east (Central and Eastern Europe), and had neither well-defined nor well-sustained high cultures, nor the necessary political skills to protect them. The cultures which exist neither have a state to educate the lower orders (as in zone I), nor merely the need to unify a multiplicity of political units (as in zone II). Instead, there is a patchwork of folk cultures, and political and religious boundaries devoid of any coherence. The task of nationalists is, then, to fuse culture and politics, beginning with ethnography which is both descriptive and normative. This zone contains both 'historic' nations (who once had, but subsequently lost, statehood), and 'non-historic' nations who require political definition in terms of culture rather than history.

Finally, Gellner argued, there is zone IV, further east still and largely corresponding to the territories of the old Tsarist empire, which shared the fate of zone III until it was replaced by secular communism in 1917. Thereafter, nationalism was kept at bay, civil society destroyed, and the social conditions which generated nationalism elsewhere – people's identification with high culture – did not materialise. In other words, it was frozen culturally and politically until the fall of communism in 1989. The small successor states which emerged from the wreckage blended with a variety of political ideologies from populism, fascism, to democracy.

It is plain from his later writings that Gellner was primarily interested in zones III and IV, for he took the formation of states in zones I and II as given and historical. In Central and Eastern Europe, on the other hand, all is still to play for. It is the time-frame here which is crucial. In his paper 'The coming of nationalism and its interpretation: the myths of nation and class' (1996), he outlined the path or stages which societies take in moving from agrarian to industrial society.

There are five stages in all. The first of these he called the 'baseline' and dates from the French Revolution to the Congress of Vienna in 1815, the beginning of the 'modern' world. This represents the post-medieval break-up, and the replacement of this universal order by a system of sovereign states. Nevertheless, ethnicity is still not recognised, and there is no link between this and political boundaries. Its outcome can most obviously be seen in zone I in which the state preceded its ethnic identity.

The second stage he refers to as national irredentism, in which ethnicity as a political principle is beginning to operate, and the former borders are under threat from this principle of one culture, one state. In this age of irredentism from 1815 until 1918 people are shaped often by force into the cultural mould, either by persuasion, violence, redrawing of territories or adjusting of frontiers. In this phase the nation is the principle of moral authority, although actual political change to fit this pattern was in practice only partly successful and certainly contentious, as the wars of this period show, culminating in the Great War of 1914–18.

Thereafter, the third stage which Gellner called 'National Irredentism, triumphant and self-defeating' takes over. The collapse of large empires ushers in a plurality of small, fragile states which struggle to survive against predatory ones, most obviously Germany and the USSR.

The fourth phase he labelled '*nacht und nebel*' to describe the reshaping of territories by force and stealth during the Second World War. Assimilation gave way to forcible repatriation and ethnic cleansing. Nationalism was often mobilised in a virulent form, asserting the mythic virtues of the homogeneous village community against pluralistic universalism and reason.

In the final stage, and in part in reaction to the excesses of the vision of nationalism in the fourth stage, post-1945, the intensity of ethnic feeling diminishes and, coupled with growing affluence, a belief in cultural convergence rather than divergence predominates. Nationalism does not disappear, but becomes an implicit ideology of the state, a taken-for-granted identity of the individual with the 'national interest'. In Gellner's words:

> People really become nationalists because they find that in their daily social intercourse, at work and at leisure, their 'ethnic' classification largely determines how they are treated, whether they encounter sympathy and respect, or contempt, derision or hostility. The root of nationalism is not ideology, but concrete daily experience.
>
> (Gellner, 1996a: 123)

On the other hand, explicit nationalism or ethnic feeling emerges where cultural differentiae become aligned with social or economic cleavages, in a manner familiar to those acquainted with Gellner's previous work. However, for most of the population, nationalism has become tamed just as religion was tamed, made routine and banal, a matter for personal, private preference rather than public, political assertion.

Gellner's periodisation of nationalist development was generated independently of the one constructed by Czech writer Miroslav Hroch, whose book *Social*

Preconditions of National Revival in Europe was published in English in 1985, but Gellner found this work 'highly influential and powerfully argued and well-documented' (1996: 132). What interested Gellner too was that Hroch's was an attempt to fuse the Marxist and nationalist perspectives insofar as he sought to marry the development of national movements with socio-economic change under capitalism.

Hroch's model of nationalism

Before we look at Gellner's critique of Hroch, let us lay out briefly what the latter was saying. In short, Hroch argued that national movements had three phases. In phase A, activists are involved in small-scale scholarly enquiry into the cultural basis of the nation. This involves collecting linguistic, folkloric, historic and social fragments and distilling them into a semblance of a national culture. This was in essence a phase of cultural nationalism, and few sought to translate that into a set of political demands. The second phase, phase B, involves a new range of activists seeking to win over as many of the same ethnic group as possible with a view to 'awakening' the nation from its slumbers, at first with little success, but progressively with more. In the final phase, phase C, a large part of the population – a mass movement – highlights its national identity, and seeks political statehood as a means of expressing the national will. In its highest form, this expression feeds through into all the political parties which thereby make implicit their national programmes.

The combination of developments of the national movements in conjunction with socio-economic change in Europe produce, according to Hroch, four types:

- *First type*: phase B occurred under the old regime of absolutism but acquired a mass character in a time of revolutionary changes in the political system, when an organised labour movement also began to assert itself. The leaders of phase B developed national programmes in conditions of political upheaval: e.g. Czech agitation in Bohemia, and Hungarian and Norwegian movements, all of which entered phase B around 1800. Norwegian patriots gained liberal constitution and declaration of independence in 1814, while Czechs and Magyars developed, in different ways, national programmes during revolutions of 1848.
- *Second type*: national agitation began under the old regime, but the transition to a mass movement, or phase C, was delayed until after a constitutional revolution. This shift of sequence could be caused by either uneven economic development, as in Lithuania, Latvia, Slovenia or Croatia, or by foreign oppression as in Slovakia or Ukraine. Phase B can be said to have started in Croatia in the 1830s, in Slovenia in the 1840s, in Latvia at the end of the 1850s, and in Lithuania not until the 1870s – reaching phase C in Croatia not before the 1880s, in Slovenia in the 1890s, and in Latvia and Lithuania only during the revolution of 1905. Forcible Magyarisation checked the transition

to phase C in Slovakia after 1867, as did oppressive Russification in the Ukraine.

- *Third type*: national movements acquired a mass character already under the old regime, and so existed before the establishment of a civil society or constitutional order. This pattern produced armed insurrections, and was confined to lands of the Ottoman empire in Europe – notably, Serbia, Greece, Bulgaria.

- *Final type*: national agitation first began under constitutional conditions in a more developed capitalist setting, characteristic of Western Europe. In these cases, the national movements could reach phase C quite early, as in the Basque lands and Catalunya, while in other cases it did so only after a very long phase B, as in Flanders, or not at all – as in Wales, Scotland or Brittany.

Gellner's critique of Hroch is made on a number of connected grounds (Gellner, 1996a). He is intrigued by Hroch's attempt to fuse Marxism and nationalism as analytical frames, but argues that Hroch treats feudalism and absolutism as one form of social order and capitalism as another. A catch-all feudalism-absolutism fails to spot the emergence of nationalism at an earlier stage, and 'inhibits the formulation of any questions concerning possible earlier roots' (ibid.: 134), and points to harbingers of nationalism in the Reformation (the Protestant use of vernacular languages) and possibly the Renaissance. Gellner argues that Hroch's schema seems to suffer from the application of too little Marxism (an understanding of historical stages) rather than too much. He acknowledges that his own view is that nationalism is in essence linked to the coming of industrialism.

However, there is something odd about Gellner's criticism, as his own account is not concerned with the pre-modern origins of nationalism. Similarly, he seems too willing to treat Hroch's 'capitalism' as a synonym of his own 'industrialism', especially as Gellner's account focuses on the latter as having different (and wider) features than the former. The other ironic aspect is that whereas Hroch's 'Marxist' account teases out in considerable detail the features of national movements (cultural and political), Gellner's non-Marxist account virtually ignores them in favour of the socio-economic conditions which require to be present for nationalism to emerge. Elsewhere, Hutchinson (1994) argues that Gellner's account is curiously functionalist, seeming to argue that nationalism and modernity are inextricably linked. This raises the problem of teleology, as nationalism is explained as a function of modernisation, and hence the role of national movements is essentially subsidiary to it. They will do its bidding as and when required. In Stargardt's words: '*Nations and Nationalism* is a frankly functionalist account of nation building, laying the stress on necessary and sufficient conditions rather than on actual historical causation' (Stargardt, 1996: 177). John Hall (1993) has defended Gellner's account from the accusations of functionalism on the grounds that many nationalist leaders themselves were aware of the need to 'modernise', but the teleology of Gellner's model is nevertheless strong.

Gellner was also critical of Hroch for reifying 'nations' as given, which struck him as an odd thing for a Marxist to do, but this is part of Gellner's broader critique that in steering clear of reducing nations to classes and vice versa, Hroch treats as separate two processes which are actually the same transition. He commented: 'What Hroch has tried to do is to confer scholarly respectability on two of the great myths of the 19th and 20th centuries, namely marxism and nationalism' (1996: 142). But, said Gellner, history is about neither the conflict of classes nor the conflict of nations, but is rich in countless kinds of conflicts. He observed: 'Neither economic tension nor cultural difference on its own achieves anything, or, at any rate, not much. The socio-economic base is decisive. That much is true in marxism, even if its more specific propositions are false' (ibid.: 143).

Gellner's points are well taken, but many of them might well be applied to his own account. If anything, Hroch's is a more explicit attempt at integrating 'national' and 'class' dimensions in accounting for the rise of nationalism than is Gellner's. It is undoubtedly true that Gellner found Hroch's analysis highly stimulating, and it is a measure of this that he uses it as a sounding-board for many of his thoughts, rather than mounting a systematic and careful defence of his own theory.

Conclusion

Gellner's theory of nationalism has been criticised on a number of grounds. We have already commented that it seems to rely on a teleological connection between modernity and nationalism. It is the role of nationalism to provide ideological functions for the modern state. Gellner got the chance to answer his critics in the comprehensive review of his social philosophy edited by John Hall and Ian Jarvie in 1996 shortly before his death. Like some grand chess master playing all his opponents at once, he took the issue of functionalism head-on. 'Functionalism', he commented, 'is a term people sometimes apply to their own position and it is not clear why it should be a badge of shame' (Gellner, 1996e: 627). He refuted the accusation that his theory of nationalism was teleological (that is, explaining its rise in terms of the needs it satisfies), and saw his own theory as 'straightforwardly causal' (ibid.). Brendan O'Leary (1996) in the same volume accepts that Gellner's argument about the 'elective affinity' between nationalism and modernity is valid (the allusion to Weber's relationship between the Protestant ethic and the spirit of capitalism is clear and justifiable in explanatory terms).

However, this single, revolutionary transition is depicted as a once-and-for-all process, and Gellner's account seems over-dependent on a particular characterisation of 'modern' society as an integrated, self-contained and well-honed organism. Just how appropriate this is in a world of 'globalisation', which, even without taking an extreme view of this process, does seem to leave societies rather exposed and less autonomous than Gellner implied. On more empirical grounds, Gellner's characterisation of 'modernity' seems to pay insufficient attention to historical facts. It is plain that nationalism frequently predated industrialisation and, more specifically, it is difficult to argue for a causal link between industrialisation and the development of mass education systems on which his theory seems to depend. For example, England did not develop a mass school system until the 1870s but there is evidence of nationalist consciousness at least as early as the sixteenth century (Greenfeld, 1992). Again, Scotland had a system of mass schooling in the eighteenth century but no mass nationalist movement until two centuries later. It seems that too much is smuggled in under the guise of 'modernisation' or 'industrialisation', which explain everything and nothing in the emergence of nationalism.

It is plain that Gellner's theory of nationalism rests on cultural and materialist assumptions, and that for many of his critics such as O'Leary he reduces the political dimension to the point of invisibility. O'Leary argues: 'Gellner's theory too readily assumes that the general case, that the political nation and the cultural nation must be one, is the universal and, in the long run, the irresistable tendency' (1996: 100). He does not, for example, spell out the mutually reinforcing relationships between nationalism, egalitarianism and democratisation, confining himself to the relationship between the first two. It is interesting that in his critical reply, Gellner (1996e) confines himself to saying that he does not reduce nationalism to social conditions, and that he has little to say beyond that about his neglect of the political dimension.

Relatedly, there is also an unexplored tension in Gellner's work between state nationalism, and oppositional nationalism. While he acknowledges that these are different, he seems uninterested in exploring the tensions between them. It is as if once oppositional nationalism has won the day and its state, little more has to be said. As we have observed, Gellner is uninterested in the emergence of neo-nationalist movements in Western Europe, not because he has not noticed them, but because they do not fit his theory very well. After all, the states in which they have grown up were deemed to have an all-encompassing and implicit nationalism of their own. Plainly, this was not as hegemonic as he made out. While it is true that one can invoke contingent and instrumental factors to explain their outcome, they do present puzzles for students of the phenomenon in the late twentieth century. Gellner's theory was geared to explaining the kind of nationalism which emerged (or not, as the case may be) in Europe in the transition to industrialism in the late eighteenth and nineteenth centuries. It is less helpful in accounting for pre-modern or late-modern versions of nationalism, and perhaps such an all-round theory simply is not possible. It is perhaps Gellner's robust claims to generality which let him down here.

In like vein, his characterisation as a modernist, as someone who sees nations as 'invented', relies on his way of stating his case. We have already alluded to his well-known aphorism that 'nationalism is not the awakening of nations to self-consciousness; it invents nations where they do not exist' (Gellner, 1964: 169). As Benedict Anderson argues, Gellner is so anxious to show that nationalism masquerades under false pretences that he assimilates 'invention' to 'fabrication' and 'falsity' rather than 'imagining' and 'creation' (Anderson, 1996a: 6). Of course, Gellner followed up his statement with the counsel that cultural raw materials had to be available, but this is lost in the brilliance of the aphorism, which in turn becomes a stick with which others can beat his back. Not one to step back from an argument, Gellner often fell foul of his own debating ploys and tripped over the loose ends. If his critics have found it relatively easy to pick up loose threads in his theory of nationalism, that is a reflection of his incisive mind and philosophical training which led him to set up an argument only to see where it would lead and how many critics it would incite. That it led in many directions and generated much heat and considerable light is a measure of the contribution of Ernest Gellner to our understanding of nationalism.

If Gellner's theory of nationalism is not without flaws, why has it had such an impact on how we see and study the subject? Certainly, his key insight that nationalism is inherent in and necessary to all modern societies transformed it from a study of history to a study of sociology and politics. It has become so much harder to dismiss nationalism as simply the memory-trace of an ethnic past. Gellner's work contains many loose ends, but this reflects the fact that he was less interested in producing a sanitised academic theory than in commenting on the world as he saw and experienced it. He had the experience of living on the edge of so many nationalisms without properly belonging to any, although he was happy to own up to its emotional power. He sought a rational theory of nationalism but recognised its capacity to move. It is revealing that in his reply to his critics (1996e), he took exception to Perry Anderson's charge that, unlike Weber, he had failed to detect the spell of nationalism (Anderson, 1992: 205). It was in response to what he saw as this unfair jibe that he commented:

> I *am* deeply sensitive to the spell of nationalism. I can play about thirty Bohemian folk songs (or songs presented as such in my youth) on my mouth-organ. My oldest friend, whom I have known since the age of three or four and who is Czech and a patriot, cannot bear to hear me play them because he says I do it in such a schmaltzy way, 'crying into the mouth-organ'. I do not think I could have written the book on nationalism which I did write, were I not capable of crying, with the help of a little alcohol, over folk songs, which happen to be my favourite form of music.
>
> (Gellner, 1996e: 624; reprinted 1997: ix)

Gellner's contribution to nationalism derives not simply from his ability to produce intellectual insights, but (*contra* Stargardt, 1996) from his capacity to understand it.

5

NATION AS STATE

Nationalism and state-building

Nation and state: we have grown used to treating these terms interchangeably. The British nation, the American nation, the Spanish nation and so on, are, of course, states, and that is largely what we mean when we say 'nation'. Those, however, who live in 'stateless nations' such as Scotland, Catalunya and Quebec, find the equating of state and nation problematic and exasperating, but it is one which is so widely used that they too have grown accustomed to it, although they are careful of and sensitive to the distinction. In contemporary Scotland, for example, the epithet 'national' is now ambiguous and has come to be prefixed by 'Scottish-' or 'British-' as appropriate. To some this sounds pedantic: 'it's only words', they say, but the women's movement has taught us that 'only' does not mean trivial, but basic. The use of male pronouns or adjectives to refer to all human beings is now widely avoided. 'Mere words' carry a basic template for seeing the world and ordering it according to a hierarchy of power.

Why, then, should the use of 'national' and 'nation-state' matter? In a large part because it frames the world as it is meant to be, not how it is. Strictly speaking, 'nation-state' implies that all self-governing political units – states – correspond with culturally distinctive units – nations – so that the world appears as a giant jigsaw of such entities. Of course, the pieces don't fit. Not only are most states not culturally and ethnically homogeneous, but many (most?) imagined communities – nations – are stateless. Charles Tilly (1992) has enjoined us to use the term 'national states' to indicate that states govern multiple cultural regions, and few are those in which people share a strong linguistic, religious and symbolic identity. Few European states, he comments, have ever qualified as genuine 'nation-states' (perhaps Sweden and Ireland), but: 'Great Britain, Germany and France – quintessentially national states – certainly have never met the test' (ibid.: 3).

State, nation and society

We might, then, ask why it is that the term nation-state has such strong currency in the Western world. It is one thing to fret about the inexactness of the term, a more interesting thing to ask why it has such hegemony in describing the modern world. The root of the answer lies in the theme of this chapter, namely, that the term was captured by the process of state-building which has shaped Western Europe over the last two centuries. If states were not actually 'nations' too, then they could be imagined as such either now or in the future. So successful has this alignment between state and nation been that it is part of our common-sense, our taken-for-granted political and cultural world. Does it matter that we align state and nation? – most certainly, because it gives a fundamental legitimacy to the modern state without which it could not function.

We can see this particularly in the comments of those who are largely hostile to forms of nationalism which threaten rather than support existing states. For example, Eric Hobsbawm cites the Polish politician Marshall Pilsudski: 'It is the state which makes the nation, not the nation the state' (1990: 44–5). This might seem a strange comment coming from a nationalist in Poland whose people more frequently than not existed as a nation rather than a state, but it underscores Hobsbawm's view that 'nations do not make states and nationalisms, but the other way round' (ibid.: 10). Here, of course, he is echoing Gellner's oft-cited view that nationalism actually creates – imagines – nations, but Hobsbawm slips in 'states' (which Gellner does not do) to imply that by and large we have to understand 'nations' as ideological constructs of the state. The explanatory legitimacy in other words runs from the political (the state) to the cultural (the nation).

There are, of course, costs to understanding if we focus simply on definitional issues. Josep Llobera (1994b) has usefully advised that the literature on nationalism is plagued by a false dilemma: either that the state makes the nation, or the nation makes the state. It appears we have to choose which side to be on. Llobera argues that this debate frequently becomes sterile. After all, some states consolidated and grew on this basis, while others disappeared, and ethno-national identities developed as a result of outside pressures even when a proper state did not exist. The key lies not in the reality that the nation-state is a hegemonic political form in itself, but instead that it is the ideology of the nation-state which is hegemonic. Further, as Cobban points out: 'during the early modern period . . . the word nation changed its significance: it lost its linguistic and acquired an almost wholly exclusively political meaning' (Hutchinson and Smith, 1994: 245).

We can see the downplaying of the cultural component in modern definitions of the state. David Held comments: 'All modern states are nation-states – political apparatuses, distinct from both rulers and ruled, with supreme jurisdiction over a demarcated territorial area, backed by a claim to a monopoly of coercive power, and enjoying a minimum level of support or loyalty from their citizens' (1992: 87). We might be surprised that the cultural component is downplayed and operates merely as a loyalty device for the state, but this view of the 'nation-state' is the dominant one. Similarly, Anthony Giddens virtually reproduces this definition, but without any cultural component being mentioned. The nation-state, he comments, is 'a set of institutional forms of governance maintaining an administrative monopoly over a territory with demarcated boundaries, its rule being sanctioned by law and direct control of the means of internal and external violence' (1981: 190). Giddens sees the 'nation' as a 'bordered power-container', which can only exist 'when a state has a unified administrative reach over the territory over which its sovereignty is claimed' (1985: 120). Max Weber who, as we have seen in chapter 1, well understood the distinction between state and nation, defined the key characteristics of the modern state as follows: territoriality – having fixed and defensible borders; control of the means of violence – both internally and externally; an impersonal structure of power – the idea of a sovereign and impersonal political order; and legitimacy – requiring the loyalty of its citizens (Held, 1992).

Does this reduction of the nation to the state matter? Our argument here is that it does, because the concepts actually operate on different planes, and lead us to imagine that modern states have captured political and cultural power. This is problematic because the ideal-typical process had always a much more messy reality lying behind it. Particularly in the late twentieth century, the concepts are coming apart. At this stage we need to inject a third, related, concept, that of 'society' or 'civil society'. If the 'state' is in essence a political concept, then 'society' is a sociological one. Broadly speaking, we can identify two ways of talking about society. Most sociologists use society in a fairly unproblematic and implicit way. It is, simply, the state. In the words of the sociologist Zygmunt Bauman: 'It seems that most sociologists of the era of modern orthodoxy believed that – all being said – the nation-state is close enough to its own postulate of sovereignty to validate the use of the theoretical expression – the 'society' concept – as an adequate framework for sociological analysis' (1992: 57).

The second sense of society is as 'Society' (capital S). This is a higher level of abstraction, and is used to refer to the broad, common patterns of human organisation, to how people relate to each other, as well as its subsets – industrial society, capitalist society and so on. In the main, however, when sociologists today talk about 'society', they are usually referring to 'nation-states'. Alain Touraine observed:

> The abstract idea of society cannot be separated from the concrete reality of a national society, since this idea is defined as a network of institutions, controls and education. This necessarily refers us back to a government, to a territory, to a political collectivity. The idea of society was and still is the ideology of nations in the making.
>
> (Touraine, 1981: 5)

This somewhat diluted image of 'society' carries its own difficulties. It implies that the conventional state is a bounded and self-contained social system. The two dominating paradigms of Western sociology in the twentieth century both adopted this convention. On the one hand, Parsonian structural functionalism has equated society with 'social system', a limited and enclosed world within which all meaningful social interaction takes place. On the other hand, Marxism has used the concept 'social formation' in much the same way. Economic and social exchange has taken place largely within the confines of a (national) market, and policed by the state. In practical terms, society was simply the state. For example, 'British society' is a term which has been in common currency as long as the sociology has had a professional foothold in these islands, and it has been used extensively since the coming of the welfare state in 1945.

In recent years there have been attempts to refine society as an analytical concept by using the prefix 'civil'. The term 'civil society' refers to 'those areas of social life – the domestic world, the economic sphere, cultural activities and political interaction – which are organised by private or voluntary arrangements between individuals and groups outside the direct control of the state' (Held, 1992: 73). In other words, whereas the state can be treated as a unitary entity which functions externally (through warfare) and internally (through law), society is composed of an extensive though bounded network of self-activated individuals and groups. State and society are not wholly independent of each other, but are largely formed and maintained within the context of the other.

The concept of civil society is not without dispute, particularly concerning its relationship between state on the one hand and market on the other. As regards the first, Salvador Giner has observed that civil society 'must be understood as the sphere of that which is relatively but autonomously private within a modern polity' (1995: 322). In other words, given the way state and civil society operate across each other today, we cannot differentiate between them easily. To take the Scottish example, institutional autonomy as regards law, education and local politics is now underwritten and managed by the state, albeit a Scottish 'semi-state'.

Neither can we reduce civil society simply to the market, not only because state and economy are now thoroughly intermingled, but because there is more to civil society than that. Within the Marxist tradition, most notably associated with Antonio Gramsci, civil society has come to stand not simply for the economic – market – dimension, but for the set of social and civic institutions, including the whole range of public institutions from courts, welfare agencies and educational bodies, mediating between the individual and the state. In Kumar's words: 'Civil society is the sphere of culture in the broadest sense. It is concerned with the manners and mores of society, with the way people live' (1993: 382–3). The fall of communism in Central and Eastern Europe has helped to boost the revival of the concept 'civil society'. Kumar is critical of commentators on Eastern Europe who, he argues, imply too much consensus in the sphere of civil society at the expense of the real degree of coercion involved in the maintenance of political power in modern societies. Others counter that civil society provides 'the space or arena between the household and the state, other than the market, which affords possibilities of concerted action and social self-organisation' (Bryant, 1993: 399).

Let us at this stage clarify what we mean by the state (Poggi, 1978). First, the state has a unity. Each state operates in its own territory as the sole, exclusive fount of all powers and prerogatives of rule. This unity is expressed through the medium of a single currency, a unified fiscal system, a single 'national' language (national culture being acquired through a powerful education system) and a unified legal system. (In passing, we might note that 'statelessness' is a question of degree.

Scotland, Catalunya and Quebec may not be formally 'states' but they have a high degree of autonomy over many of these institutions.) Second, the state is ineluctably modern. That is, it appears as an 'artificial, engineered institutional complex', a deliberated constructed framework vital for state and nation-building. Poggi comments: 'The modern state is not bestowed upon a people as a gift by God, its own geist, or blind historical forces; it is a "made" reality' (ibid.: 95). The state, in other words, is viewed as a machine, internally structured as a formal, complex organisation. He argues: 'In sum, the state is designed and is intended to operate as a machine whose parts all mesh, a machine propelled by energy and directed by information flowing from a single centre in the service of a plurality of coordinated tasks' (ibid.: 98).

The third characteristic of the state is that it embodies, in Max Weber's phrase, rational-legal legitimacy, expressed above all in Law, that is, 'positive law, willed, made and given validity by the state itself in the exercise of its sovereignty, mostly through public, documented, generally recent decisions' (Poggi, 1978: 102). In other words, rule-making is no longer conceived of as custom, or as a set of partial immunities for some but not others, nor is it the expression of the will of God or Nature or the Monarch. The legitimacy of the modern state rests on rational and open procedures of law.

The third concept in our trilogy is the 'nation'. To classical writers like Weber it referred to 'a community of sentiment which would find its adequate expression only in a state of its own and which thus normally strives to create one' (Beetham, 1985: 122). As we have seen in this book so far, the essentially ideological nature of the concept is best captured in Benedict Anderson's definition of nation (1996a: 6–7) as an 'imagined political community' with the following characteristics:

- it is imagined as a 'communion' of people (whom one has never met)
- it has finite territorial boundaries
- it implies sovereignty and self-determination of its members
- the community is viewed as deep and horizontal comradeship.

Treating state, society and nation as analytically separate concepts – as political, social and cultural frameworks respectively – allows us to see better how they inter-connect. In this respect, it is the nation which, according to the conventional model, cements state and society together. Bauman comments:

> In the course of modern history, nationalism played the role of the hinge fastening together state and society (represented as, identified with, the nation). State and nation emerged as natural allies at the horizon of the nationalist vision (at the finishing line of the re-integrating race). The state supplied the resources of nation-building, while the postulated unity of the nation and shared national destiny offered legitimacy to the ambi-tion of the state authority to command obedience.
>
> (Bauman, 1992: 683)

The conventional way of looking at state, society and nation is to see them as aligned with each other so as to be coterminous: state-society-nation coming together to form self-contained, free-standing, ethnically homogeneous 'communities'. Each state is the embodiment of these distinct communities – self-originating and self-empowering, operating exclusively in pursuit of its own interests. Note that the state is judged to have a 'will' generated by the principle of nationality.

In sum, then, although we can find analytical differences between state, (civil) society and nation, these have become fused in our models, and treated as coterminous with the 'nation-state'. As we have seen, in practice, the most common idea of the modern state is to characterise it as the 'nation-state', in which the political realm (the state), the social (society), and the cultural (the nation) are as one. Our problem is that, on the one hand, the covert influence of nation-state building in the nineteenth and twentieth centuries dominates politics, sociology and history alike. On the other hand, societies bounded in geographical and social space are less and less likely to be unified totalities in the late twentieth century when economic, political and cultural forces have eroded the homogeneity of states.

Much of the debate in the late twentieth century concerns the relationship between state, society and nation, rather than whether one, both or all is in operation. For instance, Edward Shils' argument that multiculturalism in the United States is destroying the national spirit and the nation as a unity is premised on the view that culture is expressed as the nation which in turn generates a civil society to give it voice and protection (Shils, 1995). It is, however, possible to argue that primacy lies with civil society, the institutional expression of social interaction which thus generates 'national' feelings of solidarity, which in turn is embodied in culture. There are others, such as Habermas who argues by means of his concept of constitutional patriotism that a pure civil society without the nation is possible and desirable.

The key changes which impact on the relationships between state, society and nation in the twentieth century can be characterised as follows. On the one hand, and contrary to expectations, nationalism has waxed rather than waned in importance as this century has progressed. The usual way of identifying this is to point to the rise of nationalisms from regions or territories which wish to break away from existing state formations. Hence, when we think of nationalism in the West, we think of its rise in Scotland, Wales, Catalunya and Quebec and other formally 'stateless' nations, a phenomenon which we will discuss in a later chapter. In addition, however, in the post-war period, there has also been a core form of nationalism which is frequently implicit. As the modern state became the appropriate instrument for guaranteeing the life chances of its citizens, and ironing out social inequalities, governments became major actors in economic competition between states in the quest for economic growth 'in the national interest'. This is state nationalism expressed in economic and political competition. Nationalism, in this form, became more, not less, common in this process of post-war international competition. This nationalism of the 'core' developed alongside counter-nationalisms on the periphery which sought to redraw the limits and responsibilities of central state power, and in many cases to secede from it.

And yet, just as nationalism was growing in importance, so the conventional 'nation-state' appeared to be losing its powers. The growing interest in nationalism coincides with the apparent decline in the powers of the state. How is it possible to explain this apparent contradiction? One possibility is that the sovereignty of the nation-state was always a trick of the eye. In the words of one writer, 'The era of the homogeneous and viable nation-states is over (or rather the era of the illusion that homogeneous and viable nation-states are possible is over, since such states never existed) and the national vision must be redefined' (Tamir, 1993: 3).

The second and related set of changes concerns the state–society link. We might characterise this in general terms as follows: the state has encroached on society, and society on the state, making it much more difficult for us to distinguish between the two. Just as citizens demand more of the state, so the political dimension has required legitimacy for its actions in the social and cultural spheres. In Poggi's words: 'some encroachments on the state–society line result not from the state being 'pulled over' the line, as it were, but from its 'pushing' itself over it' (1978: 131).

Why should this have occurred? The two key domains of civil society are the family/domestic sphere, and the economy. In their classical forms, both are judged to be beyond the influence of the state, defined as the public sphere. The public refers to the sphere of 'work' (employment), authority, power, responsibility and management of the world – by men. The private relates to the 'domestic kingdom', where women and feminine virtues are said to prevail. As Stuart Hall comments:

> The private/public distinction is . . . rooted in a particular sexual division of labour, and one of the principal means by which the exclusion of women from public affairs has been constructed and secured. The maintenance by the state of the public/private separation is therefore sometimes taken to exemplify the patriarchal aspects of the state.
>
> (Hall, 1992: 20)

Similarly, in its classical form, the privately owned economy stands outside the influence of the state. The breaking down of the state–society line results from economic developments (the market is no longer self-equilibrating), the extension of the franchise resulting in increased demands on the state, and the emergence of a sizeable state sector with its own interests to protect and enhance.

In the late twentieth century the domestic and the economic spheres are no longer separated from the state in any meaningful way. The boundaries of the state/civil society were, of course, never fixed, but have been constantly redrawn, with obvious implications for relations between men and women. However, in modern times, the state can no longer stand outside social, political and cultural relations and institutions which make up society. In other words, as Hall points out, the 'empty' state – without a social content – does not exist. The state constitutes society as well as being constituted by it.

'Civil society' indicates that there is a sphere which is autonomous from the state. Neither is it simply the economy writ large. Similarly, what is meant by the state and society have themselves changed over time, as well as the relationship between them. The distinction between the two was probably much more meaningful to Victorians than it is to us today. That is because, as Poggi has pointed out, the last century or so has seen an increasing fudging of the boundary between state and society. Notably, the extension of the franchise has brought to bear new political and social pressures on the state, and increasingly the state is constituted to exercise rule over society. He comments: 'the state tends to increase its power by widening the scope of its activities, but extending the range of societal interests on which rule is brought to bear' (1978: 135). The state is required to address the concerns of its citizens more directly, and this presents the task of societal management for modern governments.

Creating the 'nation-state'

From our vantage point of the late twentieth century we can see that 'state', 'society' and 'nation' do not mean the same thing; they are treated as synonyms. Let us examine, then, the 'strong' theory of the nation-state which places the emphasis on the political dimension – the state – as the engine which has driven the fusion of nation-state-society. We will focus on the works of two writers, the sociologist Michael Mann, and the political scientist, John Breuilly. This helps to give a rounded perspective without implying that only political scientists argue for the primacy of the political realm. In this respect, let us begin with Mann's sociological account.

Mann's interest in nationalism derives from his ambitious work on the history of power in modern times (1986, 1993b). His prime concern is with the ways in which the modern state came to monopolise power, and in this context nationalism became a key ideological device. Mann (1992: 138) characterises himself as a 'modernist', like Gellner, and he argues that nationalism was only capable of spreading across the Western world from the late eighteenth century onwards. The key to his account, and his understanding of nationalism, is the need for the state to communicate both across and down large social spaces. A 'rationalised' society did not emerge out of industrialisation, as Gellner had argued, because it arrived too late and too unevenly to be a prime factor. Instead, Mann argues, it had two principal causes: the emergence of commercial capitalism on the one hand, and the emergence of the modern state with its armies of soldiers and administrators on the other. Nationalism was an elaborated ideology which depended on being shared across a territory, and hence rested on an extensive communication system of what Mann calls 'discursive' literacy, the ability to read and write non-formulaic texts. This focus on 'print culture' is, of course, close to Benedict Anderson's argument about the connection between nationalism and print capitalism, and Mann builds on it by identifying the principal media for the diffusion of discursive literacy in the late seventeenth and early eighteenth centuries: the church, the state – in the forms of the armed forces, and civil administration, commerce, the profession of law, the universities, the literary media, the periodical media, and academies and literary centres.

The key to the rise of nationalism, in Mann's view, lies in the state activities of internal administration, but also in its mobilisation of military power. He comments: 'The "Military Revolution" of 1540–1660 created more centralised, yet more functionally differentiated armies and navies. Its effects on literacy were felt right through the 18th century' (1992: 143). This was the result of the standardisation of army drills and logistical support, more complex technology, drill manuals and map-reading. The increasing size of armies from the mid-sixteenth century until the early nineteenth century made them a key channel for spreading literacy, and thereby national identification (see Eugene Weber's account (1977) of the 'nationalising' of the French peasantry). Mann's interest in the role of military factors causes him to observe: 'It is rather curious that though nationalism asserts the moral virtue of one ethnic group over another, most theories of nationalism pay so little attention to geopolitical causes of its rise' (Mann, 1992: 151). This was most obvious in the generation of national identity in the French and British states who fought four major wars against each other in the eighteenth century. By this means both were turned into 'nation-states' (we might, however, call them 'state-nations', for in both, albeit in different ways, the political took precedence over the cultural in fostering national identity).

Mann, as I have said, follows the 'modernist' tendency which argues that nations and nationalism have developed in large part in response to the development of the modern state. However, he rejects materialist and culturalist theories of nationalism, and seeks to forefront the primacy of political institutions, especially in Europe where nations in the modern sense first surfaced and predominated. The emergence of nationalism first took proto-nationalist phases in the sixteenth century where religion first shaped the concept of the nation ('cuius regio, euius religio' was its obvious expression, as the state's religion reflected that of the monarch), and in the late seventeenth century when it passed through a commercial/statist phase. From the late eighteenth century, nationalism took three fully fledged phases: militarist, industrial and modernist. As each of these phases occurred serially, the relation between state and nation took different forms. Nations could reinforce the state, leading to their correspondence as in France and Great Britain (in his writings Mann takes the view that to all intents and purposes, the UK is in essence Greater England). Second, as in the old empires – Austrian, Ottoman and Russian – nations acted to subvert the state. Finally, nations could actually create the state, as in Germany and Italy. In other words, Mann argues that how the state and nation came together was problematic and unpredictable, and depended on the particular needs of the state. Nationalism, then, did not emerge out of capitalism which was mainly trans-national, nor out of industrialism which in itself was too attenuated to be a direct cause.

Of the three phases which Mann identifies, he places greatest weight on the first, the militarist one. The role of warfare, he argues, is a key but neglected aspect in theories of nationalism. For example, by around 1700, European states were spending about 5 per cent of their GNP on the military in peacetime, and 10 per cent in wartime. By the 1760s the range was 15 to 25 per cent, by 1810 it was 25 to 35 per cent, and by that date around 5 per cent of the population was being conscripted into the armed forces, figures virtually comparable with the twentieth century. This militarist phase helped to mobilise populations on the grounds that they were fighting for 'the people' and 'the nation', and the French Revolution had an effect well beyond its frontiers in setting popular expectations about the nature and purpose of warfare. Reformers focused on transforming the central state to make it more representative and responsive, leading to a more integrated and 'national' state. The old empires which were confederal and multinational found it especially difficult to cope, and national revolts occurred among provincial elites who mobilised cultural markers such as language and religion, reinforced by the nationalising of economic markets, thereby cementing ethnic solidarities. Linguistic nationalism reinforced public as well as private communication channels, and laid down the networks for greater democratisation which the empires found impossible to withstand.

The second, industrial, phase lasted from the mid-nineteenth century to the Great War, and shifted state responsibility in two ways. First, the notion of popular sovereignty took hold, and second, the functions of the state expanded, notably in communications. These helped to 'naturalise' social life, and led to the growth of state functionaries – administrators, teachers and public sector workers – who became, both in practice and belief, nation-statists.

The final phase, what Mann describes as the 'modernist' one, commenced with the post-war peace settlements after 1918, and was reflected in the redrawing of maps and boundaries. The concept of popular sovereignty was firmly embedded in the new democratic national states as well as by authoritarian rightist regimes who used nationalism as an aggressive way of extending state power. Mann's is a politically driven model of nationalism in both its democratic and authoritarian manifestations, and nationalism evolved in both manifestations to rally citizens behind the regimes. While state-subverting forms of nationalism, notably in the territories of the crumbling empires, seem to have taken an ethnic form, Mann considers that the driving force is in essence political rather than cultural or economic. In other words, nationalism is to be understood as a means of state-building either of democratic or authoritarian regimes in Europe. The state became important in the modern world for providing key services: it alone was capable of waging massive and routinised war; it supplied communication infrastructures for both militarism and capitalism; it was the main site of political democracy; it guaranteed social citizenship rights; it participated in macro-economic planning which it largely invented (Mann, 1993b).

If Mann's is the sociological account which emphasises the salience of political factors, the most elaborated 'political' account of nationalism is given by John

Breuilly. His book *Nationalism and the State* was first published in 1982 and updated in 1993. His aim is to show that in essence nationalism is 'politics', and he argues that interpreting nationalism either as an expression of cultural identity or as the outcome of materialist forces is misleading. Nationalism is a political doctrine built on three basic assertions: that a nation exists with a distinctive and unique character; that political identity with and loyalty to the nation take precedence over other interests and values; and that the nation should have political sovereignty in the form of a separate state.

Breuilly, like Mann, is a modernist, arguing that political movements making these claims are essentially modern, and have helped to embed the notion that statehood is the natural and inevitable goal of all nationalist movements. This makes the primordial approach an inappropriate way of understanding nationalism as politics. Modern nationalism is inherently institutional, with legal, economic and political identities. Second, while there are past myths and symbols which are mobilised, the discontinuities with the way these are mobilised and constructed are far greater than the continuities.

Nor, according to Breuilly, can we explain nationalism in terms of its various functions, whether psychological, materialist/Marxist, or in terms of the requirements of modernisation processes. The problem with functionalist accounts, he observes, is that they are better at answering 'how' questions, rather than 'why' questions, for they assume intentionality either by individuals or institutions which they are unlikely to have. 'Historical' accounts of nationalism fall into the trap of description masquerading as explanation, and they are prey to teleological reasoning. Because there is an outcome, it is assumed that narrative processes lead up to and cause it, and contingent outcomes are factored out.

The key to understanding nationalism is, according to Breuilly, setting it in the context of theories of modernity. Such theories focus on the centrality of transformations, and these provide the focus of three sets of accounts. Benedict Anderson's account is concerned with the transformation of consciousness and ideas in the nationalist canon. Here we encounter familiar problems with accounts which attribute analytical power to ideas beyond their material context, or, reflecting Breuilly's own predilections, beyond the political framework. On the other hand, Gellner provides a theory of transformation which stresses social aspects, notably in the context of industrialisation. The problem is that such accounts fail to make a temporal or spatial connection between nationalism and industrialisation.

Breuilly's own preference is for a theory of modernisation which lays the stress on political modernisation – nationalism as politics. This allows political movements to be connected to political doctrines like nationalism. Modernisation involves a generic (rather than a narrowly economic) division of labour, and works within the general context of a separation of 'political' (state) and 'social' (civil society) arrangements. The connection between state and society was also necessary and this was made first by the political solution of citizenship, so that the nation – its 'civic' conception – was simply a body of citizens. Society was also seen as a collective entity, with a common 'national' culture – an 'ethnic' conception – which was expressed in shared cultural characteristics.

Here, says Breuilly, we have the two conceptions of the nation. 'Logically the two concepts of the nation – a body of citizens and a cultural collectivity – conflict. In practice, nationalism has been a sleight-of-hand ideology which tries to connect the two ideas together' (Breuilly, 1996: 166). As a result, nationalism can and does take many different forms and emphases. In the first instance, political movements were oppositional to established power systems and to processes of political modernisation. Three basic political strategies emerge according to whether the nation in question is part of the territory of the existing state, in which case separation is the political strategy; whether or not it is identical with the territory – in which case, reform; or whether the nation is larger than the territory – leading to unification nationalism. Nationalism ideology can also serve to co-ordinate common interests among elites; to mobilise groups hitherto excluded from the political process; and finally, to legitimate the goals of the nationalist political movement.

The focus in Breuilly's work is on the two main forms of nationalist struggles in Europe, 'unification' nationalism, notably in Germany and Italy, and 'separatist' nationalism, also in nineteenth-century Europe. With regard to the former, Breuilly argues that nationalism was not so much a cause as a product. 'Their major contributions to unification were to provide legitimation for unity in the eyes of outsiders and essential elite coordination for the effective running of the new state once the initial act of unification had been carried through' (1993: 96). The key was that nationalism had little popular appeal as such. While it played no part in the resistance to Napoleonic invasion, the legacy of political-administrative organisation of the territories in question provided the framework in which nationalist consciousness emerged. In this regard, the German confederation was a more effective seedbed than Italy, especially as it had to come to terms with adjacent spheres of influence in the form of the French and Russian states. It was precisely the organisational effectiveness of the confederation after 1815 which made it the focus of nationalist opposition. The state system in the form of the *Zollverein* – Customs Union – acted to shape economic and political national consciousness.

In Italy, on the other hand, the lack of organisational unity made radical nationalism under Mazzini the more likely form, although the fragmentation of the territory into statelets delayed the formation of 'national' consciousness. However, in neither Germany nor Italy was nationalism a popular force in 1848, and its appeal was limited and its character divided. From both cases, Breuilly draws out a more general principle that nationalism is not primarily a movement of sentiment or ideology, but dependent on mobilising interests, and on their territorial organisation. In other words, national ideology has an important mobilising and co-ordinating function, but is not the 'cause' of nationalism as such. The political movement is more important. Breuilly is critical of the view that radical nationalism actually led to the unity of Germany and Italy, and prefers to see it as a means by which liberal elites legitimated their new states, especially in the eyes of powerful allies and neighbours. However, nationalism did play an important part in the unification of the historic territories of Poland which could be 'imagined', although these could not be imagined as ethnically or linguistically homogeneous.

In short, Breuilly's argument is that unification nationalism was an elitist movement with little popular base, although in Poland for historic reasons it was stronger. Nationalist movements in the three countries expressed nationhood in historical-territorial terms as a means of reinforcing state integrity and of overcoming centrifugal forces. The gist of his argument is that these states were 'made' as political-administrative units first, and cultural-national ones later, for 'politics' is the key to unification nationalism.

As regards 'separatist' nationalism in the Habsburg and Ottoman empires of nineteenth-century Europe, Breuilly argues that the initial nationalist responses tended to come from culturally dominant groups, and that nationalism took quite different forms in each empire. Whereas in the Habsburg empire co-ordination and mobilisation were important in nationalist movements, legitimacy mattered in the case of the Ottoman empire. The Habsburg empire had been a feudal state in the eighteenth century in which noble landowners had formal and extensive political rights. As a consequence, elite control of institutions and an ongoing process of modernisation created the bases of nationalist organisation, so that national opposition to imperial power developed through these privileged groups and was expressed in historic territorial terms, something of special benefit to linguistic communities. On the other hand, the Ottoman empire was organised by means of a system of bureaucratic and military control from the centre combined with informal agreements with local power groups (as in Greece), but by and large there were no local institutions to give a clear focus to political resistance, nor local language divisions. In the Habsburg empire, however, economic and linguistic divisions often coincided, and overlapped with religious ones.

The key to the ways in which nationalist movements emerged, according to Breuilly, depends on the structure and organisation of the states to which they were opposed. There are similarities between the way nationalism developed in the Habsburg lands and the way it developed in France and England, but what mattered was the existence of ethnic divisions, the fact that state power could only be secured by territorial separation rather than reform, and that the language used to justify it was couched in terms of cultural identity rather than historic or natural rights. It fits his general argument that the legitimating function of nationalist rhetoric is secondary to the functions of co-ordination and mobilisation. In other words, it is opposition to a modernising state – a political function – which is the key to the emergence of nationalism out of the nineteenth-century European empires.

Is nationalism simply politics?

Both Mann and Breuilly start from the premise that nationalism is an essentially political phenomenon tied in with state formation in nineteenth-century Europe. Hence it is the process of political modernisation which matters, and nationalist politics emerge as a reaction to this process. In essence, both Mann and Breuilly are arguing that too much is made of culturalist accounts of nationalism, when in fact political rather than economic accounts (be they the outcome of forces of industrialism or capitalism) have primacy.

Let us examine the key points of criticism of this 'political' explanation. In the first place, 'state-building' accounts tend to ignore the variety of kinds of states which develop, or at least imply that while there are deviant outliers, it is democratic, Western states which matter. This seems to be the assumption which lies behind Hans Kohn's well-known distinction between 'Western' and 'Eastern' forms of nationalism. He argues that the former is largely a political occurrence which was preceded by the formation of the future nation-state in England, France, the Netherlands, Switzerland, the US and the British Dominions. Eastern forms of nationalism, on the other hand, were cultural rather than political in essence according to Kohn, and 'generally at a more backward stage of social and political development'. Eastern forms of nationalism 'extolled the primitive and ancient depth and peculiarities of its traditions in contrast to Western rationalism and to universal standards' (Hutchinson and Smith, 1994: 164). The distinction may have empirical value insofar as the 'mix' of ethnic and civic aspects of nationalism clearly varies, but whether we should elevate it into a generic and dichotomous principle is another matter. We might argue that ethnic forms of nationalism tend to become routinised into civic forms in order for the state to operate. Having high levels of emotional identification and conflict endemic in the state does not permit the routinised and taken-for-granted quality of much political organisation and state practices. If we take to extremes the view that, for example, Western states have essentially non-ethnic – territorial – forms of nationalism underpinning them, and that only 'ethnic nationalism' is the 'true' form (often connived at by these states with the claim that theirs is patriotism not nationalism) then we rule out perhaps the most significant variant of nationalism that there has ever been, namely, classical Western state nationalism.

We also risk, perhaps, ignoring the varieties of 'nation-state' in modern history, notably the liberal, imperialist and fascist forms. Mommsen (1990) has pointed out that in the late nineteenth and early twentieth centuries the nation-state lost its emancipatory features and took on anti-liberal ones in which national homogeneity became the ideal. The new integralist version of the nation-state was also strengthened from the 1880s by the policy of high imperialism, notably in Germany, France and the UK, whereby political and cultural traditions were extended abroad via the expansion of empire. The transition from a liberal to an exclusivist version of the nation-state reached its acme in the fascist period in the second quarter of this century, but far from the Second World War leading to disenchantment with the idea of the nation-state, its liberal variant re-established itself on a global scale in the second half of the century. Mommsen comments: 'the age of the nation-state is far from over; rather we observe a revival of the nation-state, notwithstanding the increasing interdependence of the world which could suggest that transnational forces of political and economic organisation are increasing in importance. . . . The nation-state is still with us as an essential principle of political organisation, but it is to be hoped that it will not resemble too closely its forerunners of the late nineteenth and early twentieth century' (1990: 226).

The second reason why we should be wary of treating nationalism as essentially a political project directed towards state formation and state building is that recent work on the origins of the classical European nation-state shows a considerable diversity of origins. The routes to 'nationhood' of the major European states – Germany, France, Britain and Italy – are all distinctive and 'unusual' to the extent that the conventional model does not apply. In recent years the old assumption of the alignment of state and nation has been called into question, and scholars are beginning to explore the circumstances and contingencies which were once taken for granted. Britain's peculiarity derives from the fact that the state was formed in the 'pre-modern' period – 1707 – and in such a way that a unitary political system lay alongside distinctive civil societies which were largely autonomous and self-governing. Italy is, of course, a much younger state, but it too had a weak sense of nation-ness to go with its statehood. Both might be called state-nations rather than nation-states.

It is an interesting aspect of the literature on nationalism that there is far more emphasis on the latter than the former. Perhaps the most obvious, and certainly the most successful, example of a state-nation is the US. By this we mean that it was first and foremost a political rather than a cultural concept insofar as its population which was so ethnically diverse had to be taught how to be American. It is, of course, the case that a common sense of nationality was successfully created so that imagining a 'nation' came almost naturally. The US like France, its eighteenth-century republican *confrère*, equated the state with the 'people', and helped to create the revolutionary concept of the 'nation' as constituted by the deliberate opting-in of its citizens. In Hobsbawm's words: 'Americans are those who wish to be' (1990: 88). The making of Americans, as Billig points out, is a matter of daily ritual, such as the pledge of allegiance. He comments: 'the sacral has become part of everyday life, instead of being confined to a special place of worship or particular day of celebration' (Billig, 1995: 51), and so the state-nation enters the private lives of individual citizens.

One interesting feature of recent writing on nationalism is the exploration of the relationship between state and nation in terms of their historical development. In his study of citizenship and nationhood in France and Germany, Rogers Brubaker (1992) argues that definitions of citizenship in these key European states result from the fact that whereas in France the unitary state was established before the concept of nation took hold there, in Germany it was the other way round; the 'nation' preceded the 'state'. In France, the monarchy held sway over a fairly defined and gradually expanding territory, and promoted the concept of citizenship based on *ius soli*, the law of soil or territorial jurisdiction, in such a way that whatever their ethnic or geographical origins, all residents on French soil could in principle be subjects, later citizens, of the French state. Peasants had, of course, in Eugene Weber's phrase, become Frenchmen, but this formulation expresses nicely the prior existence of the state over the sense of nation, at least in popular terms. In Germany, by contrast, the unitary state did not arrive until 1871, and the nation had to be defined differently. Since members of the German nation might be subjects of different kings – Bavaria, Saxony, Prussia, even Austria and Russia – national identity was based on *ius sanguinis*, the law of blood, so that anyone with German blood was German, and thus after 1871 eligible to be a citizen of Germany whether or not they actually lived on German soil.

As a result of these different routes to 'nation-statehood', the interpretation of nationality differs. In France, according to Brubaker, it is state-centred and assimilationist, whereas in Germany it is volk-centred and differentialist. He comments:

> The state-centred assimilationist understanding of nationhood in France is embodied and expressed in an expansive definition of citizenship, one that automatically transforms second-generation immigrants into citizens, assimilating them – legally – to other French men and women. The ethnocultural, differentialist understanding of nationhood in Germany is embodied and expressed in a definition of citizenship that is remarkably open to ethnic German immigrants from Eastern Europe and the Soviet Union, but remarkably closed to non-German immigrants.
>
> (Brubaker, 1992: 3)

There are, of course, issues which are beyond the scope of this chapter, having, for example, to do with racism and immigration in these states. But for our purpose here it is important to note that the historical and ideological routes to modern citizenship are quite different, making problematic the assumption that state and nation in the West have been fused in a similar and unproblematic way as if nationalism operates simply to make the state. Even in the classical European heartlands there is no single route for the state to take, and this should sensitise us to the orthodoxy that nationalism is about state-building.

A third criticism of this orthodoxy relates to its overly rationalist assumptions especially about the normality of cultural homogeneity. We might say that if the aim of nationalism has primarily been to bring this homogeneity about, then it has not done a very successful job. It is the lack of correspondence between nation and state in Europe as well as elsewhere which is striking. We have many states which are not 'nations' insofar as their citizens have a variety of ethnic identities, and there are nations which are not states in the conventional sense of the term. Josep Llobera's comment is apt: 'state and nation make strange bedfellows basically because they are organised on very different principles' (1994: 121).

Finally, the 'state-building' theory of nationalism can be criticised for reducing cultural nationalism to the role of cover for political nationalism rather than a phenomenon in its own right. Its critique often takes on a robust, even aggressive, dismissal of 'national' traditions as fabricated, epiphenomenal and derivative, and is linked with the view that cultural nationalism is frequently regressive and romantic. This is the stance taken by Hobsbawm and Mann, for example, who in their different and competing ways treat nationalism as subordinate to wider economic or political projects respectively. While it is proper to be sceptical of the claims of nationalists for the essentialist character of their traditions, a similar stance might be adopted to its opponents.

Conclusion

In this chapter we have explored the dominant thesis that nationalism is essentially about the process of state formation and maintenance. This is a variant of a 'modernist' approach which sees nationalism as instrumental to wider concerns of a largely materialist nature. Hence, modernist explanations can focus on the relationship between nationalism and industrialism (Gellner), nationalism and capitalism (Hobsbawm) and, as we have seen in this chapter, nationalism and state-building. In each of these types of account, cultural and ethnic aspects are downplayed to the role of secondary and ideological aspects of the wider project. In the next chapter we will focus on 'liberation' nationalism as it emerged in opposition to colonial regimes and in the post-colonial period, and we will once more encounter the dialectic between ethnicity and state-building.

6

DIALECTIC WITH THE OTHER

Liberation nationalism in the twentieth century

For much of the twentieth century it seemed that anti-colonial nationalism was its 'last wave', that Third World nationalisms represented the end of a long process of liberation against colonial powers begun in Latin America in the previous century. Indeed, the 'last wave' was the description of Benedict Anderson in his classic study *Imagined Communities* first published in 1983. The second issue was published in 1991, and by 1996 it was in its seventh impression. By this point Anderson had acknowledged that this description was premature, not only because plainly other waves of nationalism had followed it, but because the 'periphery' played a much more active and involved part in its oppression, and hence liberation, than previous theories had suggested.

In this chapter I will argue that this revisionist way of looking at 'liberation nationalism' provides much greater insights into the nature of nationalism itself, and helps us to break out of the tendency to see it as a separate, catching-up form of nationalism. Above all, I will seek to show that the key insight is in the construction of the 'other', that there is an interaction, a dialectic, between imagining self and other in such a way that while both colonial power and anti-colonial reaction ostensibly were engaged in defining each as different, their very essences actually carried that of the other. Hence, the contribution of liberation nationalism is not that it completes the puzzle begun in Europe centuries before – the belated catching-up process – but that it makes us see that nationalism and national identification is a game played with reflecting mirrors wherever it occurs.

The salience of identity also highlights the importance of gender relations in nationalism. This chapter will focus explicitly on the ways in which these have played a crucial role in how nationalist movements have developed and how the nation is imagined. This is not to imply that gender relations only operate with regard to liberation nationalism, but is to acknowledge that the role of women in particular has been especially important in these struggles. Liberation nationalism has focused on women in important and by no means straightforward ways, and that is the justification for looking at gender relations in this chapter.

Around the 1980s, a major change of focus occurred with regard to how liberation nationalism was understood, hence Anderson's self-revisionism for his second edition in the early 1990s. If our understanding of liberation nationalism reached its culmination in the work of writers like Emmanuel Wallerstein (1979) and Andre Gunder Frank in the 1960s and 1970s, then the watershed of the 1980s produced the insights of Edward Said (1993), Homi Bhabha (1990) and Partha Chatterjee (1986). It may seem that in part this change marked the end of materialist and Marxist accounts, and their replacement by more 'cultural' approaches, but this would be altogether too crude. After all, the revisionists retained an interest in the ways in which economic and cultural power interacted, and writers such as Frank and Wallerstein operated in a fairly unorthodox, albeit Marxist way. Other writers such as Franz Fanon provided an important bridge between the old and the new accounts.

The decline of post-colonialism

Part of the reason for the change of approach clearly lies in the ostensible failure of the post-colonial regimes themselves. In other words, if these regimes were meant to be the epitome of economic, social and cultural liberation, then something went horribly wrong. This was not simply a matter of Western liberal distaste and conservative vindication, but the realisation that many of the regimes were ill-equipped to harness nationalism in a liberating way for their populations. This was to imply a failure of will, for often the oppressive structural conditions of world trade carried through implications for how regimes could operate and legitimate themselves. Instances abounded: the post-colonial regimes of India and Algeria, founded on a version of Western secular socialism, were outflanked by counter-risings which mobilised culture and religion. Even where new states were created out of the wreckage of empire as in Turkey in the post-Ottoman period, ideological and political stability was hard to find. Much of the Middle East and Africa saw post-colonial regimes which had won independence swept away by cultural forces. The Western response to these forms of 'politicised religion' (Jeffery, 1998) was to reach for explanations in terms of 'fundamentalism' which described much but explained little, or to fall back on essentialist accounts which argued that these new states were basically unstable because they had been drawn arbitrarily and hurriedly by fleeing colonial powers. Readers will recognise by now that such essentialist explanations and implied solutions – redraw the boundaries to make the states ethnically homogeneous – beg more questions than they answer.

What was an intriguing problem, and one much more difficult to explain, was that in many parts of the Third World secular nationalism as represented by the post-colonial regimes in India, Algeria and much of Africa, was withering away under the challenge of a much more culturalist nationalism which sought to rally under a politicised form of religious expression. More established secular regimes such as that established by 'Ataturk' – Mustafa Kemal – in 1920s Turkey were losing a battle with a more generic Islam in the 1990s. In India, Hindu nationalism aligned itself with the territory under the control of the state (even/especially those parts occupied by non-Hindu – particularly Muslim – peoples who were judged to be there illegitimately and 'unnaturally', the result of some kind of historical accident).

Elsewhere, the picture was complicated by the growing politicisation of Islam, which appeared to be a supra-national force but which was quite capable of becoming a 'national' ideology as in Iran after the fall of the Shah. In the Middle East, the picture was further complicated not only by Islam but by the vestiges of Arabism, itself a supra-national ideology, and one which arose in the nineteenth century not as a reaction to Western rule but as a critique of the Ottoman empire which had been dominant since the sixteenth century (Kramer, 1993). The Arab awakening in Arabia and the Fertile Crescent both generated and fed off an Arabic cultural and literary revival, and was mobilised by Western powers against Turkey during the First World War. It became a truism that the territories were then divided in an arbitrary way by Western powers to reflect geo-political interests. As Kramer comments: 'None of the new states was commensurate with the political community. Syria, Lebanon, Iraq, Transjordan, Palestine – these names derived from geographical or classical history, and their borders largely reflected the imperial jostling for strategic position on oil' (ibid.: 179).

The problem was that few thought of themselves as 'Arab' first and foremost, and the lands of the Fertile Crescent became a complex of religious, ethnic and dynastic identities. What became known as 'Arab nationalism' took an anti-imperialist twist after 1920, and a revolutionary mode after 1948, most obviously in Nasserism in Egypt and Baathism in Syria. Sami Zubaida (1989) has pointed out that Arab, Egyptian and Islam jostled for position much of the time, and that the epithet 'Egyptian' only acquired political resonance in the nineteenth century under a dynasty which separated Egypt from the Ottoman empire while retaining Turkish personnel and language in government and the army. 'Arabism' came much later, and latterly was challenged by Islam which attacked Arab nationalists for betraying fellow Muslims (in Turkey) in favour of the West. Zubaida makes the important point that different identities could be mobilised as the need arose (as Muslims against the 'Christian' West, or as Arabs against the Jewish state, for example, and as Egyptians against neighbouring states – or Britain in the 1956 Suez debacle). In other words, which identity was claimed and mobilised depended on the geo-political circumstances of the conflict to hand, and often more than one could be used – witness the Arab–Israeli wars of the 1960s and 1970s. Zubaida is critical of Anthony Smith's notion that ethnic-based solidarity was a key component of pre-modern history, and argues that modern states are not determined by this pre-modern history.

What is undoubtedly clear is that Arab nationalism (we should properly call this pan-Arabism, as it is strictly not 'nationalist', just as pan-Africanism, another casualty of post-colonialism, is not) has succumbed to a broader 'religious' identity of Islam, so that mobilising people as Muslims rather than Arabs has greater play in the late twentieth century. We should perhaps beware of concluding that this has more to do with religion than with politics, and the term 'politicised religion' seems an appropriate hybrid in this respect. Elsewhere, it is clear that what passes for 'inter-ethnic' conflicts has taken over from anti-colonial struggles, and that 'funda-mentalism' and 'nativism' are used less as explanations and more as labels. The old accounts of liberation nationalism seem less and less relevant at the end of the twentieth century.

Liberation and underdevelopment

These accounts were premised on the dominance of the colonial axis. They reached their apotheosis in the 1970s neo-Marxist accounts of Wallerstein and Frank. Wallerstein (1974, 1979) is best known for his 'world system theory' which we might compare and contrast with the more orthodox Marxist variant as follows:

ORTHODOX	NEO-MARXIST
production relations	exchange relations
class relations	relations of dependence
internal causation	external causation
capitalist mode of production	world system of capitalism
social formation derived from mode of production	territorial or national unit as sub-system of global system
exploitation within the labour process	transfer of surplus value

As this model indicates, Wallerstein focused on the relations of exchange gener-ated by capitalism rather than on defining it essentially as a mode of production. Exchange takes place between territories and what he calls 'ethno-nations' rather than simply by class divisions, that is, according to how they are structured by core–periphery relations. He comments:

> Core and periphery are simply phrases to locate one crucial part of the system of surplus appropriation by the bourgeoisie. To oversimplify, capi-talism is a system in which the surplus value of the proletariat is appropriated by the bourgeoisie. When this proletariat is located in a different country from this bourgeoisie, one of the mechanisms that has affected the process of appropriation is the manipulation of controlling flows over state boundaries. This results in patterns of 'uneven develop-ment' which are summarised in the concepts of core, periphery and semi-periphery. This is an intellectual tool to help analyse the multiple forms of class conflict in the capitalist world-economy.
>
> (Wallerstein, 1979: 293)

Wallerstein is broadening the concept of class struggle to include not only conven-tional social class structured around the mode of production, but territorial units, and especially ones in which people have a shared identity – what he calls 'ethno-nations'. By these he does not mean 'status groups' in a Weberian sense. He comments 'I believe "class" and what I prefer to call "ethno-nation" are two sets of clothing for the same basic reality. However, it is important to realise that they are in fact two sets of clothing, so that we may appreciate how, when and why one set is worn rather than the other. Ethno-nations, just like social classes, are formed, consolidate themselves, disintegrate or disaggregate, and are constantly re-formed' (ibid.: 224–5). By focusing on territorial relations between core and periphery, Wallerstein is pointing out that there are two dimensions of class relations in the broadest sense, and that it is the transfer of resources from periphery to core, from poor to rich, that generates social conflict. Anti-colonialist struggles, then, are waged by 'nation-classes'. The great revolutions of the twentieth century, Cuban, Vietnamese, Chinese, Russian, have been as much national as social. Similarly, it is 'not at all accidental that oppressed lower strata in core capitalist countries (Blacks in the US, Quebecois in Canada, Occitanians in France etc.) have come to express their class consciousness in ethno-national terms' (ibid.: 230).

Wallerstein saw no real difference between ethno-national struggles in developed capitalist economies as indicated above, and those in the Third World, although in the latter case, class and ethnicity coupled with territorial exploitation generated a more revolutionary strain. He himself sought to apply his thesis to the case of Scotland, arguing that its relationship to the English core was one essentially of colonial exploitation which helped to explain the rise of nationalism in the second half of the twentieth century. Some writers, notably Michael Hechter (1975), applied the term 'internal colonialism' to the relation of the 'Celtic countries' to England, while others pointed to the limitations of this model in a country which played the role of 'junior partner' in British imperialism rather than colonial underdog (McCrone, 1992). Wallerstein (1980) himself entered into a debate with the Scottish historian Christopher Smout about the extent to which Scotland pursued economic development by English 'invitation' rather than by free-market forces.

His foray into the territorial politics of 'developed' societies was probably less successful than his analysis of Third World countries (Wallerstein himself began as a historian of Africa). Nevertheless, his key insight was that the world as a whole should be treated as a single 'world system' rather than as a segmented one in which the 'underdeveloped' territories strove to catch up with the developed. Wallerstein observed:

> A developmentalist perspective assumes that the unit within which social action principally occurs is a politico-cultural unit – the state, or nation, or people – and seeks to explain differences between these units, including why their economies are different. A world-system perspective assumes, by contrast, that social action takes place in an entity within which there is an ongoing division of labour, and seeks to discover empirically whether such an entity is or is not unified politically or culturally, asking theoretically what are the consequences of the existence or non-existence of such unity.
>
> (Wallerstein, 1979: 155)

Wallerstein, then, regarded the world-economy as a single system with one division of labour, and a variety of cultures with no overarching political structure for redistributing surplus beyond the market. Territories related to each according to their structural positions *vis-à-vis* development in the world-system

In similar fashion, Andre Gunder Frank (1971) derived his notion of systematic 'under-development' from his work on Latin America. That is, less developed territories were structurally prevented from catching up because the developed world needed their raw materials and cheap, captive markets, rather than because their populations did not have the proper attitudinal need for achievement or work habits. Frank's notion, like Wallerstein's, also provided a rich framework for analysing economic exploitation and concomitant nationalist reaction. Both accounts were essentially materialist insofar as they started from an analysis of the economic relations between territories, and derived political and cultural responses from it. Their accounts could handle with little difficulty the rise of nationalist-anticolonialist challenges to colonial regimes. They were, however, less able to avoid other problems. Theda Skocpol (1977) has suggested that Wallerstein fell into the 'mirror-image' trap of trying to set up a paradigm in contradistinction to the one it opposes, in this case, modernisation theory of the 1950s and 1960s. She argues that he set out to break away from the over-emphasis on national states and ahistorical model-building, but ended up assuming strong states and international political domination as the basic premise of his theory.

It is also plain that under-development theorists such as Wallerstein and Frank have very little to say about nationalism and ethnicity as such, for they take for granted the existence of these, and they are treated as unproblematic. How an 'ethno-nation' is constructed and maintained is not defined as a problem in their accounts, and hence, they would seem to have little to offer by way of explanation for the collapse of post-colonial regimes and the rise of alternative politico-cultural codes. With hindsight, we can see that theories of under-development of this sort grew out of a debate with more orthodox Marxist and modernist accounts of social and economic change in the 1960s and 1970s. The neo-Marxist strain which Wallerstein and Frank represented owed more to the writings of the 'early' Marx than to the later one, and for a decade or two provided a new and fresh way of analysing colonialism. It seems, however, ill-suited to the more political and culturalist approaches of the 1980s and 1990s. We see, then, in Benedict Anderson's recanting of liberation nationalism as the 'last-wave', a recognition that another dimension is needed, and it is to this that we now turn.

After the last wave

Let us start with Anderson's own way out of the problem. He adopts the challenging position that the new American states, north and south, of the late eighteenth and early nineteenth centuries developed understandings of nation-ness well before most of Europe, and hence were the progenitors of nationalism in the modern age. These, including the US, were 'creole' states, that is, they were 'formed and led by people who shared a common language and common descent with those against whom they fought' (Anderson, 1996a: 47). 'Creoles' referred to people of European extraction but born in the Americas. The puzzle, according to Anderson, was why such a population made common cause with large, indigenous native populations against their fellow-ethnics in Spain or Portugal (or England/Britain in the case of the US). His answer is that while the American states (North and South) had been administrative units from the sixteenth to the eighteenth centuries, they had been excluded from power precisely on the grounds that they were irremediably creole. The logic of exclusion was clear: 'born in the Americas, he could not be a true Spaniard; ergo, born in Spain, the *peninsular* could not be a true American' (1996a: 58). This was as true of north Americans as of those in the south, and it was the northerners – Protestant, English-speaking creoles – 'who were much more favourably situated for realizing the idea of "America", and indeed eventually succeeded in appropriating the everyday title of "Americans"' (ibid.: 63).

It is Anderson's argument that the framework for new national consciousness was uniquely provided by these creole cultures rather than, as orthodoxy has it, liberal and Enlightenment movements in Europe itself. In other words, creole nationalism was 'foundational' precisely because it conveyed the contradictory condition of 'being between'. In many respects, nationalism should be seen as the outcome of these contradictions, as a condition of political and cultural dissonance. The problem with characterisations of nationalism as 'Western' and 'Eastern' is not simply that they carry assumptions about the former being more 'developed' than the latter (usually contained in the 'civic' versus 'ethnic' distinction, for example), but that they miss the crucial point that constructing the national 'self' intimately involves constructing the 'other'. One is not only a mirror of the other, but involves a complex dialectic between the two ('me watching you watching me', and so on). That is similar to what Said means by a 'structure of attitude and reference' (1993: xxvi) whereby the experience of the oppressor and the oppressed is largely a common one. That is the point he is making when he argues that imperialism and resistance actually advanced together, that, in essence, there is no 'us' and 'them'. It is this dialectic of identity to which Said points, and not, as some of his critics have it, that the colonised simply inculcate their image from the coloniser.

Just how that was brought about is the subject of Anderson's 'revisionist' account published in his second edition in 1996 (Anderson, 1996a). There he identifies three key institutions of power which profoundly shaped the way in which the colonial power imagined its dominion, and which also set up the framework for its anti-colonial successor. These institutions were: the census, the map and the museum. The common aim of all three was, to borrow Said's term, to codify difference, to turn it into a taken-for-granted piece of knowledge. Anderson argues that these provided a totalising classificatory grid, a 'warp' as well as a 'weft'. The warp refers to a way of classifying peoples, regions, religions, languages, products, monuments and so on. 'The effect of the grid was always to be able to say of anything that it was this, not that; it belonged here, not there. It was bounded, determinate, and therefore – in principle – countable' (Anderson, 1996a: 254). The weft refers to the serialisation, that the world is made up of 'replicable plurals': 'the particular always stood as a provisional representation of a series' (ibid.: 254–5).

The census was used, in Anderson's words, to create a new demographic topography which became the basis for organising education, the law and the police, bureaucracy and the organs of the state. From the late 1870s, he argues, the census categories became more visibly and exclusively racial (rather than religious), and their importance lay less in the construction of ethnic-racial classifications and more in their systematic quantification. As a result, 'the flow of subject populations through the mesh of differential schools, courts, clinics, police stations and immigration offices created "traffic habits" which in turn gave real social life to the state's earlier fantasies' (ibid.: 246). Classifying populations in this way provided a degree of visibility and control for the colonial state, but one which crucially employed cultural markers which became embedded in identities in the post-colonial situations. The most infamous example of such practices might be the division into Hutus and Tutsis by the Belgian colonial regime for the purposes of social and political control in what is now Rwanda. What started out as a fairly arbitrary distinction (owning cattle or not) has taken on not only cultural but even physiological characteristics (Tutsis became taller because they were more affluent and better fed). Once the colonial power left, the distinction became 'naturalised' and took on an awful life of its own. Classification and counting are based on systems of implicit power which are all the more powerful for being that.

The map, not only the census, shaped the 'grammar' of post-colonial states. The mercatorian map, which European colonisers used to divide up the surface of the globe into parallel lines of longitude and latitude, replaced other ways of understanding space. The mercatorian map happens to over-emphasise the size of the colonising countries, and under-emphasises that of the colonised. This was not a deliberate strategy, but a function of the mathematics of projecting a sphere onto a plane, but it became a convenient representation of political power and difference. (Other versions of maps such as the Phillips projection which preserves area not distance are less useful in this political respect.) In general, a map is to space what the clock is to time, namely the essence of the thing rather than simply a way of representing it. (Indeed, we speak of the clock 'charting' time.) So powerful, in fact, is the map that what was originally a map 'for' has become a map 'of', even though it actually never ceased to be a map 'for' – that is, a purpose – of defining and charting systems of power. Anderson points out that maps stood as property spaces, as 'sovereignties', and also as 'logos' – as pure signs of a country which we could recognise by its shape. He comments:

> In this shape, the map entered an infinitely reproducible series, available
> for transfer to posters, official seals, letterheads, magazines and text-book
> covers, table cloths and hotel walls. Instantly recognisable, everywhere

> visible, the logo-map penetrated deep into the popular imagination,
> forming a powerful emblem for the anticolonial nationalisms being born.
> (Anderson, 1996a: 175)

This was especially important as a rallying emblem for subordinate groups. For dominant ones it was often enough to colour the territory an appropriate colour (pink-red for the British imperial territories, purple-blue for the French ones). There is an irony that as these colonial territories have been lost, so the capacity of the core to 'map' itself becomes increasingly problematic. In the 'British' Isles, for example, the geography (the archipelago of islands) does not map onto sovereignty (two states – the United Kingdom, and the Republic of Ireland). How many, for example, would recognise a map of England without Scotland to the north and Wales to the west? While the inhabitants of these 'Celtic' countries would have little problem in recognising the relevant map-logos, the ambiguity and confusion about 'England' is represented in and compounded by its lack of a recognisable map-identity.

Finally, the job of recovering and recharging the 'past' is the task of the museum. Anderson points out that until the early nineteenth century, the colonial rulers of Southeast Asia had little interest in antique monuments, but came to appreciate their ideological possibilities in the face of indigenous challenge. Archaeology could be used to 'prove' that natives were indubitably natives, and hence education would be wasted on them. Second, ancient monuments could be used in the ideological battle against the anti-colonialists to say: 'Our very presence shows that you have always been, or have long become, incapable of either greatness or self-rule' (ibid.: 181). This monumental archaeology also allowed the colonial state to take on the role of guardian of 'tradition' in such a way that its ancient prestige enveloped the natives in a diffuse way. Thus museumised, the colonial state could legitimate itself as the protector of the 'heritage' over which it ruled in a benign way.

Anderson's point is not simply to show how census, map and museum were legitimatory devices of colonialism, but how they became key emblems of the anti-colonial movement in turn. The nation could be imagined and reproduced without much difficulty because the spadework had already been done; the task was simply to transfer ownership to the 'people'. Hence, the 'traffic-habits' of the old regime could be redirected but not radically altered by the new one, for the basic categorisation of peoples had already been done. Similarly, the people's territory could be easily charted because its logo-map was already to hand. Anderson points out, for example, that what brought quarrelling Papuan nationalists together in the 1960s was the shared map over which they squabbled. Finally, the nation's heritage was re-appropriated rather than radically redefined by the new nationalists. The issue was one of ownership rather than content, for the album of the nation's ancestors had already been assembled. Thus, Angkor Wat which had been restored by the French colonialists became a central symbol in turn for Sihanouk's royalists, Lon Nol's militarists, and Pol Pot's jacobins (ibid.: 183). So the census, map and museum shaped the grammar and syntax of the new post-colonial regimes, which then sought legitimation within the series of other similarly defined post-colonial 'nations'. Their collective logo 'by its emptiness, contextlessness, visual memorableness and infinite reproducibility brought census and map, warp and woof into an inerasable embrace' (ibid.: 185).

Culture and colonialism

We can now begin to see more clearly why post-colonial regimes faltered in the longer term. Their first step was to take over the syntax of governance from colonialism, along with its hidden rules of political and cultural grammar. More fundamentally, the very conception of the anti-colonial nation as the antithesis of colonialism was actually its mirror. In the words of Eley and Suny:

> Nationalism in the colonial world borrowed from European nationalism even as it attempted to liberate itself from the nationalist discourse of the colonisers. Without completely freeing themselves from the structure of power of imperialism, colonial nationalists nevertheless adapted the discourse to their own requirements, eventually even using nationalism as a new form of state ideology.
>
> (Eley and Suny, 1996: 29)

Here Chatterjee's work on India (1986, 1996) is most illuminating. His argument is that nationalism declared that it had domain over the spiritual, cultural level, and refused to allow the colonial power to intervene in that domain. He argues that colonial nationalism first created its own domain of cultural sovereignty within the colonial society even before it began its struggle with the imperial power. It did this by dividing the world into material/secular and cultural/spiritual domains, and in such a way that the West was dominant in the former, and colonial nationalism in the latter, in which, crucially, the essential marks of cultural identity were to be found. In this way colonial nationalism was empowered, and refused to allow the imperial power to penetrate its own inner world. Chatterjee is critical of writers like Anderson and Gellner for seeing Third World nationalisms as 'modular', based like so many templates on the European experience, whereas they are in essence defined by their difference from the West and in the context of the colonialist experience.

We have here a similarity between two sets of arguments. On the one hand, the conventional media wisdom for the collapse of post-colonial states such as Sri Lanka, Algeria and Rwanda is that 'nativism' has taken over, that older forms of ethnic identity have reasserted themselves and choked the younger, more secular and 'civic' forms of state nationalism. On the other hand, if Chatterjee is right, then anti-colonial nationalism always had as its essence an inner, ethnic and 'spiritual' form into which it could retreat and out of which it could sally to attack.

There is little doubt that the post-colonial regime which gained independence for India in 1947 sought to build a civic form of nationalism, rather than the 'communalism' which was deemed to be reactionary and backward-looking. Prime Minister Nehru made this plain:

> The day of even national culture is rapidly passing and the world is becoming one cultural unit. The real struggle in India is not between Hindu culture and Muslim culture, but between these two and the conquering scientific culture of modern civilisation . . . everywhere religion recedes into the background . . . we have to come to grips with this life, this world, this nature which surrounds us with infinite variety. Some Hindus talk of going back to the vedas, some Moslems dream of an Islamic theocracy, idle fantasies. For there is no going back, even if this was thought desirable. There is only one-way traffic in time.
>
> (Matossian, 1994: 222)

Nehru's hopes, fifty years on, seem time-bound and misplaced. There has been a rise of pan-Indian Hindu nationalist movements who seek to redefine India's national identity in line with the Indian state. *Hindutva* – 'Hindu-ness' – is a major threat to the secular post-colonial order, and seeks to make Indian identity synonymous with Hindu-ness. Here is a counter-view to Nehru's secular one:

> The Hindu *rashtra* (nation) is essentially cultural in content, whereas the so-called secular state pertains to the state and is limited to the territorial and political aspect of the Nation. The more territorial-cum-political concept divorced from its cultural essence can never be expected to impart any sanctity to the country's unity. The emotional binding of the people can only be furnished by culture and once that is snapped then there remains no logical argument against the demand by any part to separate itself from the country.
>
> (H.V. Sheshadri, quoted in Varshney, 1993: 240)

The irony is that both the Western media and Hindu nationalists would recognise this 'natural' animosity as the basis of communal violence in modern India and elsewhere. As far as the former are concerned, the rise of communalism in India and elsewhere is a reflection of the 'essential' importance of tribe, culture, religion and caste in Eastern nationalism. In this view there is something natural about the bloodiness and violence of politics in the 'East' (conflict in the former Yugoslavia can be included as it is on the fringe of the 'East' and liable to its cultural and social forces). On the other hand, there is also the tendency among nationalists to see nationalism, at least in its 'civic' form, itself as a Western import, to be put into practice by Western-educated intellectuals and politicians (like Nehru). Of course, as we have argued in this book, the discourse on nationalism has always been caught up with the European discourse on modernity, and theories of nationalism are sometimes little more than neo-modernisation theories. Chatterjee is critical of writers like Gellner and Anderson who universalise Western experience for the rise and diffusion of nationalism, and underplay the experience of colonialism. He complains:

> History has decreed that we be perpetual consumers of modernity. Europeans and Americans have thought out not only the script of colonial enlightenment and exportation, but also that of our anti-colonial resistance and post-colonial misery. Even our imaginations, it seems, must remain forever colonised. The most powerful as well as the most creative results of the nationalist imagination are posited not on the identity but on difference with the 'modular' forms propagated by the West.
>
> (Chatterjee, 1993: 73)

Chatterjee and others, including Edward Said, have challenged conventional theories and explanations as to why anti-imperialism took on the form of nationalism. They are critical of overly political accounts, which underplay the importance of cultural resistance. Conventional histories of nationalism tend to focus primarily on the political contest, constitutional or violent, with the colonial power, whereas anti-colonial nationalism captured the cultural space within the colonial state. Chatterjee comments: 'it is here that nationalism launches its most creative and historically significant project, to fashion a "modern" national culture which is nevertheless not "Western". If the nation is an imagined community . . . then it is here where it is brought into being. In this "true" and "essential" domain the nation is already imagined even when the state is in the hands of the colonial power' (ibid.: 524).

The problem is in large part that much of the literature on nationalism assumes, in Anderson's words, that the dawn of nationalism was also the dusk of religion (1996a: 11), and so religion is factored out of modern nationalism. However, in India and elsewhere the original fight for independence was not secular, nor did it represent the dusk of religion. Rather it was steeped in Hindu religious and cultural traditions so that the Indian dreams of the nation take religion as one of the main aspects of national identity (Van de Veer, 1994). The point is that there were many competing forms of nationalism on offer, all claiming to represent the essence of India. *Hindutva* and communalism on the one hand, and anti-colonial nationalism on the other were not competing forms. Similarly, there are many different strains of Hindu nationalism, moderate and extremist, as well as shifting meanings of Hinduism as 'culture' and/or as 'religion', and India as 'sacred geography' (Varshney, 1993). 'Moderate' nationalism emphasises Hinduism's 'natural' syncretism and pluralism, with India perceived as a federation of different communities and religions, a version of 'unity through diversity', as 'many flowers, one garland; many rivers, one ocean' (T. Basu *et al.*, 1993: 6). From the 1920s, however, a more extreme version of nationalism emerged, the *Hindutva*, which took one religion as the basis of Indian national identity. Hindu nationalism as expressed in the actions and ideology of organisations like

Rashtriya Swayamsewak Sangh (RSS) in the 1930s and 1940s now meant, according to Basu, that all the flowers 'make up the single garland of *Hindutva*, the many rivers flow into one Hindu ocean' (ibid.: 7).

The next stage in the argument is to remind ourselves that there is no automatic relationship between, on the one hand, how the nation was imagined and imperialism resisted and, on the other, the form which political nationalism took after independence. Chatterjee and Fanon both argued that if anti-colonial nationalism began as a revolutionary movement, it often was soon reduced at independence in the post-war period of 'modernisation' and 'development' to state-building based on the kinds of models on offer from the West. While it is important not to conflate the very different historical experiences of many post-colonial states, there is an argument that they had little option but to adopt the forms of state framed by the logic of the world system. Chatterjee (1993) points out that India was governed not by prophets and romantic rebels, but by Nehru, a pragmatic moderniser and state builder. To him the peasants and the urban poor were ruled by passions not reason. Nehru did not properly appreciate that Gandhi's ability to mobilise the nationalism of India was based in large part on his status as a Hindu holy man.

Similarly, Fanon writes of the anti-colonialist struggles in Algeria, and describes the way post-colonial nationalism often started off as patriotic, antagonistic and progressive, but quickly deteriorated into an ideological tool for the elite. He saw that unless national consciousness was turned at the moment of its success and changed into social consciousness, the future held an extension of imperialism, not liberation. As a result, 'autonomous forms of imagination of the community are overwhelmed and swamped by the history of the post-colonial state' (Chatterjee, 1993: 525). In the Third World the history of the nation and the history of the state seem to be particularly at odds, with the effect that the state struggles to legitimate itself. As these post-colonial states failed in this exercise, and as the programmes of development and modernisation came to little, the ascendency of 'cultural' versions of nationalism came to the fore. We should not be surprised, then, at the assertion of *Hindutva* and Islam from the 1980s. Some states, such as Turkey, have an older and, until recently, seemingly more robust stance *vis-à-vis* Islam. The success of Mustafa Kemal in holding Turkey together out of the remnants of the Ottoman empire in the aftermath of the First World War brought him the title '*Ataturk*', father of the nation (Delaney, 1991). His determinedly secular state exploited the idea of the nation as coterminous with the people living on the soil, and so the key to legitimacy for Turks became 'origins' whereas the key for Islamists was the 'divine'. The tensions have become more and more obvious. Delaney comments:

> The symbolics of political geography reinforce the belief that secularisation in Turkey cannot mean merely a separation of religion and state. Rather, the state has taken over the symbols and structure of the authority of Islam but changed the referents. The secularism Turks are

confronted with is a mirror image of the religious worldview reflected back into this world. But is the nation a sacred state or a secular religion?

(Delaney, 1991: 282)

More generally in the Third World these politico-cultural reactions are embarked on their own programmes of invention and mobilisation, which themselves essentialise cultural difference. Communalism is taken as the antithesis of the otherness of secularism which is defined as part of the Western project of modernity, with its reliance on rationalism and science. Secularism (India and Algeria are good examples) is viewed by cultural nationalists as a Western import derived from Judaeo-Christian thought with roots in the Enlightenment, Reformation and the Protestant ethic. Colonialism then became the vehicle for transporting secularism, with its assumption of state–church separation, into the Third World. This critique views the post-colonial regimes of Nehru and his successors in the Congress Party as constructed on an inappropriate foreign vision of development, democracy and urbanism. Secularism, science and democracy can be attributed to Western influences and foreign to the native communal culture, which, as we have seen, is deemed to be the preserve of the people themselves.

Such assertions that Indian culture is synonymous with Hindu culture, narrowly defined by *Hindutva*, allow the construction of a national(ist) essence which views animosity between Hindus and Muslims as 'natural', especially as the latter are deemed to have been not native to India but a remnant of a previous colonial age of conquest. The primordial people who have withstood this and later conquests are the 'true' inheritors of the culture and territory now that the usurpers have gone. Said's analysis of Orientalism has made us aware of the ways in which the colonial power has written the history of the subject nation, which in turn has been internalised into post-colonial accounts. Writing the Hindu history of India, Pandey (1992) has suggested, has involved building on the colonialist account of Muslims as outsiders, as part of another civilisation centred elsewhere. He argues that *Hindutva* history has two phases: first, the glory of pre-Muslim India, and second, the increasing troubles which have come to pass since the Muslims came to the sub-continent. He comments:

> There is a general view of Muslim history as a catalogue of conquests and cruelty which is widely propagated by Hindu historians and considerably aided by colonialist accounts which remain influential in text books and in much popular Indian history. Over time this history has come to establish itself as a kind of popular 'common-sense', which has produced myths about the marital and sexual practices of the Muslims, their perverse characters and violent temperament.

(Pandey, 1992: 13)

What we see here is a good example of the active making of anti-colonial history out of the colonial power's own accounts, and one which essentialises an inner core of culture for modern political purposes. The rise of Hindu nationalism and communalism is a modern phenomenon with its roots in anti-colonial resistance in which the nation came to imagine itself as essentially different from the imperial other. Once this process of imagining had constructed the nation as different, then *Hindutva* was always to hand, existing as a more extreme version of the more moderate form of nationalism propagated by the new post-Independence state, and ready to become more salient when its political project began to fail. In the Indian case, there is a matching form of majoritarian politics in the post-Partition state of Pakistan. Thus Indian Islam has been marginalised both by Partition and by the political-cultural shift of the Pakistan state away from the Indian sub-continent and towards the Middle East (Ludden, 1996). So Hindu and Islamic nationalism provide distorting mirrors of the cultural enemy derived from the assumption of homogenised and alien peoples. Basu has pointed out that in the Indian case at least Hindu nationalism has both encouraged and yet mystified the expression of deep-seated conflicts based on class, caste and gender (Basu, 1996).

At this point, we can see that the failure of Western thinkers to predict the rise of what we might call religious nationalism or politicised religion reflects the prevailing view that nationalism is in essence the master narrative of modernism in which religion has no place. At the same time these 'cultural' forms of nationalism seek to claim a primordial and essentialising identity but in a thoroughly modern way. The appeal is not religious so much as political despite the denial of the centrality of the state to its project. It is also mobilised to exclude Muslim and other 'minorities' (a term of political rather than statistical relevance) from participation. In turn, as Brass (1990) has pointed out, Muslim elites in Northern India have also indulged in symbolic selection so that they have emphasised divisive rather than composite symbols. Seeing themselves as losing the privileges as a distinctive community, they chose to emphasise a special sense of history incompatible with Hindu aspirations and a myth of Muslim decline into backwardness. In other words, organising on the basis of Muslim-ness is a way of gaining or holding on to power.

The ways in which identities are essentialised and yet contested have been explored by Edward Said in his classic studies of 'Orientalism'. His key point is that imperialism and resistance advanced together, are mirrors of each other, and did not develop in isolation. They share the same structure of attitude and reference (1993: xxvi). Nationalism has particularism built into it; hence every 'us' needs to have a 'them'. 'In time, culture comes to be associated, often aggressively, with the nation and the state; this differentiates "us" from "them", almost always with the same degree of xenophobia' (ibid.: xiii). Said's project is to show how two of the greatest binary oppositions – Occident and Orient – do not correspond to a stable reality, but are stereotypes which function to confirm our own identity against 'otherness'. All empires, says Said, 'all cultures are involved in one another; none is single and pure, all are hybrid, heterogeneous, extraordinarily differentiated, and unmonolithic' (ibid.: xxix).

Why then do so many people appear to be duped into believing in the binary divide? The point is not that they are fools, but that identification requires knowing that one is not the other. Binary distinctions are not unique to issues of nationalism, but are endemic to any system of knowledge, and through knowledge, we come to dominate the cognitive and material worlds. Of course, this perspective is essentially Western, and we may be dealing here with two incommensurate epistemologies. The world of power involves a complex dialectic of us and not-us, of which nation and not-nation is but one expression. This divide is replicated within the nation itself: male/female; urban/rural; high/low cultures, and so on. The role of binary opposites operates especially in relationship to knowledge, most obviously in Western rationality in contra-distinction to Eastern traditionalism. As we have seen in the Indian case, this dichotomy is not simply foisted on the subordinate by the dominant partner, but is actively pursued and mobilised by the former in creating and mobilising the native core. Of course, these are ideological antinomies in the main, and Michael Herzfeld (1992) has argued that the Western view of bureaucracy as a perfectly honed, rational tool is but one expression of a system of values.

If Said's contribution had merely been to show that nationalism operates with a binary system of knowledge and value, then it would have been fairly unremarkable. His contribution has been to show that while colonialism has obviously ended, imperialism lingers in a kind of general cultural sphere, and is mobilised by the oppressed as well as the erstwhile oppressor. Its power rests in the taken-for-granted, and especially in cultural forms like the novel. Defoe's *Robinson Crusoe* is an allegory of a European (the author masks out and so renders unimportant the Scottishness as well as the personal identity of his model, the shipwrecked sailor Alexander Selkirk) who creates a fiefdom for himself on a distant island in a faraway sea. (We might also note in passing that the author Daniel Defoe had a well-developed political sense, operating as an English agent or spy at the time of the Union with Scotland which his government was keen to see carried out.) Crusoe without 'Man Friday' (identity reduced to gender/servant status, and day-of-the-week) is unthinkable because it would not be possible to highlight self-characteristics otherwise. Above all, the novel is an allegory about nationalism, for it is about land, its very essence. Said comments:

> Underlying social space are territories, lands, geographical domains, the actual geographical underpinnings of the imperial, and also the cultural contest. To think about distant places, to colonise them, to populate or depopulate them: all of this occurs on, about, or because of land. The actual geographical possession of land is what empire in the final analysis is all about.
>
> (Said, 1993: 93)

Literature is not peripheral to this endeavour, says Said. In nineteenth- and early twentieth-century English and French literature, allusions to facts of empire are everywhere, and empire everywhere provides the crucial setting even where it is seemingly invisible (as in Austen's *Mansfield Park*, and *Jane Eyre*). E.M. Forster's *Passage to India* also conveys the mysterious 'otherness' of that country, as well as being an identity tale about the foreigner, the Raj. In writers like Joseph Conrad we find both imperialist and anti-imperialist sentiments. He seems to say, comments Said: 'we westerners will decide who is a good native or a bad, because all natives have sufficient existence by virtue of our recognition. We created them, we taught them to speak and think, and when they rebel they simply confirm our views of them as silly children, duped by some of their Western masters' (ibid.: xx). The key lies in fiction because that is where the 'other' is imagined, created and mobilised. 'We' are what 'they' are not.

The novel as a genre is also important because of the significance of 'narrative' in imagining the nation. Homi Bhabha's work – nation as narration – is the most relevant here. He shows how people come to be constructed within a range of discourses as a 'double narrative movement'. That is, they are not simply historical events, but 'a complex rhetorical strategy of social reference' (Bhabha, 1990: 297). They are both historical objects, and subjects of signification, a double hermeneutic, to use Habermas' term. It is the process of cultural production and reproduction which is the focus of Said's as well as Bhabha's work, and it marks a significant analytical shift away from the macro-economic/political level which operated in the work of writers like Wallerstein and Frank, discussed earlier in this chapter, to a focus on the 'micro-physics' of power in which self-construction plays a crucial and active part in cultural reproduction. Said is critical of Western intellectuals for accepting too readily the essentialism of national and ethnic identity, and seeks to refocus attention of the process of active self-identification at the cultural sphere.

The point he is making is that the development and maintenance of every culture requires the existence of another different and competing alter ego. Each society creates and recreates its 'others', for the process of identification involves the identities of these different 'others'. In other words, the process of identification is a dialectical one, it is contested and not essentialist except in its cultural outcomes. Creating ontological distinctions between, for example, West and East is not the result of faulty logic or analysis, but a key device for constructing identity for ourselves, whoever we are and who we want to be. The problems arise when we treat their boundaries as absolute, as given and fixed, whereas the 'Orient' is largely a construction of, a mirror for, the West. The sciences of classification, biological and social, contributed to the codification of difference, and helped to build a culture of superiority and inferiority embedded in both sides. At its height, imperialism, especially in its expansionist age, had the scope and authority to create and impose its own version of culture on the natives. Said comments that Verdi's opera *Aida* represented a construction of 'Egypt' derived from the fashion for Egyptology. It represented a kind of 'curatorial art' evoking an imperial spectacle designed to alienate as well as impress an almost exclusively European audience (Said, 1993: 156). The Pyramids, then, could be imagined as the property of the West rather than of modern Egypt, just as the Acropolis of modern Greece does not 'belong' to that state in cultural terms.

In similar fashion, resistance to imperialism was not simply a reaction to it, but also its counter-culture which was formed as a crucial part of its own image. In Said's words, 'the history of all cultures is the history of cultural borrowings' (ibid.: 261). Nationalism is the mobilising force that coalesced into resistance against an alien and occupying empire, mobilised according to a perceived common history, religion and language. Too often, however, it is hijacked as the vehicle for national bourgeoisies and elites, and deteriorates into an equation of nationality with nativism. This is to fall into the trap set by colonial cultures, for, says Said, imperialism's worst and most paradoxical gift was to allow people to believe that they were only, mainly, exclusively white or black, or Western or Oriental. 'No one today is purely one thing. Labels like Indian or woman, or Muslim, or American are no more than starting points, which if followed into actual experience for only a moment are quickly left behind' (ibid.: 407). All cultures are hybrids, and all identities created in dialectic.

It is difficult, some would say impossible, for Westerners to grasp these essential differences and complexities. Our basic epistemology imposes on us a linear understanding of processes. Let us take the example of language which lies at the cultural root of so much of our understanding of nationalism. 'One language, one people' is such a pervasive equation that it leads such an eminent scholar as Edward Shils to imagine that American national identity would unravel if monolingualism was given up. 'One culture, one nation, one society' is still the *leitmotif* of Western thought. And yet not only do we know that linguistic pluralism is the norm in virtually every Western society, we also build our old assumptions into the bedrock of our theories. Karl Deutsch's thesis of nationalism and social communication derives from the middle of this century (Deutsch, 1953), and its basic tenet that nationalism is associated with mass mobilisation of people via a common language is well known and accepted. Deutsch's theory of nationalism was in fact based on a wider cybernetic theory of politics which argued that states only survived if they successfully transmitted and processed information so as to create cultural unification.

Such a view of language and monoculturalism is highly ethnocentric. More recently, David Laitin's on language repertoires and state construction in Africa shows just how much more complex these are. Laitin (1992) argues that the most common pattern of state building in Africa involves what he calls a '3 + 1 language outcome'. To meet the needs of the modern world, citizens of these states need to have (a) knowledge of a European language, which will be in use in central bureaucracy and educational establishments; (b) a national language which may or may not replace the European language in a wide range of language domains; and (c) their own vernacular language which is the medium of education for the early years of education and the language of administration in the home region. It may be that (b) and (c) become the same $(3 - 1 = 2)$, or that migrants from one titular state living in another will feel compelled to learn a fourth language $(3 + 1 = 4)$.

These language outcomes mean that multiculturalism will remain the norm for most African citizens, and is not to be mistaken for linguistic 'backwardness'. Neither, says Laitin, does the resurgence of language politics necessarily mean the breakdown of frail multinational states into tribal homelands (1992: 163). After all, he points out, language issues may have the power to bring down fragile governments in the West too (such as Belgium and Canada), but do not erode the integrity of state boundaries.

Women and nationalism

If identities are created in dialectic, then women's relationship to nationalism is doubly engendered. Much of the literature on nationalism – reflected in this book so far – ignores gender. So why discuss it in a chapter on liberation nationalism? Perhaps that term gives an explanation, for women have a double hurdle to jump in the quest for freedom. There is, of course, a more optimistic view which points out that in much of the Third World women and men received the franchise together, and as a result citizenship, nationality and gender have been much more closely connected than in the West where the gendering of citizenship rights has been obvious from the outset (Jayawardena, 1986; Walby, 1996; Yuval-Davis, 1997). There is also the fact that in many of the liberation struggles of the twentieth century (notably those of a secular and socialist disposition – South Africa, Algeria, Eritrea, Vietnam), women have fought alongside men as more-or-less equal partners. The problem seems to arise once independence has been achieved, at which point gender roles revert to type.

Much of course depends on the general ideology and social circumstances under which liberation struggles occur. Under generally right-wing forms of nationalism, gendering is more obvious. For example, Patricia Jeffery argues that where nationalism takes the form of politicised religion, as in India, it poses an overt threat to feminist activism and to women's rights generally. She comments:

> Politicized religious organizations represent the idioms used to mobilize adherents as founded on natural primordial loyalties. Yet such idioms are socially constructed frameworks for thinking about peoplehood and identity, despite often being 'naturalized' by reference to genetic and racial purity or to claims that a people's culture, language and religion are in their bones, blood, or genes. Hindutva or Islam are imagined communities . . . in direct competition with 'woman' as idioms for laying claim to people's primary allegiances. And politicized religious organizations assert a truth and authenticity that they refuse to concede to countervailing feminist claims.
>
> (Jeffery, 1998: 224)

This is brought about in a number of ways. First, role models can be found in female deities, something which politicised religious movements can turn to

120

advantage for transcendental reasons by stressing self-sacrifice and devotion to duty. Further, by bearing and rearing children, women maintain the racial purity of the stock, and transmit its culture. Jeffery comments: 'The glorification of women's selflessness in the home may be paralleled by the iconized mother serving the nation, aggressively defending national honor as she would her children, or released from domestic duties to become an activist for the nation' (ibid.: 225). Third, in stressing allegiances politicised religion implicitly separates women from each other. The Hindu Right, for example, has used worship of Hindu goddesses to advantage in mobilising women against Muslim women and men, especially as it can present itself as an oppressed minority in its own land. Feminists find themselves in a difficult position: as women against patriarchy, as Third World women against Western feminist agendas, and as educated Indian women in a position of relative privilege in their own country (Jeffery, 1998). As a consequence, they find their voices muted or, worse, subverted, as for example over the protest at the Miss World contest in India in 1997 which was organised by the Hindu Right. Women found that by and large the agenda was set by the religious Right and not by feminism.

Other powerful movements of the Right have also mobilised to limit the political and cultural agenda for women. The Afrikaners in South Africa, for example, constructed and elevated the figure of the *volksmoeder*, the mother of the nation. Anne McClintock (1993, 1996) shows how 'commodity spectacle' such as the commemoration of the Great Trek (*Tweede Trek*) is a vital component of nationalism. Its power lies in its capacity to organise popular displays of belonging, to inhabit the world of fetishes. She comments: 'More often than not, nationalism takes shape through the visible, ritual organization of fetish objects – flags, uniforms, airplane logos, maps, anthems, national flowers, national cuisines and architectures as well as through the organization of collective fetish spectacle' (McClintock, 1996: 274). These fetishes (akin to Billig's icons of 'banal nationalism') 'embody crises in social value, which are projected onto and embodied in what can be called impassioned objects' (ibid.).

McClintock's analysis of women in Afrikanerdom shows the complexity of their position within nationalism. Their role as *volksmoeder* is not one imposed on them as unwilling victims, but acknowledges the power of white motherhood. McClintock comments: 'it is a retrospective iconography of gender containment, containing women's mutinous power within an iconography of domestic service. Defined as weeping victims, white women's activism is overlooked and their disempowerment thereby ratified' (ibid.: 276). The point is that women are not hapless victims but 'both colonised and colonisers' and so accomplices both in their own right and in the dispossession of black people. In a parallel analysis of black women in the African National Congress (ANC), McClintock shows how, unlike their Afrikaner counterparts, they transformed the ideology of motherhood into a revolutionary mode: as 'mothers of the revolution'. In that context, black women put revolutionary struggle above their feminism. McClintock is also suspicious of the fact that, since *apartheid* was overthrown, the institutionalisation of patriarchy would take place, and that black women would drop down the hierarchy of social and political power in the new South Africa, just as nationalist and socialist revolutions generally have a poor record of ushering in equality of the sexes. This, of course, is not inevitable, as in the case of Finland, where a social revolution accompanied national liberation, and which is reflected in the high percentage of women in the national parliament (30 to 40 per cent in recent years).

McClintock makes the point that there is no more one kind of feminism than there is one form of patriarchy. Her analysis of two very different and competing forms of nationalism in South Africa underscores the point that simple conclusions about the progressive or reactionary nature of nationalism *vis-à-vis* women's rights cannot be made. Seeking to forefront gender identity over national identity, to give one primacy over the other, tends to ignore the important and unpredictable interactions between them. Feminism and nationalism can enmesh positively or negatively, as we see from McClintock's work. Subordinating one to the other misses the complexities of their 'interactive effects', as well as undervaluing the capacity of women (as well as men, for that matter) to construct and mobilise their identities in an active manner.

Women's relationship to nationalism and national identity has been largely ignored by writers. One looks in vain to the works of Gellner, Anderson, Smith and others for a sustained analysis of gender issues in nationalism. This is odd, for as McClintock points out, 'nationalism is thus constituted from the very beginning as a gendered discourse and cannot be understood without a theory of gender power' (1996: 261). Nevertheless, it is one of the growing areas in the field. A useful starting point is provided by the five major ways identified by Yuval-Davis (1993) in which women are connected to nationalism:

- as biological reproducers of national collectivities
- as reproducers of the boundaries of national groups through restrictions on sexual relations
- as active transmitters and producers of the national culture
- as symbolic signifiers of national difference
- as active participants in national struggles.

The centrality of gender to nationalism can be gauged by the vocabulary used to describe the nation: it is a 'motherland' (only rarely a 'fatherland'); it is imagined as a 'family' in a wider 'family of nations'; 'blood' and lineage figure prominently in its iconography; it is imagined as a domestic space. In her study of Turkish village society, Delaney shows how Mustafa Kemal Ataturk capitalised on the peasants' deep relation to the soil and land ('*Memleket*'). She comments: 'They did not have to understand the concept of the nation-state to be motivated to protect their own threatened soil, conceived as a mother who was being raped or sold into captivity' (Delaney, 1991: 272–3). National emblems cleverly insinuated themselves into national consciousness. The red and white of the flag (white crescent moon and star on a red ground) symbolised not only the spilling of Turkish blood in battle (especially the battle of Malazgirt in 1071), but key aspects of procreative sexuality. The red proclaimed *kizlik*, virginity and creative potential; white was the colour of milk, purity and honour. The second symbol, the hearth or *ocak*, stood for the household and the continuity of the patriline. So strong is masculinity in the identity of Turkey, that the leader of the military coup in 1980 proclaimed that 'Turkey is a nation of men, not women' (ibid.: 275).

In the iconography of nationalism, by and large, women are locked into relatively passive and iconographic roles. This is in part a division of public and private spheres, as well as temporal ones – women as keepers of history; men, of the future. McClintock points out:

> Women are represented as the atavistic and authentic body of national tradition (inert, backward-looking and natural), embodying nationalism's conservative principle of continuity. Men, by contrast, represent the progressive agent of national modernity (forward-thrusting, potent and historic), embodying nationalism's progressive, or revolutionary, principle of discontinuity. Nationalism's anomalous relation to time is thus managed as a natural relation to gender.
>
> (McClintock, 1996: 263)

Women are also crucial boundary markers for nationalism, outlining the limits of the nation. They become its repository, and the personification of its defence. That is why, in the case of Afrikaner women, they are represented in the iconography as suffering and self-sacrificing. The domestic sphere was the engine of cultural production and, like India, was kept by Afrikaner society out of the hands of British control and away from the imperial gaze. The nationalist regime which took power in Iran after 1979 identified women as the bearers of cultural identity and therefore they became the main targets of cultural reform. Women were 'hailed as prospective mothers of martyrs, and the clergy and media have joined forces to convince them of their obligation to marry and return to the sphere of domesticity' (Afshar, 1989: 239). A more extreme and recent version of this strategy has occurred in Afghanistan where the Taliban have systematically excluded women from schools and from the labour market.

Women's sexuality and reproductive role become a symbol of the nation because their sexuality is also used as a border guard. These border guards often involve control over women's sexuality and rules about who they should marry. 'Mixed marriages' may be tolerated but when the nation is threatened, the offspring of such engagements are deemed less than trustworthy. The child's citizenship may even be questioned if it ensues from a mixed marriage. The most obvious and brutal transgressing of national/sexual borders is in systematic wartime rape. In the Bosnian war of the 1990s, for example, it was recognised that there was a clear political purpose behind the rape of Muslim women by Serbian men, often urged on by Serbian women. Adam Jones argues that 'rape is a double-edged weapon in war. It is aimed not only at the exploitation and humiliation of the victim, but at the morale of the population as a whole' (1994: 117). He interprets them as instruments of revenge on the menfolk of the Muslim community. As women are constructed as the safeguards of nationality through the restriction of sexual behaviour, sexual assault on women can be interpreted as a direct assault on the identity of the entire community. The Serbian intentions seem to have been to inflict the humiliation of carrying the enemy's children onto Muslim families, as well as to infiltrate the Muslims with enemy 'blood' so as to impurify their national 'stock'. Such attacks were devastating because women's sexuality is considered the property of the nation. Women who conceive a child of 'mixed' nationality may themselves be perceived as violating the boundaries of the nation by producing 'impure' offspring, which in consequence may result in difficulties in establishing full citizenship rights for the children and the family.

Conclusion

In this chapter we have examined the character of liberation or Third World nationalism. The aim has been to draw it into the mainstream of nationalism studies and away from the political and intellectual fringes which it has inhabited for so long. Rather than seeing it as a special but unusual case requiring peculiar explanations, liberation nationalism forces us to confront the central issue of nationalism generally – *the* issue of identity: self and other. To put it simply, much of conventional writing on nationalism treats the West as the seedbed of nationalism, and 'Western' forms as superior to 'Eastern' ones. Much of this is underpinned by an implicit model of development which sees Western ways as diffused to the periphery, without recognising that there is a complex dialectic involving West and East, self and other, First World and Third World.

At the same time and for much the same reasons, conventional wisdom has quite ignored the gendering of nationalism, a feature which only in the 1990s is being addressed. The relationship between feminism and nationalism is now being tackled, and we are moving away from the well-worn and somewhat patronising wisdom attributed to Virginia Woolf, from her novel *Three Guineas* published in 1938: 'As a woman I have no country. As a woman I want no country. As a woman my country is the whole world.' Although Woolf was putting these words into the mouth of a female pacifist, there can be little doubt that they were her own sentiments. We might contrast them with the Quebec feminist slogan of the 1990s: 'No women's liberation without the liberation of Quebec; no Quebec liberation without the liberation of women' (Fidler, 1991: 163). Sixty years on, Woolf's statement seems distinctly *passé*, for women are playing a key role in nationalism not only in the Third World, but in the West where new forms of nationalism and autonomism are emerging. It is to these that we now turn our attention.

7

IN AND OUT OF THE STATE

The rise and rise of neo-nationalism

In the second half of the twentieth century there has arisen one of the most para-doxical forms of nationalism of all; 'neo-nationalism', a new territorial politics in Western states. There are few in which it has not occurred: Scotland and Wales in the UK; Catalunya and Euskadi in Spain; Flanders in Belgium; Brittany and Occitanie in France; Quebec in Canada, and so on. 'Neo', that is 'new', forms of nationalism are paradoxical because they were largely unpredicted, and conven-tional theories of nationalism have found them difficult to accommodate. After all, was not nationalism in the West well and truly over? Had it not served its purpose in ushering in the modern state during the nineteenth century?

Neo-nationalism as 'nationalism'

The unexpected and untheorised nature of neo-nationalism can be gauged by the way it is treated in the literature. If we examine the key writers on nationalism, we find that their explanations are contingent and *ad hoc*, on the one hand, and neutral to hostile in tone on the other. Ernest Gellner, as seen in chapter 4, had little to say about it beyond, in his own words, a 'feeble' suggestion that nationalism in late twentieth-century Scotland is contingent and instrumental. The discovery of North Sea oil, coupled with historical and cultural means for expressing identity, has allowed Scotland to try to renegotiate its relationship with the UK state which it joined in 1707. Like Gellner, Anderson is more interested in the failure of nationalism to 'take' in Scotland in the nineteenth century. Anderson's explanation is that 'already in the early 17th century large parts of what would one day be imagined as Scotland were English-speaking and had immediate access to print-English, provided a minimum degree of literacy existed' (B. Anderson, 1996a: 90). The migration of Scottish intellectuals to England after 1707, together with open access to English markets, meant that a rising bourgeoisie had little need to mobilise nationalism for its political or economic ends. Catalunya and Quebec figure not at all in Anderson's account, and the latter warrants only a passing mention in Gellner (1983: 70) as an instance of voluntary incorporation into a federal state.

Anthony Smith sees what he calls the 'third wave of demotic ethnic

125

nationalisms' since the 1950s as specific to the political-cultural conditions of the well-established industrial states to which they belong. They are to be judged as 'autonomist' rather than 'separatist', with particular emphasis on maintaining or developing cultural, social and economic autonomy, but remaining within the political framework of the state into which they were incorporated. They are persuaded of this by the economic benefits to be had, by which means Smith seeks to explain the devolution debate in Scotland in the 1970s: the triumph of economic self-interest over cultural sentiment. It also suits him to be able to show, in his desire to establish the pre-modern character of nationalism, that many of the recent movements after the 1960s have been built on older ideals and identities. He comments: 'In all these cases [Wales, Scotland, Catalunya, Euskadi, Brittany] a cultural renaissance, literary, linguistic, and historical, preceded the formation of political movements demanding ethnic autonomy' (Smith, 1991: 141).

Eric Hobsbawm, who is undoubtedly the most hostile to neo-nationalism, commented that 'the characteristic nationalist movements of the late 20th century are essentially negative, or rather divisive' (1990: 164). Most of this hostility is directed at ethnic-linguistic forms of neo-nationalism such as is found in Wales and Quebec, where, he asserts: 'the stance of Quebec nationalism is that of a people in headlong retreat before historical forces which threaten to overwhelm it; a movement whose very advances are viewed in terms of potential weakness rather than as success' (ibid.: 165). Scottish nationalism, on the other hand, is, according to Hobsbawm, the outcome of adverse *political* processes. It is, he comments, 'plainly a reaction to an all-British government supported by only a modest minority of Scots, and a politically impotent all-British opposition party' (ibid.: 179), such a state of affairs no doubt to be redressed by the election of a Labour government, when support for nationalism will, he assumes, ebb away.

This touches on a favourite explanation for the rise of neo-nationalism, that it is not actually 'nationalism' at all, but something akin to 'regionalism', the mobilisation for instrumental ends of territorial identity, but stopping well short of separatism. Peter Alter, for example, comments that 'regionalism', 'resistance to the state's centre from peripheral areas' (1991: 135) results from inadequate political incorporation. The 'political nations' of France, Spain and the UK, he argues, were never completely unified or homogeneous, and failed to develop the requisite conditions for a successful political system: a common political-cultural identity, a high degree of allegiance to the centre, and shared political aims. Parties like Plaid Cymru in Wales and the Scottish National Party (SNP) are mere 'regionalist organisations' 'not serious about complete political separation' (ibid.: 138), and 'regional economic differentiation as a generator of regionalism can also be fruitfully offered as a thesis to explain the situation in Catalonia and the Basque country' (ibid.: 141).

The sense that regions are playing the nationalist card for political reasons but without being true believers also fits into the general approach that territorial politics are at work. John Breuilly, for example, concludes that 'what has developed [in Quebec] as in the Basque and Scottish cases, is a rather tough-minded, frequently radical nationalism which is very different from the anti-modernist, rather romantic nationalist movements of "peripheral" regions in many 19th century European countries' (1993: 333). In other words, Breuilly sees these late twentieth-century movements as quite different from their nineteenth-century counterparts insofar as they have a much more 'political' orientation driven by largely economic concerns on the part of key social groups, especially upwardly mobile managerial and technical workers in these territories. Their emergence fits in with Breuilly's overall thesis on nationalism that 'there is no valid explanatory theory of nationalism, only a number of ways of describing and comparing various forms of nationalist politics' (ibid.: 338).

What this brief review of perspectives on neo-nationalism shows is that it is usually subordinated to the overall framework of the authors, and that by and large it is not central to that framework. Hence, we find a preference for contingent explanations, and for 'political' accounts of territorial relationships between core and periphery. The centre of interest is usually in another place (the Third World, for example), or at another time (the nineteenth century).

Where the analysis of core–periphery relations is applied, as for example, in the work of Michael Hechter (1975) and his 'internal colonialism' thesis, there is strain on the historical and empirical evidence to hand. Internal colonialism was a framework which Hechter borrowed from Latin America by way of analysis of race relations in the US and applied to what he calls the Celtic periphery in the UK. Drawing on the sociology of development, Hechter rejected the assumption that all territories are equally incorporated into the culture and economy of the core, and argued that an exploitative and unequal relationship develops between peripheries and core in such a way that the internal colony produces wealth for the benefit of areas closer both geographically and economically to the core-state. The internal colonies are differentiated by particular cultural variables such as religion, language or ethnicity which exclude them from superior social and cultural positions. Hechter argues that for internal colonialisation to exist there must be a 'cultural' division of labour so that the colony contains low-status occupations and positions, and the core gets the high-status ones. Nationalism is generated as a form of territorial 'class' reaction to this concentration of power and resources at the centre.

The obvious problem with Hechter's account is that it does not fit historical facts. In particular, territories such as Scotland, Catalunya and Quebec all developed relatively high degrees of institutional and cultural autonomy and, if anything, the spur to neo-nationalism lay in their relatively privileged rather than their relatively disadvantaged relationship to the central states in question. Peripheral regions of this sort are prosperous and enjoy a large degree of autonomy. Neo-nationalism seems to occur in regions with a relatively strong economic base, whose relationship with the central state has undergone significant economic or political readjustment. Similarly, it is difficult to speak of the primacy of 'ethnic' factors in these instances. Rather, 'civic' identity in terms of membership of a territory seems to be preferred. In Linz's words:

> Ethnic peripheral nationalism will move from an emphasis on primordial elements to a definition based on territoriality. That is, definition would change from an emphasis on common descent, race, language, distinctive cultural tradition, in some cases religion, to one based on 'living and working' in an area, on a willingness to identify with that community.
>
> (Linz, 1985: 205)

In ideal-typical terms, these new civic nationalisms forefront their national identity over those of the state identities to which they belong. In so doing, they mobilise their history and culture by calling up the flags, hymns and icons which are available to them. This, of course, they share with other forms of nationalism. In Tom Nairn's words, 'A new political movement . . . it is in a number of ways analogous to historical or mainstream nationalism. But a more careful consideration shows its different place in history and its different character and potential. It deserves to be called "neo-nationalism" rather than nationalism' (1977: 127).

Neo-nationalism in stateless nations

This, then, is the starting-point for our examination of late-twentieth-century forms of neo-nationalism which have emerged in Western industrial states. This chapter focuses on three examples in which neo-nationalism is reckoned to be most advanced (Keating, 1996): Scotland, Catalunya and Quebec. These cases have similarities as well as differences. They are all what we might call 'stateless nations', territories in which identification with the nation is greater than that with the state of which they are currently a part. The differences are obvious, but the comparative leverage we get is positive. For example, both Scotland and Catalunya are nested within states which are members of the European Union, which has an embryonic political project *Europe de Patries* to which these nations aspire. On the other hand, Quebec operates within Canada which participates in the North American Free Trade Association (NAFTA), which is more of an economic than a political project. Catalunya and Quebec appear to have stronger cultural politics than Scotland, notably regarding language, and with a capacity to mobilise Catholic religious identity. Both Catalunya and Quebec also have formally autonomous assemblies to manage domestic affairs, whereas Scotland has, as we write, none, although one is planned for the year 2000. Finally, Scotland and Quebec share a common British imperial legacy, and while they have different relationships to it as coloniser and colonised respectively, they have in common the general context of progressive economic liberalism since the eighteenth century.

The argument of this chapter is that there are a number of key characteristics of neo-nationalism, which are outlined first and then developed around case studies. These are as follows:

- Neo-nationalism occurs in *coherent civil societies* which are not independent states, but with ostensible but varying degrees of political autonomy.

- In each there is a *complex relationship between cultural nationalism and political nationalism*, and these have converged in recent years. 'Civic' rather than 'ethnic' nationalism is emphasised; a stress for political purposes on territorial *residence* rather than lineage and *blood*.

- *Multiple national identities are a feature of political identity*, rather than a mono-cultural one. Hence, Scots are also British, Catalans are also Spanish, and Quebecois are also Canadian, when it suits them. This plurality is a political resource which can be played in appropriate circumstances rather than a fixed characteristic.

- It tends to occur in relatively rich regions rather than the poorest. '*Relative gratification*' is more important than relative 'deprivation'.

- *Progressive political and economic aspects outweigh reactionary ones*. Movements appear as social-democratic or as neo-liberal, reflecting 'niche nationalism'. Attempts are made to align leftist and rightist elements (learning to love – or live with – the global market in a social-democratic or liberal way).

- *Different ideological elements are mixed and mobilised*: right/left; ethnic/civic; past/future; local/global; corporatist/neo-liberal; separatist/autonomist.

- These shifts in ideological messages relate to *changing and diverse social constituencies*. Unlike 'bourgeois' nationalist movements of the nineteenth century, the social base is more free-floating and unpredictable.

- *The 'movement' for self-government is not simply aligned with support for the party*. The voters are adept at giving only contingent support at certain elections, and voting in ostensibly 'unionist' ways in others.

- *Political movements/parties are of relatively recent origin*, that is, mainly in the second half of the twentieth century. The Scottish National Party, Convergença i Unio, and Parti Quebecois are in essence modern creations.

- There is *ambiguity about their aims*. Are they seeking independence or autonomy? Ambivalent terms are used in political debate, such as '*Home Rule*', '*Autonomisme*', *Souveraineté-Association* or *Consociation*.

- This ambivalence is reflected in terms used by analysts to describe the movements: such as '*regionalism*', or '*regional nationalism*' or '*neo-nationalism*'.

- The *variable geometry of power*: political debates take place within three dimensions not simply two dimensions: the nation, state and supra-state such as the European Union and NAFTA.

Civil society

In chapter 5 we explored what is meant by 'civil society', and how it relates to the concepts 'state' and 'nation'. Plainly, Scotland, Catalunya and Quebec are not states in the conventional sense that they do not have independent legislatures. Can we refer to Scotland, Catalunya and Quebec as 'civil societies'? Scotland did not cease to be a civil society in 1707, nor was it incorporated into greater England. Instead, the political settlement which was the Treaty of Union (note the word Treaty) was, in Tom Nairn's phrase, a settlement between two patrician classes for economic and political gains. On Scotland's side, it gave its merchants access to English markets at home and abroad. For England, it healed the running sore of Scotland's historic and troublesome alliance with the old enemy, France, by closing the backdoor to Gallic intrigue.

This settlement took place in 1707, long before what we now know as 'modern' processes began, and well in advance of the French and American Revolutions in the last quarter of the eighteenth century which were to give political change a democratic impetus. As Linda Colley (1992) pointed out, the 1707 Union did create something new. Greater England it was not. Instead, Scots took full advantage of the opportunity which England and the Empire provided, and were in no way confined to the subaltern tasks.

A genuine sense of Britishness was created with reference to two related aspects: war with France, and Protestantism. The invention of Britishness was forged in the long period of virtual or actual warfare with France from 1707 until 1837. As Colley points out, Britain:

> was an invention forged above all by war. Time and time again, war with France brought Britons, whether they hailed from Wales or Scotland or England, into confrontation with an obvious hostile Other and encouraged them to define themselves collectively against it. They defined themselves as Protestants struggling for survival against the world's foremost Catholic power. They defined themselves against the French as they imagined them to be, superstitious, militarist, decadent and unfree.
>
> (Colley, 1992: 5)

Britishness sat lightly on top of the constituent nations as a kind of state-identity which is the key to understanding state–society relations in the UK and elsewhere. The British state was quite unlike later state formations which sought to integrate political, cultural and economic structures in the classical 'nation-state'. These formations demanded the alignment of state, nation and society, and even economy and culture in such a way that 'national identity' ran through all of these institutions as a connecting thread. Being a citizen in these modern states formed in the nineteenth century demanded allegiance, and in return the state was made accountable, and its sovereignty limited, often by means of the doctrine of popular rather than Crown/Parliamentary sovereignty as in Britain.

All in all, the Anglo-Saxon state, especially in its British form, was viewed, as Poggi points out, as a 'convenience', a *gesellschaftlich* reality. In contrast, the continental European state was seen as an 'entity', as The State. Comments Poggi: 'There is little *gesellschaftlich* about that' (1978: 100). The point here is that the British state sat lightly upon civil society, whereas continental European states were thoroughly interwoven with theirs.

It is this relationship between state and civil society which is touched upon by commentators like Tom Nairn and Neal Ascherson when they speak of the British state as an *ancien régime*. In Ascherson's words: 'It is closer in spirit to the monarchy overthrown in 1789 than to the republican constitutions which followed in France and elsewhere in Europe' (1988: 148). The doctrine of the Crown-in-Parliament underpinned the British state at that crucial period in its formation in the late seventeenth and early eighteenth centuries – between the self-styled Glorious Revolution of 1689 and the Treaty of Union in 1707. On paper, from the vantage point of the late twentieth century, it looked authoritarian, although in the context of the early eighteenth century, Britain was counted among the most liberal of the age.

This, then, is the context in which the Union took place between Scotland and England (and, to all intents and purposes, Wales and Ireland), well before the period now characterised as 'modern'. With hindsight, we might argue that the only kind of state which allowed the Scots to retain a high degree of civil autonomy was a 'pre-modern' one in which the links between high and low politics were tenuous indeed. It is doubtful if the Scots would have agreed to submerge their institutional autonomy into the British state if it had been a thoroughly modern formation. A 'modern' state formation would have required the integration of the 'nation' into the state, and with it the formation of a unitary – British – civil society. There were attempts especially in the nineteenth century to fashion a British imperial identity, and while this met with some success, especially at the popular level, by the second half of the century the Scottish agenda had begun to assert itself (R.D. Anderson, 1995; Morton, 1996).

What effect did the Union have on Scottish civil society? The short answer is probably not much. The lives of ordinary people were untouched and, crucially, the middle classes continued to run Scottish institutions which were largely in the hands of the lawyers, ministers and teachers who have done so much to shape modern Scotland and its values. When Scotland negotiated away its formal statehood in 1707, it retained much of the institutional apparatus of self-government. At the core was the 'holy trinity' of institutional autonomy – the law, the church and the education system. Scotland remains that legal anomaly – a society with its own law-making system and no parliament of its own. (There remains a debate in Scotland about whether one can consider semi-state bodies such as these as constituting 'civil society' or whether they are actually state institutions – see Paterson, 1994; Morton, 1996, 1998b). At the core of civil society was the Kirk, which essentially constituted the local state, closely linked to the education system through 'parish' schools – the legacy of Scotland's Protestant revolution in the sixteenth century (Paterson, 1994: 39). In Paterson's words:

> The Union had left intact all that really mattered to daily life in Scotland in the eighteenth century. . . . The Union was, in Angus Calder's words, 'a rational solution to very dangerous economic and political problems', involving the abandonment of an already highly constrained foreign policy in the interests of maintaining independent control over domestic policy.
>
> (Paterson, 1991: 105)

The efflorescence of Scottish intellectual development, the Enlightenment, can also be traced to the relative autonomy of Scottish civil society. The removal of its aristocratic elite to the London court left Scottish cultural life very much in the hands of its professional classes who gave their imprint to this rich intellectual development at the end of the eighteenth century.

Day-to-day life remained in the hands of Scots, and this was consolidated in the 1832 Scottish Reform Act and in the setting up of *ad hoc* boards to administer prisons, poor law, healthcare, schools and crofting counties. The history of Scotland in the Union is one in which control over its civil society remained firmly in Scottish hands. By 1885, the diverse boards were consolidated under the control of the Scottish Office. That was to mark an important development in Scottish affairs because it saw the beginning of an explicitly political solution to the issues of Scottish autonomy. In Paterson's words:

> If Scotland had had a fully separate state, the only significant extra it would have had would have been an extremely circumscribed foreign policy, which no doubt might have provided an alternative for those who emigrated to positions of power in the Empire, but which would hardly have made much difference to the way that Scottish society evolved.
>
> (Paterson, 1991: 107)

The irony, of course, is that the British state used the devolving of administrative power to the Scottish Office as a way of deflecting the demand for greater direct democracy in Scotland, and that this policy in turn has helped to reinforce the sense of grievance. The more a Scottish semi-state was created with devolved bureaucratic powers, the more obvious the democratic deficit became.

The shifting relationships between state and civil society were, of course, not unique to Scotland and Britain. As Poggi pointed out, the last century or so has seen an increasing fudging of the boundary between state and society. Notably, the extension of the franchise has brought new political and social pressures to bear on the state, and increasingly the state is constituted to exercise rule over society. He comments: 'the state tends to increase its power by widening the scope of its activities, but extending the range of societal interests on which rule is brought to bear' (Poggi, 1978: 135). The state is required to address the concerns of its citizens more directly, and this presents the task of societal management for modern governments. In the post-war period, the state became the appropriate instrument for guaranteeing the life chances of its citizens, and ironing out social inequalities. Governments became major actors in economic competition between states in the quest for economic growth 'in the national interest'. Nationalism became more, not less, necessary in this process of international competition. This involvement had direct implications for the relationship between Scottish civil society and the British state.

By the 1990s, the delicate balance between Scottish civil society and the British state had been transformed. It had begun on the implicit understanding that

Scotland would retain a high degree of self-governance of its social institutions. Parliamentary politics was a fairly unimportant side-show for much of the history of the Union. However, the pre-modern and largely unreconstructed British state had retained the doctrinal incubus of parliamentary sovereignty which became a central element in politics in the second half of the twentieth century. The ushering in of the welfare state after 1945 was an attempt to modernise British state structures in the light of demands for reform from civil society. This project, which represented the high-point of Labour power in Britain, required state-led social change but without major reforms of the British state itself. The state was required to do more, but did not have the legitimating mechanisms to carry out these reforms.

To what extent do Quebec and Catalunya share Scotland's characteristic as civil societies? In general terms, their histories suggest that they are weaker in this respect although they have formal political autonomy within their respective states whereas Scotland does not. Scotland's negotiated compromise in 1707 established it as a distinct civil society without a parliament. Catalunya's geographical position between the French and Spanish kingdoms gave it a degree of cultural and political distinctiveness, and by the sixteenth century it had a high degree of institutional autonomy reflected in its parliament, the *Corts*, and its government, the *Generalitat* which was responsible for the management of taxes raised for the Crown (Balcells, 1996: 9). Catalunya developed a complex system of negotiated compromises which came to be known as *pactisme*. In Keating's words: 'There was little space here for absolutism, or the unilateral imposition of authority. Monarchical prerogatives were strictly limited by custom and countervailing powers. Sovereignty was divided. Public life was dominated by a civic and commercial spirit' (Keating, 1996: 116).

This system of political autonomy largely came to an end in 1714 following the War of the Spanish Succession, reinforced by the so-called decree of *Nueva Planta* issued by the king two years later. Royal authority and rule by the king's appointees replaced local autonomy, and the fiscal privileges were abolished. While Catalunya never regained its previous character as a distinctive civil society, the process of indigenous industrialisation in the nineteenth century helped to reinforce the power of the Catalan bourgeoisie, which was socially conservative and Catholic. Nevertheless, the fact that Catalunya was developing ahead of Spain 'inspired the Catalans with a feeling of superiority which prompted them to rebel against their political subservience and cultural dependence on Castilian, or Castilianized, Spain' (Balcells, 1996: 21).

This was the foundation on which the *Renaixença*, the mid-nineteenth-century cultural revival was built. Drawing upon the Romantic movement, it injected a new interest in arts and language, notably the *Jocs Florals* (Floral Games), the revival of an ancient literary contest. This gave a cultural basis to Catalan civil society, but it had its limitations. In Balcells' words:

> While a Catalan literature had been created, a Catalan culture was still required, and that meant Catalanizing education and securing official-

language status for Catalan. In order to achieve this, it was necessary to bring about the political autonomy without which cultural autonomy was impossible.

(Balcells, 1996: 27)

While political autonomy was briefly restored in 1932 under the Republican government in Madrid, its abolition under Franco in 1939 and the suppression of the language in public places including schools meant that it was not until the restoration of democracy in Spain in the 1970s that the *Generalitat* was reintroduced.

Today, Catalunya has a strong civil society fostered by its political autonomy, and built around its language base. Keating points out that the *Generalitat* lists more than 25,000 associations legally constituted to pursue public interest affairs; there are nearly 500 private foundations, and a strong co-operative movement. He concludes: 'Catalan civil society remains a bastion of Catalan values and identity and an important arena for nation-building' (Keating, 1996: 150). In many ways the Catalan political project is seen as a means of protecting and developing language and culture, and giving them political expression. By 1997, a controversy had opened up concerning further legislation (*Ley Catalan*) which would give priority to Catalan over Castilian and, at the time of writing, it is not clear whether this legislation will go ahead.

What of Quebec? Its foundation as *Nouvelle France* gave it an obvious identity, which was reinforced by the social, cultural, economic and political organisation of the colony. As a result, following the Conquest of 1763, the British were confronted by an established civil society. As Jean-Guy Lacroix points out:

French-Canadian civil society had already been organised and structured by a set of specific institutions (among others, the family, religion and schools) providing it with a self-sufficient, internal socio-cultural force. Having already taken root, its cultural hegemony was strong enough to resist assimilation and impose and reproduce its specificity in the political field.

(Lacroix, 1996: 65)

However, as a conquered territory, Quebec was forced by the Royal Proclamation of 1763 to surrender its seigneurial system of land holding, to accept English laws, the submission of the Catholic church to British royalty and the state, and English as the official language of state. Following social unrest, the Quebec Act of 1774 did reinstate the French civil code and the seigneurial system, lifted the restrictions on the church, and helped to reinforce the homogeneity and social cohesion of the colony, and to reproduce its civil society over time. Over the next 200 years the tension between this politically integrated territory yet distinctive civil society has been the dominant theme of relations between Quebec and Canada. This has been aggravated by the development of the state and territory of Canada, from a distinction between Upper and Lower Canada, to a thoroughgoing federal state in which Quebec's demand to be acknowledged as a 'distinct society', one of the two co-founders of the Canadian state, is overridden by its status as simply one province among many.

Language is not only a cultural marker for Quebecois society, but is also a key institution of civil society through which most other things are translated and given meaning. The role of the Catholic church was not only a distinctive aspect of this society, but a means for helping to integrate Quebec into Canada, as the state recognised its special privileges and concerns. In a social and political context, the church underpinned the rural, conservative society – '*la survivance*' – which was largely swept away in the 1960s by *la révolution tranquille*. This process of social and political modernisation ended the church's special status as well as the system of patronage politics under the control of right-wing parties, and ushered in a new kind of politics which was more leftist and secular. This process has also had economic implications as business has become indigenised, developing close links of a corporatist kind with government often referred to as 'Quebec Inc.'

Much of Quebec society is self-contained, with a high density of local associations and organisations, much like Scotland and Catalunya. As Keating observes: 'Quebec has a dense network of non-governmental institutions and voluntary organisations, which take as their reference point the province rather than the federal level' (1996: 97). It is the tension between this civil society and its development on the one hand, and the governance of the state on the other which is reflected in political demands for greater autonomy to the point of formal independence. Indeed, in all three societies, we can observe the tensions between civil society and the state, between social and economic developments on the one hand, and the political framework on the other. It is the survival and development of civil societies that have confronted the states in question with the problem of how to accommodate their demands.

Cultural and political nationalism

The second aspect of neo-nationalism which is worth noting is the relationship between cultural and political nationalism. We have grown used to the notion that these are closely connected, that one leads to the other, yet it has been a feature of nationalism in the countries we are dealing with that the relationship is complex. Simply put, it seems that until recently culture was an alternative, an antidote, to political nationalism in these stateless nations, rather than an integral part of it. If people could realise their cultural aspirations, then what need did they have of political nationalism? Cultural nationalism could be seen as a safety valve which let off the steam of nationalism lest it take a more challenging political form. That was the sentiment behind the comment by the Scottish nationalist Jim Sillars that the Scots were 'ninety-minute nationalists', happy to cheer on their sporting team, but unwilling to translate that identification into voting for the nationalist party.

The relationship between cultural and political nationalism has been one of the key defining themes of the debate on Scotland's future in recent years. The distorted or deformed nature of Scottish culture – its tartanry and kailyard imagery – is blamed for ingraining in Scots a sense of their inferiority and dependency (Nairn, 1977; Beveridge and Turnbull, 1989), and is reflected in what is referred to as the 'Scottish cringe', a lack of personal and political confidence in people's capacity to take charge of their lives. The critics of tartanry/kailyardism saw Scotland as suffering from 'sub-national deformation', or neurosis, a divided consciousness in which the cultural and the political were destined to remain apart. In Nairn's words:

> It was cultural because of course it could not be political; on the other hand, this culture could not be straightforwardly nationalist either – a direct substitute for political action like, for example, so much Polish literature of the 19th century. It could only be 'sub-nationalist' in the sense of venting its national content in various crooked ways – neurotically, so to speak, rather than directly.
>
> (Nairn, 1977: 156)

The debate, then, about 'real' Scottish culture is almost always going to be about historical excavation of the 'golden age', or attempts to construct a pure national character free from alien and inferiorist influences. The search for a truly Scottish culture is inevitably retrospective and romantic, a celebration of the past. There is a growing amount of Scottish historiography which argues that history took a funny turn after the Union of 1707. As Scotland lost its formal statehood, so it appropriated that which had flourished in the currency of the Romantic movement, the Gaelic vision, for example (Chapman, 1978). More recently, Colin Kidd (1993) has argued in similar vein that Scottish Whig historians of the late eighteenth century looked to the Anglo-British state to offer a more progressive and liberating vision of society. This was not another example of the Scottish 'cringe' but a rational assessment of the opportunities for liberty and progress set against those offered by Scotland alone.

The novelist Walter Scott is often taken to task for inflicting on Scots this cultural divide between head and heart, being British versus being Scottish. Scott was a central figure in romanticising Scotland, and is held responsible by many opposed to the 'deformation' of Scottish culture. He is credited (or blamed) with creating a Scotland divided between the heart (its romantic Scottish past) and the head (its rational British future). This Caledonian antisyzygy, the battle between unrestrained fantasy and dour realism, is judged to be at the heart of the Scottish psychiatric-political condition (Nairn, 1977: 150).

Because Scottish identity could not take a 'state' form of expression, it was judged to have been subverted into a cultural backwater of a deformed nationalism. The key to this critique lies in the relationship between culture and politics. 'Normal' societies are deemed to be those in which national culture and politics are fused. In recent years, the discourse which sees Scotland as locked into a choice between reason and emotion, being British or Scottish, between political and cultural nationalism, has been fast eroding. It has become clear that the cultural renaissance of the 1920s and 1930s which produced new works of art in literature (Craig, 1987) was not independent of the stirrings of modern political nationalism, most obviously the creation of the modern Scottish National Party, and the broad movement for Home Rule. Both cultural and political developments reflected the decline of the English imperium. The second twentieth-century revival in the late 1960s and 1970s saw cultural and political nationalism developing apace so that it is now much more difficult to argue that being culturally Scottish but politically British is consistent. By the 1990s the connections between culture and politics are plain and powerful, but still not entirely straightforward.

In both Catalunya and Quebec, a similar re-connection has occurred, although the paths have been different, reflecting the historical trajectories of these societies. In the former, *Catalanisme* took its early expression in a cultural form in the *Renaixença*, which was the prelude to its political expression (Balcells, 1996). Catalan culture was both religious and linguistic, features which did not alienate a developing bourgeoisie in the middle of the nineteenth century. It was, however, obvious by the end of the century that without political autonomy there could be no long-term cultural independence. This was given special force following the victory of Franco's Spanish nationalists in 1939 when the defeat of the republicans pushed Catalan cultural expression into the undergrowth or into exile. Between 1939 and 1975, nearly 200 periodicals and 650 books in Catalan were published abroad (Balcells, 1996). From the 1950s a complex network of social and cultural organisations grew up in Catalunya itself, ostensibly non-political but able to give expression to being Catalan. Survival gave way to recovery and regeneration in the 1960s, and there was an explosion in literature, song, folklore, film and cultural studies. The stage was set for the assertion of political rights in the early 1970s, which developed into the *Assemblea de Catalunya* in 1971 under the auspices of the always-Catalan Catholic church. Based as it was on the Catalan principle of *pactisme* – co-operation – its task was not to overthrow Francoism but to effect its peaceful democratic transition when its end came.

In Quebec, *la survivance*, the survival of cultural identity, was an expression of conservative nationalism dominated by the Catholic church which was to the Right as its Catalan counterpart was to the Left. This clerical conservatism had underpinned the petit bourgeois politics of Duplessis and his *Union Nationale* which governed Quebec from 1936 until 1959. The church and business groups supported Duplessis, and nationalism was kept as a means of expressing this rural, small-town conservative ethos. This world which had channelled cultural nationalism into a narrow political mould was blown open in the 1960s by *la révolution tranquille*. This involved modernising not simply the economy but a whole range of social and political attitudes. A new Francophone middle class was emerging with strong public-sector and technocratic interests, whose political aspirations found their way into new political formations, notably the Parti Quebecois which appeared in 1968. A few short years later, it won control of the provincial assembly in 1976, and so began a programme of politicising the language issue, most notably in Bill 101 which prioritised French over English as the public language of state. Nothing spelled out more obviously the re-connection of culture and politics than this. 'Language politics' became the essence of nationalism in Quebec. The language was not merely a means of expression and communication, but the public assertion of political identity, a connecting of the personal and the public around 'possessive individualism' (Handler, 1988).

Multiple identities

If a single and homogeneous national identity is a key feature of classical nationalism, then plural and shifting identities characterise neo-nationalism. Built into the classical model is the assumption that cultural identity is constructed in terms of a single, shared culture, in Stuart Hall's words, a 'sort of collective, one true self' reflecting 'common historical experiences and shared cultural codes which provide us as "one people" with stable, unchanging and continuous frames of reference and meaning beneath the shifting divisions and vicissitudes of our actual history' (S. Hall, 1990: 223).

Identity in the late twentieth century is obviously far less clear-cut than this. It is not something which is achieved and constantly reinforced. We should think of cultural identity less as an accomplished fact and more as a 'production', never complete, always in process, and closely linked with how it is (re)presented. Further, there is no single representation, but a variety of ways of constituting 'who we are', and 'what we have become'. In essence, it is a matter of 'becoming' not 'being'. Hall comments:

> It belongs to the future as much as to the past. It is not something which already exists, transcending place, time, history and culture. Cultural identities come from somewhere, have histories. But like everything which is historical, they undergo constant transformation. Far from being eternally fixed in some essentialised past, they are subject to the continuous 'play' of history, culture and power.
>
> (S. Hall, 1990: 224)

The task, then, is not to recover the past, as if it – a unified essence – is waiting simply to be found, a sort of touchstone of national identity, but it is necessary instead to have a debate with the past about who we are now and who we want to become. National culture is a discourse, a way of constructing meanings which influences and organises our actions and our conceptions of ourselves. The idea of the nation is a 'narrative' (Bhabha, 1990) whose origin is obscure, but whose symbolic power to mobilise the sense of identity and allegiance is strong. By looking at national identity in this way, as multifaceted and plural, we begin to see that it cannot be taken for granted, that it will reflect social power, and that competing identities will emerge and challenge each other. We are better able to recognise that national cultures and identities are not fixed and immutable. They are subject to processes of translation and change. Hall's term 'cultures of hybridity' refers to the ways in which identities are subject to the play of history, political representation and difference, and are very unlikely to be pure or unitary.

In the Scottish case we find that people consider themselves many things in terms of political identity. The resolution of 'national identities' was, for much of the twentieth century, relatively straightforward. To be Scottish (or English, or Welsh) was a complementary aspect of being British, which in turn had two aspects – a UK one, and an overseas one – both reflected in rule from a Westminster 'imperial' parliament. These were nested identities in the main, to be seen as a set of concentric circles moving outward from the local to the (Scottish) national to the British to the imperial and so on.

The late twentieth century has seen new challenges of a more overtly national-istic kind. 'Britishness' in these islands has waned as older 'national' identities have grown. Hence, the contest between 'state' and 'national' identities in these islands seems particularly fertile ground in which to examine identity politics.

It takes little to persuade us that people living in Scotland think of themselves these days as Scottish (their national identity) rather than British (state identity). For example, in the 1997 Scottish Election Survey 86 per cent of respondents opted for 'Scottish' and 46 per cent 'British', with 12 per cent 'European' (multi-choice was possible). These forced-choice responses of course are crude, and in the last decade they have been refined in scalar terms by the Moreno question, which provides the consistent findings given in Table 7.1.

We may argue about what these labels mean – can we be sure, for example, that the same terms 'Scottish' and 'British' evoke the same thing? – but there is little doubt that the results are consistent. In all the surveys to date between 59 and 69 per cent of people living in Scotland give greater emphasis to being Scottish over being British (categories 1 and 2), whereas the percentage prioritising their Britishness (categories 4 and 5) is 10 per cent or less. At the same time, most Scots –

Table 7.1 National identity in Scotland

	July 1986	*Sept 1991*	*April 1992*	*SES* 1992*	*SES* 1997*
Scottish not British	39%	40%	32%	19%	23%
More Scottish than British	30%	29%	29%	40%	38%
Equally Scottish and British	19%	21%	29%	33%	27%
More British than Scottish	4%	3%	3%	3%	4%
British not Scottish	6%	4%	6%	3%	4%
None of these	2%	3%	1%	2%	4%
Sample size	*1021*	*1042*	*1056*	*957*	*882*

Source: Brown *et al.* (1996: 198), and preliminary data analysis for 1997 general election (*Scottish Election Study).

between half and three-quarters – claim dual identity, as Scottish and British (categories 2, 3 and 4). These responses are broadly consistent with social characteristics – age, gender, class. For example, young people, and manual workers opt for the 'Scottish' end of the spectrum, with older people, women and the middle classes being more 'centrist' in their identities, while no social group opts for identities at the 'British' end.

In Catalunya, given the history of recent dictatorship from the centre, and the fact that an autonomous government has existed for nearly twenty years, we might expect that *Catalanisme* would be stronger. In fact, using the same scales as for the Scottish data above, fewer people in Catalunya feel Catalan and more feel Spanish than we might expect.

Comparing these data with their Scottish equivalents, we can see that whereas the ratio of Scots prioritising their Scottishness over their Britishness is of the order of 6 to 1, among Catalans the balance is about equal as regards national (Catalan) and state (Spanish) identity. The number of Catalans claiming dual identity is also high (over 60 per cent), but in this regard they are comparable with their Scottish counterparts. The modal responses are, however, different. Whereas among Scots the mode lies in the category 'More Scottish than British', among Catalans the norm is to claim to be 'equally Catalan and Spanish' (ranging from 36 per cent in 1990 to 44 per cent in 1995). Given rates of in-migration from the rest of Spain since the 1950s, it is not surprising that place of birth is an important determinant of national identity. People born in Catalunya are more likely to claim to be only Catalan (18 per cent) or to have dual identity (42 per cent), and while around one-third of those born outside Catalunya say they are Spanish only, a degree of Catalan-ness is claimed by the rest.

Surveys of this sort are indicative only, but they do suggest a complex relationship between state (British or Spanish) and national (Scottish or Catalan) identities. It could be that having established autonomy over their own domestic affairs, the Catalans can afford to be more relaxed about their national and state identities, and are more likely to see them as nested within each other, or at least not in

Table 7.2 Self-identification in Catalunya, 1990–5

	1990	1991	1992	1993	1994	1995
Only Catalan	6%	15%	17%	12%	11%	10%
More Catalan than Spanish	23%	21%	17%	18%	21%	17%
Equally Catalan and Spanish	36%	37%	37%	42%	42%	44%
More Spanish than Catalan	10%	7%	6%	9%	15%	16%
Only Spanish	22%	18%	21%	19%	11%	12%
Don't know	3%	2%	1%	1%	1%	1%
Sample size	*557*	*2191*	*1684*	*1695*	*1704*	*1297*

Source: Moreno and Arriba (1996: 85).

current competition in the political marketplace. The Scots on the other hand have not, at the time of writing, achieved an autonomous parliament, and asserting Scottishness over Britishness is an important weapon in a political struggle. It is interesting that the survey results we have referred to above for Scotland are on a par with those for Euskadi where the ratio of Basque to Spanish is also of the order of six to one.

In Quebec, we do not have data comparable to those for Scotland and Catalunya, but those we have suggest that over the last few decades there has been an assertion of being Quebecois over being (French-) Canadian. This is reflected in data showing that the percentage of francophones calling themselves 'Canadiens' has fallen from 34 per cent in 1970 to a mere 9 per cent in 1990, whereas the description 'Quebecois' has risen from 21 to 59 per cent over the same period. As Keating observes: 'Between 1980 and 1991, the percentage feeling profoundly attached to Canada fell from 56 to 30%, and this correlates with support for sovereignty' (1996: 83). Nevertheless, we can surmise from these figures and from the political debate that some identification with Canada has not atrophied entirely, and that mobilising national and state identities in each case is part of the weaponry in the struggle for greater autonomy. In all three nations, there undoubtedly has been a move to assert national identity, but it seems that there is a degree of manipulation and instrumentality about it, reflecting the negotiated and attenuated character of territorial politics in the Western world.

The politics of economic opportunity

One of the key features of territories in which neo-nationalism has emerged is that they broadly belong to the world of the economically privileged rather than the disadvantaged. In recent years, one of the most obvious and explicit examples of this in the Western world has been the *Lega Nord* in northern Italy which has made much of its opposition to what it sees as a poor and parasitical South. Such explicit examples of 'beggar my neighbour' have been rare, and are less strong in the political agendas of Scotland, Catalunya and Quebec, though no doubt present. Nevertheless, we cannot ignore the fact that the politics of relative deprivation have played a part in their relationship to the centre, and that in recent years they have perceived that this relationship has altered so that the old one has to be renegotiated. This is the sense in which we encounter what Tom Nairn (1975) has called the nationalism of the elect rather than nationalism of the damned.

In the case of Scotland, it is important to remember that the Union of 1707 which joined it to England was in essence a marriage of convenience. As Clive Lee observes: 'While the short-term economic effects of the Union were disappointing to some Scots, historians have generally agreed that in the longer term Scotland gained substantially from it' (1995: 13). For the Scots, access to English markets at home and abroad was in many ways the *raison d'être* of the Union, and for much of the subsequent 260 years the economic balance sheet produced a positive effect for Scotland. It was of course the discovery of oil in the North Sea which altered the political calculus in Scotland's favour, and this almost immediately coincided with the rise of the SNP as a strong force in Scottish politics. Much of the subsequent thirty years has seen the constitutional debate focus on the balance of trade and payments between Scotland and London rather than on the classically romantic themes of nineteenth-century nationalism. The fact that the SNP is currently led by a bank economist is perhaps testament to the instrumental and economistic character of nationalism in modern Scotland. It is more a battle about the pocket-book than it is about the prayer-book or the song-sheet. The transformation of the Scottish economy away from its heavy industrial base, selling to imperial or British markets, to an international one based on hi-tech and services in a European market is a reflection of both the political and the economic transformation of Scotland's relationship with the British state, and the possible end of the negotiated compromise begun almost 300 years ago.

It has long been recognised that Catalunya is one of the economically advanced parts of Spain, and from the middle of the nineteenth century it, along with Euskadi, represented the vanguard of industrialisation. Catalunya had developed early trading links with much of the Mediterranean for much of its history, but it was excluded from establishing colonies in Spanish America by Madrid. However, it seems that the reasons for early industrialisation *vis-à-vis* Spain as a whole rested on certain social structural features. In the eighteenth century the possession of land (through long-term leases rather than outright ownership) was widespread, and Catalan law encouraged primogeniture (Balcells, 1996: 20). Specialised agriculture, wine exports and the development of textiles, coupled with the key role of an indigenous Catalan bourgeoisie, all helped to give Catalunya an early and continuing economic advantage.

Since the fall of the Francoist dictatorship, the role of this native bourgeoisie in both economy and politics (via the ruling coalition of Christian Democrats (*Unio*) and the smaller Liberal party (*Convergençia*)) has been extended. Big business is well-represented at the Spanish level and Spain represents Catalunya's biggest market (helping to explain the reluctance of nationalists in the *Convergençia i Unio* coalition to head for an independent Catalunya), while smaller business groups such as those affiliated to PIMEC (*Patronal de la Petita i Mitjana Empresa de Catalunya*) are more reliant on local Catalan markets. ˙

In general, Catalunya has a higher level of economic development, reflected in the in-migration of unskilled and semi-skilled workers from the rest of Spain over the last forty years. This helps to explain why, especially in the growing context of the European Community/Union since 1986, Catalan capitalists are ambivalent about the political project. On the one hand, Catalunya is relatively 'over-developed' *vis-à-vis* Spain and does more business with the European Union, while on the other hand there is reliance on Spanish markets which full independence would threaten.

Just as the relative economic situations of both Scotland and Catalunya *vis-à-vis* their respective states helps to account for the rise of neo-nationalism, so the modernisation of Quebec's economy is a key aspect in its political development.

The political economy of Quebec has moved from having an indigenous agricultural economy and an industrial and financial sector dominated by anglophone interests, to one in which local ownership has grown, especially in manufacturing and finance (Keating, 1996: 93). This transformation has been aided by local state leverage via quangos and agencies to encourage indigenous development. The crossover from public to private sectors is actively encouraged, and large state projects such as Hydro-Quebec have helped to open up the northern parts of the province.

The effect of this economic transformation is to generate a Quebecois business class, and a growing confidence that the wider North American market, notably through NAFTA, will help to lessen dependence on the Canadian one. As Michael Keating points out: 'Deregulation, neo-liberalism and free trade have not destroyed the Quebec model of development but they have transformed it. It is geared now to the interests of large corporations, based in Quebec but increasingly continental or global in their scale of operations' (1996: 6). The social tensions deriving from this project of 'market nationalism' have impacted on the capacity of the Parti Quebecois government to pursue social democratic and welfarist policies, a feature which is shared in Scotland and Catalunya. In all three cases, however, the changing relationship of the political economy to the nationalist project is a key defining feature of neo-nationalism.

Changing political ideologies

Are neo-nationalist movements on the Right or the Left of the political spectrum? The inherited conventional wisdom is that nationalism is *petit bourgeois* in its politics and ideology, at odds with labourist or social democratic forces. This, however, tends to be more a matter of contingency and history rather than ideology, reflecting the fact that the industrial working class were brought into the industrial and political process by trades unions and 'socialist' parties at particular conjunctures. Hence, later political formations like neo-nationalism have had to fight for political space in a crowded field in which 'class' politics defines the agenda.

This is certainly the case in Scotland, where Labour took longer to establish itself as the working-class party than it did in England. For ethnic and religious reasons it was not until after 1918 that Labour became the party of the Scottish working class, and even then, large sections of the Protestant working class did not lose their adherence to the Conservative Party until after 1945 (Brown *et al.*, 1996). By the late 1960s the Scottish National Party found itself accused of being 'tartan Tories', an accusation based on the seeming fact that it did best in Conservative seats, a feature which reflected its capacity to mobilise the anti-Tory vote in these constituencies rather than its political conservatism. In the post-war years, the SNP positioned itself in the centre of Scottish politics, and it was not until the 1980s that it set out an overtly social-democratic agenda in large part to combat Labour as Scotland's majority party (in terms of seats but not in terms of votes). This was in part tactical as the SNP stood in second place to Labour in many seats, and saw its chance of political breakthrough in challenging Labour for a working-class vote. Hence, while in the October 1974 election (its best performance to date in a general election) the SNP did well across all social classes – especially among skilled manual and intermediate professional workers – by 1992 its change of tactics and ideology produced a better electoral performance among manual workers generally. In this way, the party recognises that it has a capacity to tailor its appeal according to political contingencies, and to naturalise itself as the party of 'all the nation', a category which can be redefined as the moment allows.

This ability to occupy 'niche' nationalism can also be seen in the cases of Catalunya and Quebec. Of course, in the case of *Convergençia i Unio* (CiU), its historical origins are on the centre-right, but we should not forget other nationalist groupings such as the older *Esquerra Republicana de Catalunya* (ERC) which is much more to the Left, but is far less electorally successful. However, ERC does provide a leftist nationalist challenge to CiU which it cannot ignore. Hence, neo-nationalism in Catalunya also has to play across the ideological range, challenged as it is on the Right by the Spanish *Partido Popular*, and on the Left both by ERC, and by the Socialists and Communists. The latter parties, while they have local Catalan forms (*Partits dels Socialistes de Catalunya* – PSC; and *Iniciativa per Catalunya* – IC), find themselves pulled between their Spanish and their Catalan electorates, in much the same way that the Scottish Labour Party is likely to find when it establishes a Scottish parliament in Edinburgh.

The nationalist groupings have no such problems, but have to counter the argument that local parliaments have less power than the *Cortes* centred in Madrid. Much then depends on the tactical skill of nationalist politicians, and none is as consummate as the Catalan leader Jordi Pujol, whose longevity and ubiquity in Catalan politics is reflected in the fact that he is known simply as 'Jordi'. (The son of the Dutch manager of Barcelona football club – as '*Barça*', itself a carrier of considerable nationalist identity – was referred to in the Catalan press as '*l'altre Jordi*', the other Jordi). The fact that the CiU along with moderate Basque nationalists is in *de facto* alliance with the *Partido Popular* in Madrid, just as Pujol's CiU kept Gonzales' Socialists in power for much of the 1990s, gives Pujol and his fellow nationalists considerable leverage. It also indicates their capacity to work with both Right and Left, and to adopt appropriate political ideology as and when the need arises.

In the case of Quebec, we can see there too the capacity of the Parti Quebecois (PQ) to mobilise along the political spectrum. The PQ came to power after the petit bourgeois party, *Union Nationale*, had been discredited in the early 1960s, and was a vital part of the social and cultural '*révolution tranquille*'. This process of modernisation had both a liberal and a social democratic strand, and the PQ fought the Liberal Party at provincial level for this constituency. As Keating (1996) points out, nationalism in Quebec has ranged at various times from extreme Right to revolutionary Left. The problem for the PQ in recent years is that while its modern social base is urban and working class, it has been forced to adopt programmes of fiscal austerity and pro-capital policies. Being able to range across the ideological spectrum has its disadvantages as well as its advantages.

In general, then, what characterises the main political forms of neo-nationalism, at least in Scotland, Catalunya and Quebec, is that while they have different social and political histories, they all confront the opportunities and constraints of 'niche' nationalism. As appropriate, they can present themselves on the Left as well as the Right, as in favour of neo-liberalism as social democracy, as civic as well as ethnic, depending on the circumstances. In these regards, they have to be understood as quite different kinds of animals from those nationalist movements and parties which ushered in the modern Western state in the nineteenth century.

What is neo-nationalism for?

At the beginning of this chapter, we saw that much of the conventional wisdom as regards neo-nationalism is to see it merely as a way of exerting political pressure on the centre: 'voice' in lieu of 'exit', to use Hirschman's metaphors (1970). This focus on parties as pressure groups rather than part of a broader movement is also reflected in the terms used to describe it. As Lynch points out: 'A plethora of terms has developed to define the phenomenon of minority nationalism. Substate nationalism, regionalism, ethnonationalism . . . new nationalisms . . . ethnic separatism . . . and stateless nationalism . . . have all been used to define minority nationalism' (Lynch, 1996: 4).

This raises a basic question about neo-nationalism: is its aim independence or something less than that? The short answer is that we find a variety of goals, some short-term, others long-term, and this is expressed through the declared aims. In Scotland, for example, the term 'Home Rule', coined initially by the Liberal Party at the end of the nineteenth century to refer to devolved assemblies throughout the United Kingdom of Great Britain and Ireland as it then was, took on an ambiguity in the twentieth century and is used both as a generic term for any form of self-government and in the narrower sense of devolved government. Those who prefer the term 'Home Rule' to 'devolution' are often making a nationalist point. The former term implies Scottish sovereignty, while the latter acknowledges that sovereignty resides with the British state. In Catalunya, and Spain more generally since 1975, '*Autonomisme*' is the achieved goal of the CiU, who are coy about outright independence at least in the short term. In Quebec, the political debate of the last twenty years is indicative of this ambiguity: 'sovereignty-association' and 'consociation' implying that something less than full- or old-style independence is called for. Part of this is tactical, but the parallels are clear. Jordi Pujol, for instance, commented to a Quebec journalist: '*Nous aspirons a un statut similaire a celui de Quebec actuellement, c'est-à-dire une reconnaissance de personalité differencié . . . je ne suis pas fédéraliste parce que le fédéralisme recouvre un critère homogeneisateur. Cependant, nous pourrions essayer la voie du fédéralisme asymetrique tel qu'il existe au Canada*' (Jordi Pujol, 'vice-roi d'Espagne'). To muddy the waters further, he has spoken positively of the shift to a

'Europe of the Regions', while pointing out that 'this term was chosen to serve as a common, generic name that would be acceptable to nations such as Catalonia where the word "region" is not acceptable' (Jordi Pujol, 'Regional Power in the New Europe', lecture given at Complutense University of Madrid, El Escorial, 18 July 1991). In his manifesto 'Construir Catalunya', published in 1980, Pujol is careful to define being Catalan as someone 'who lives and works in Catalonia and wants to be Catalan' (quoted in Guibernau, 1997: 91). The 'will to be' (*voluntat de ser*) is what defines nationalism for him rather than pre-ordained ethnic factors.

In like manner, the relationship between devolved government and independence is complex. In neo-nationalist parties there is a debate about whether or not devolution leads to independence ('the thin end of the wedge' to supporters and opponents alike), or is a barrier to it, buying off separatist support. This debate is especially important in the context of supra-national governmental bodies like the European Union where old-style nineteenth-century independence as 'sovereignty' is no longer possible. Hence, the SNP can campaign for 'Independence in Europe' (the models being Ireland, Denmark and so on), albeit that a significant minority of its support in opinion polls (around a quarter) wishes for Independence outwith Europe. In the 1992 election survey, for example, while 43 per cent of SNP supporters favoured Independence within the European Union, 14 per cent supported Independence outwith the EU (Brown *et al.*, 1996: table 7.11).

Nevertheless, there is a good case for saying that the development of European integration has facilitated regionalist and nationalist movements in part because they recognise that full economic independence is no longer feasible in the late twentieth century, and also because it seems easier to persuade the electorate that what is envisaged is a difference of degree not of kind. Peter Lynch puts it this way:

> In the late twentieth century party goals now favour independence in Europe, a Europe of the regions and the creation of a decentralized and federal European Union. Autonomy and European integration have therefore become intertwined, and this process has occurred over the long term and looks set to continue
>
> (Lynch, 1996: 197)

While it is true that Quebec does not have the advantage in these respects of being within the European Union, and that NAFTA is essentially an economic and not a political concept as such, it too has the capacity to operate within the new variable geometry of power between nation, state and supra-state. Hence, it can operate *de facto* within its wider continental trading area (with regard to the selling of hydro-power to the US, for example), as well as using the wider framework for rhetorical purposes, that is, to show its electorate that it is behaving as an 'as if' government. Quebec's relationship with the US is already important: the US takes 75 per cent of its foreign exports and provides 46 per cent of its imports (Keating, 1996: 104). Keating cites opinion poll data which suggest that a majority of Quebecois think that sovereignty and separatism are not the same thing (ibid.:

82–3), and while most people want Quebec to have full control over education and cultural affairs, few are willing to shoulder the burden for defence and foreign affairs. Keating observes: 'it is unlikely that Quebec would be excluded from NAFTA, *pace* some commentaries in the rest of Canada. NAFTA, however, is not a unitary regime, to which a state can simply adhere. It is a complex system of bilateral, trilateral and sectoral agreements, and Quebec's place within this would have to be negotiated' (ibid.: 110).

Further evidence that neo-nationalism is different from its more orthodox predecessor comes from the fact, it seems, that the electorate is quite prepared to play the political system, and if this means voting for the nationalist party without committing oneself to its central tenet of independence, then so be it. Hence, in Scotland it is now well established in election surveys and opinion polls that around one-third of SNP voters prefer devolution to independence, while a significant minority of Labour voters (whose policy devolution is) are in favour of independence. For example, in 1997, 31 per cent of SNP voters favoured devolution, and 22 per cent of Labour voters independence (Scottish Election Study).

A similar capacity to play the system is reflected in Catalunya where it has become established that voters often behave differently in elections for the Spanish Cortes (where the socialists got 40 per cent of the vote in the 1996 general election, and the CiU 30 per cent), and in the autonomous elections for the Catalan parliament (in 1995 the CiU took 41 per cent of the vote, and the socialists 25 per cent). When a Scottish Home Rule parliament is created in Edinburgh, we are likely to see similar strategic voting behaviour. For example, in an opinion poll during the 1997 general election campaign, 47 per cent said they would vote Labour, and 28 per cent SNP, but that in an election of a domestic parliament, these figures would narrow considerably to 39 and 38 per cent respectively. Most of these transfers were from Labour supporters, and some from the smaller Liberal Democrat party (*Scottish Affairs*, 20, 1997).

As regards Quebec, the PQ does not even stand in federal elections. In 1996 this allowed a loose coalition of nationalists operating as *Bloc Quebecois* to win so many seats that they became for a time the official Canadian opposition in the federal parliament, while the Progressive Conservative government of Brian Mulroney was only elected because nationalists opted for him as 'favourite son' and against the Liberal party, the PQ's main opposition in the province. In other words, 'nationalist' voting is likely to be greater in Home Rule/autonomous/provincial elections where 'domestic' issues are especially salient.

Conclusion

This chapter has explored the emergence of 'neo-nationalist' movements in advanced industrial countries in the West. By and large, they adopt a civic rather than an ethnic focus – 'demos' not 'ethnos'. We can, of course, find instances of the latter in all three societies where communal solidarity verges on the racist, focusing on the politics of exclusion rather than inclusion, born of being a minority in a larger state territory. Anti-English sentiment in Scotland, hostility in Quebec to anglophones or allophones (those whose first language is neither French nor English), and overly discriminating in favour of Catalan speakers in Catalunya would be instances of this.

Nevertheless, I have argued that conventional accounts of nationalism either treat these examples as a throwback to atavistic or ethnic forms of nationalism, or reduce them to mere forms of pressure group politics simply aimed at wresting more resources from the centre – in other words, that they are not 'real' forms of nationalism at all. In this respect, they are mistaken. It is a feature of nationalism in general that it is a multifaceted and adaptable ideology, and that it reflects not simply the historic memory of separate identities in certain territories – what we might call its 'vertical' significance – but connects with key current issues of economic, political and cultural power in societies of the late twentieth century – its 'horizontal' significance. We cannot dismiss neo-nationalism as simply an historical ethnic memory-trace, nor as something 'epiphenomenal' which ought to be explained in terms of other social forces such as social class. It is the confluence of both vertical and horizontal sets of processes which gives neo-nationalism its power and significance in the territorial politics of Western states. In like manner, nationalism has generic as well as specific meaning in post-communist countries of Central and Eastern Europe, as the next chapter will demonstrate.

8

THE UNFORESEEN
REVOLUTION

Post-communist nationalism

When Gorbachev became General Secretary of the Communist Party of the Soviet Union in March 1985, no-one, least of all Gorbachev himself, expected nationalism to rise from the ashes. And yet, a mere decade later, the political and cultural landscape of Central and Eastern Europe had been transformed. Four states, including his own, have disappeared – USSR, East Germany, Czechoslovakia and Yugoslavia; former national states like Hungary, Poland, Lithuania, Latvia and Estonia have become independent of Soviet influence; and new states have emerged seemingly out of nothing, especially in the non-Russian federation, the Central Asian republics, the Caucasus including Chechnya, and many more. A process of fusion has rejoined East and West Germany in unification nationalism. Fission has created the Czech Republic and Slovakia in a process which was so relatively painless that it became known as the Velvet Revolution. On the other hand, Yugoslavia imploded in a series of bloody wars, and gave the language of nationalism a new, chilling euphemism, '*etnicko ciscenjie*' – ethnic cleansing.

As we can see from the chronology of events at the end of this chapter, the unpredictability and speed of political change in Eastern and Central Europe, especially since the fall of the Berlin Wall in 1989, caught virtually everyone unawares. No-one expected or predicted it, largely because it did not fit into the set of conventional explanations. Some analysts like Francis Fukuyama (1989) saw it as 'the end of history' whereby the grand narrative of capitalism versus communism had suddenly lost its *raison d'être*. In fact, *contra* Fukuyama, history was only beginning. Territories were rediscovering their histories and connecting them into their futures, often determined to go their separate ways. The monochrome of the Cold War gave way to the kaleidoscope of cultures rediscovered and reinvented.

Many did not like what they saw. Eric Hobsbawm, who was suspicious of nationalism in East and West, voiced admiration and regret for the passing of the old order: 'It was', he commented, in melancholic retrospect, 'the great achievement of the communist regimes in multinational countries to limit the disastrous effects of nationalism within them' (Hobsbawm, 1990: 173). The Russian and Yugoslav revolutions had, he judged, at least prevented the nationalities killing each other. There was method in the madness of the old communist regimes which allowed the nationalities merely to dance. Hobsbawm predicted that the end of communism was likely to lead to greater oppression against and discrimination of minorities in new democratic states, and he pointed out that anti-Semitism in the Baltic states and Ukraine was at least the equal of Nazi Germany.

Much of this analysis sought to juxtapose nationalism and internationalism, and this brought former communists like Hobsbawm to question the liberal tenet laid down by Woodrow Wilson after the Great War: 'In the early 1990s, perhaps for the first time, rational observers irrespective of politics (other than those of some specific group of nationalist activism) began publicly to propose the abandonment of the "right of self-determination"' (Hobsbawm, 1994: 567). It might seem odd to propose the abandonment of a principle never actually operational in much of Europe, but it indicated a key perspective on the fall of communism: the rise of nationalism. Terms like 'balkanisation' re-emerged with added vigour as the phenomenon took shape before our eyes, and a new conventional wisdom emerged, shared by Right and Left alike: the theory of the ethnic abyss.

Put simply, this argued that the achievement of communism had been to hold nationalism in check, but the genie had escaped from the bottle. Ancient ethnic hatreds were deemed to have bubbled to the surface once more. It ensured that the 'deep-freeze' theory of ethnic conflict, namely that totalitarianism had blocked off political expressions of rivalries, became the dominant perspective. Nationalism was seen as both the cause and the effect of the fall of communism. It was, of course, much more complex than that, and there were at least three sets of congruent but distinct processes – ideological, political and economic – at work in the former Soviet empire to bring about the end of communism. To be sure, nationalism was a mould into which discontents were flowing, notably in territories which had a memory of historic nationhood however brief, especially Poland and the Baltic states. However, communism had also been destroyed by a quest for democracy, a popular rebellion against the arthritic system of power which vested one party with supreme authority. Similarly, communism as an economic system manifestly had failed to satisfy its people who yearned to become consumers on the Western model. In other words, command economies had reached the end of their road.

Nevertheless, it was nationalism – it was harder to be against democracy or the market – which attracted the attention and opprobrium of its Western critics who belatedly discovered one of the few virtues of communism. When the communist regimes fell like dominoes from 1989 until 1993, it was nationalism which became the focus.

The image to emerge via the media was the outbreak of historic ethnic and racial conflicts, suggesting that something nasty was going on in the woodshed and, like all self-respecting woodsheds, it was somewhere at the end of the garden, well away from the big house but close enough to make walking in the garden a bit of an ordeal. To imply, however, that it was a problem which originated in the woodshed rather than the big house was misleading. Since 1989, we have found

150

what Ernest Gellner called the 'dark gods' theory of nationalism becoming more popular. This implies that nationalism is about mobilising atavistic and irrational instincts, that it belongs to peripheral regions which history somehow has passed by, and as Tom Nairn (1993) has pointed out, there is the view that nationalism is upsetting everything. No sooner is communism dead, than nasty, racial conflicts break out in this new world disorder.

Conventional theories find it hard to cope with the rise of nationalism. Fukuyama's 'end of history' which was premised on the universal victory of Western liberal democracy as the final form of human government began to look a little silly in the context of nations' rediscovering their own histories. His thesis was premised on the final victory of universal liberalism; he observed at this time: 'it matters very little what strange thoughts occur to people in Albania or Burkina Faso, for we are interested in what we could in some sense call the common ideological heritage of mankind' (Fukuyama, 1989: 9). While recognising that nationalism had been given a new lease of life by the fall of communism, Fukuyama defended his thesis by claiming that nationalism in its modern forms was simply an arrested form of political development: 'certainly a great deal of the world's ethnic and nationalist tension can be explained in terms of peoples who are forced to live in unrepresentative political systems that they have not chosen' (ibid.: 15). Ultimately, he felt, liberal values and the 'common marketisation' of international relations would win out.

This distrust of nationalism and its predicted demise exists on the Left as well as the Right. The Spanish political scientist, Pi-Sunyer, pointed out: 'liberal scholarship has tended to look at nationalism, when it has done so at all, as an antique evil to give way to progress. Marxist theories generally treat nationalism as an ideological manifestation of some less-evident infrastructure' (1985: 254).

The 'deep freeze' theory of nationalism did have a certain plausibility. After all, communist regimes in Eastern and Central Europe had carefully counted and documented their 'national minorities' while at the same time implying in their political ideology that internationalism, not nationalism, was their driving force.

It was comforting too to the West which had its own cosmopolitan version of internationalism, capitalist liberal democracy. However, accounting for the outbreak of nationalism in Central and Eastern Europe in terms of age-old ethnic and religious hatreds was, in Hroch's words, 'closer to the world of fairy-tales than of historical processes' (1993: 14), and was soon replaced by a more 'political' theory which focused on the decline of communism and the vacuum it left.

Nationalism and post-communist politics

A variant of this theory was that nationalism provided a convenient ideology for politicians striving to hold on to power. The obvious case was the former Yugoslavia. There, the former communist Slobodan Milosevic was able to mobilise the appeal of nationalism especially among the minority Serbs in Kosovo where ethnic Albanians predominated, and then spread it into Serbia itself. The influential television series by Silber and Little, and its accompanying book *Death of Yugoslavia* (1995) took as its general thesis: 'Yugoslavia did not die a natural death but was deliberately and systematically killed off by men who had nothing to gain and everything to lose from a peaceful transition from state socialism and one-party rule to a market-based economy and multi-party democracy' (Silber and Little, 1995: xxiii). Serbian nationalism, they argued, had been reinvented by Belgrade intellectuals in the 1980s, before being harnessed by politicians like Milosevic.

Explaining the rise of nationalism in the Balkans in political terms became influential. Focusing on the international-relations aspect of the fall of Yugoslavia, the Brookings Institution writer, Susan Woodward, argued that 'nationalism became a political force when leaders in the republics sought popular support as bargaining chips in federal disputes' (1995: 380). More generally, the fall of communism and the end of the Cold War had led to political disintegration which politicians exploited. Woodward argued that the real origin of the crisis in the former Yugoslavia and elsewhere was not ethnicity as such but the disintegration of governmental authority and the breakdown of civil and political order. For this, in Woodward's view, the West was much to blame. It defined the problem as 'an unpleasant reminder of old ethnic and religious conflicts that modern Europe had left behind, rather than as part of their own national competition to redefine Europe and respond to the end of the cold war' (ibid.: 20). The broad thrust of such analysis was shared by leftist writers like Catherine Samary (1995) who focused on the role which free market economics and reforms played in under-mining the political and social order.

The importance of political factors obviously fitted with the analysis of writers on nationalism such as John Breuilly who extended his book *Nationalism and the State* in its second edition (1993) to take account of these developments. He was critical of the 'ethnic' accounts of nationalism because they imply the 'naturalness' (if irrationality) of the phenomenon. He commented: 'Indeed, its "naturalness" is sometimes taken to be the main way of explaining the irrationality: people so "naturally" take up a national identity that they will do so even if this appears to threaten economic stability and growth and to bring grave political and military dangers in its wake' (1993: 342–3). Breuilly argued that this approach is misleading, for in general it is not inevitable that nationalism leads to separatism, and in the case of the Soviet Union 'nationalism' has to be decoded as a rational political response to the unravelling of state power. The key, he argued, lay in the breakdown of the Soviet system so that state power was decentralised under *glas-nost* (freedom of information) and *perestroika* (political and economic restructuring) in such a way that regionalised power bases were formalised around republics each of which had a 'national' character. 'In this way "nationality" . . . was built into the political structures of the USSR' (ibid.: 347).

This was especially true of the Baltic states where there was a recent memory of independence, as well as an urbanised and well-educated population which could be mobilised in defence of the 'national' culture and its language. Similarly in the western Russian republics such as Ukraine where nationalism developed in the western part of the territory in the context of economic development. In other words, observed Breuilly, 'one should not see the break-up of the USSR in terms of the rise of nationalist oppositions; rather one should see the rise of nationalist oppositions as a rational response to the breakdown of USSR state power' (ibid.: 350).

The communist regimes in the buffer zone which contained Poland, Czechoslovakia and Hungary came progressively to realise that Soviet military intervention would not re-occur as time went on, and speeded up the processes of political and economic reforms. What marked out the reform movements in these countries was their ability to mobilise alternative sources of power (such as the Catholic church in Poland), and Breuilly argues that economic and political liberalisation rather than nationalism marked out the new politics of protest. Only in the former East Germany did a form of nationalism emerge, but it took the curious form of reunification nationalism (from 'Wir sind *das* Volk' to 'Wir sind *ein* Volk'). In his words, 'it is the nature of communist state power, how it broke down, and how successor states developed out of that breakdown which provides the key to understanding how nationalist conflicts could arise' (Breuilly, 1993: 364).

Even in the apparently most obvious expression of nationalism, the break-up of the former Yugoslavia, Breuilly argues that its key weakness lay in the yoking of the original Serb core to more advanced western peripheries of the former Habsburg empire, like Slovenia and Croatia. Ethnic conflicts were generated out of uneven economic development and regional disparities, coupled with the incompatibility of highly centralised communist state control and regional autonomy. Nationalism and ethnic separatism became the ideological means of expressing fundamental political and economic contradictions. In the Yugoslav case, ethnic identities which had been embedded in ethnic-religious forms and encouraged through regional autonomy were given political expression as nationalism through the breakdown of communist state power and the ensuing power vacuum, especially after the death of Tito. Breuilly's argument is that ethnicity is the means but not the primary cause of the death of Yugoslavia. This resulted from the collapse of the political state coupled with the failure of command communism, even in its more 'liberal' forms.

The politics of culture

The focus on political and economic processes which lead to civil breakdown cannot be gainsaid, but such an approach does tend to downplay or treat as epiphenomenal the role of ethnic or cultural factors to the point where they become proxies for what are deemed to be 'real', usually material factors. It is more complex than this. Writing on the Serbs, Tim Judah comments: 'Only with a solid understanding of the past can we understand how the Serbs could be induced to make such catastrophic decisions about their future. After all, the Serbs could not be manipulated if there was no material with which to manipulate them' (Judah, 1997: 24). Of course, ill-remembered history could not simply be blamed for war in the 1990s; what mattered was 'a determined and cynical leader being able to harness historical memory for his own political ends and succeeding' (ibid.: 43).

The unpredictability of form and content is nicely expressed in the so-called 'velvet divorce' which sundered the old Czechoslovak state in two (Nairn, 1994). It was so named because of its unexpected as well as non-violent character. No-one 'decided': it just occurred. Those who wish to argue for the 'primordial' quality of nationalism can use it as an example whereby ethnic faultlines will out. It was as if nationalism came bubbling to the surface because people were inalienably 'ethnic', and the separation of the Czech Republic and Slovakia became 'inevitable'. To the reply that there was always something artificial about the state of Czechoslovakia (it had been a political convenience forged following the collapse of the Austro-Hungarian empire after 1918), primordialists would reply that the reason it took so long to collapse as a state owed much to the geo-political circumstances of Central Europe, first, up to and including the Second World War, and later, the grip of communism.

To those who put primacy on 'political' factors, the explanation for the Czech–Slovak split is that while Slovak ethno-religious bonds were a necessary condition, the sufficient one came from the Czech side in the form of the economic push for liberalisation. In other words, key politicians in Prague wanted the shortest possible route to capitalist integration, whereas the Slovaks wanted a more phased approach. As Tom Nairn has pointed out, this usually meant that the Czechs denied that they were nationalists (Petr Pithart describes their nationalism as 'regional egoism'), whereas the Slovaks' political reaction came in the form of ethno-nationalism. Nairn observes: 'Western comment over the whole period [1989–93] overlooked the low-profile nature of Czech nationalism and unduly emphasised the high-profile sins and antics of Bratislava [the Slovak capital], but in reality the latter partly derived from the former' (1994: 16).

We are helped in understanding the underlying character of this conflict by Ladislav Holy's study of Czech nationalism. He comments that since 1918 Czech nationalism was largely implicit, and the awareness of being Czech mainly tacit. Nevertheless, there was a rich reservoir of historical memories and a narrative of past events which were drawn on. At the heart of these narratives were the symbolic spaces occupied by St Wenceslas, the founder of the Czech state, and Jan Hus, the Protestant reformer, the symbol of Czech nationhood. Hence, 'we' was ambiguous, referring either to the Czech state or the Czech nation. Ironically, given that communism had been voted in by the population in 1945, opposition to communism expressed itself in terms of national (rather than state) identity. In other words, what was mobilised was an ethnic-cultural model rather than a civic-territorial one. Icons like the little Czech man, better known by his literary representation, the good soldier Schweik, became part of the cultural weaponry used against communism, a process described as 'inner migration'. In Holy's words, 'under communism, charity did not begin at home; it ended there' (1996: 24). This was the political-cultural context which generated a focus on the Czech nation so that after communism the 'natural' state structure was a Czech state, whereas Czechoslovakia was deemed to be 'artificial'. The collapse of communism made the Czech-Slovak split (at least on the Czech side) virtually inevitable.

To juxtapose 'ethnic' and 'political' explanations for the collapse of communism and the rise of nationalism in Eastern and Central Europe is to simplify a complex process, and in particular to give primacy to politics. This only works, in Tom Nairn's words, 'if politics are removed into an abstract sphere' (1994: 18), for understanding nationalism requires a much more complex explanation. The Czech historian, Miroslav Hroch, has re-engaged his attentions with what he calls the 'new nationalisms' of Central and Eastern Europe (Hroch, 1996). These, he says, should be understood not as the expressions of long-suppressed ethnic rivalries, but as analogous to nineteenth-century forms of nationalism, with some significant differences. He argues that the clear parallels include:

- the prominence of linguistic-cultural demands at an early stage of post-communism such as the Estonians making knowledge of the language a condition of civil rights, and the campaign in Croatia to establish Croat as a full and independent language from Serb;
- the call for political democracy corresponding to the demand for civil rights in nineteenth-century nationalism;
- its use by social and economic elites as a means of transition to becoming a dominant capitalist class.

After half a century of dictatorship, Hroch argues, linguistic and cultural appeals in particular may be acting as substitutes for political demands in the absence of a developed civil society: 'The vernacular of any small nation fighting for its independence is automatically regarded as the language of liberty' (Hroch, 1996: 92). Nevertheless, although there are similarities with nineteenth-century nationalism, he argues that there are crucial differences. In the first place, the new ruling class has grown up in a political-economic vacuum so that the *nomenklatura*, the former communist elite, are well-placed to make the transition. Second, the economic and social conditions of the late twentieth century are much more negative and hostile than they were in the nineteenth when economic growth and social improvement were the norm. Third, in the nineteenth century, nation-building was generally the norm throughout Europe, while it is the exception in the context of the late twentieth century, where European integration is the prime agenda. Finally, Hroch points out that today ethno-nationalisms do not destabilise the world in the way they did last century. His account reminds us of the dangers of reading simplistic assumptions into the emergence of 'new nationalisms' in the former communist countries, either because we assume that 'ethnic hatreds' are the cause, or because they are simply a manifestation of a political catching-up process with the 'developed' West. In short, we need ways of explaining them which capture their complexity, especially as regards their similarities and differences.

Competing nationalisms

One such account which takes a strongly sociological approach is that of Rogers Brubaker whose book *Nationalism Reframed: Nationhood and the National Question in the New Europe* (1996) promises to be as significant as his earlier study of Western European routes to national citizenship (*Citizenship and Nationhood in France and Germany*, 1992). Brubaker approaches 'nation' as a category of practice rather than analysis (1996: 7), and hence, he argues, it follows that nationalism is not a 'force' which surges and recedes, but 'a heterogeneous set of "nation"-oriented idioms, practices, and possibilities that are continuously available or "endemic" in modern cultural and political life' (ibid.: 10). His general approach to the study of nationalism is hostile to primordialism, 'a long-dead horse that writers on ethnicity and nationalism continue to flog' (ibid.: 15). Instead, he argues, it is important to decouple the study of nationhood and nation-ness from the study of nations as substantial entities, collectivities and communities. His focus is on 'nation-ness' as a conceptual variable. 'We should not ask "what is a nation", but rather: how is nationhood as a political and cultural form institutionalised within and among states?' (ibid.: 16). In other words, in a sociological account it is more important to focus on its institutionalisation than its substance. He gives the example of the Croat writer Slavenka Drakulic who complained about being 'overcome by nationhood' in an involuntary way:

> Being Croat has become my destiny. . . . I am defined by my nationality, and by it alone. . . . Along with millions of other Croats, I was pinned to the wall of nationhood – not only by outside pressure from Serbia and the Federal Army but by national homogenization within Croatia itself. That is what the war is doing to us, reducing us to one dimension: the Nation. . . . One doesn't have to succumb voluntarily to this ideology of the nation – one is sucked into it. So right now, in the new state of Croatia, no one is allowed not to be a Croat.
>
> (from S. Drakulic, *The Balkan Express: Fragments from the Other Side of War*, quoted in Brubaker, 1996: 20)

The key to understanding nation-ness in post-communist countries, Brubaker argues, is to see that they contain distinct sets of mutually antagonistic nationalisms, reflecting the complex history of Eastern and Central Europe. Here, we can recall Gellner's model of the 'time zones' of Europe, discussed in chapter 4, that in the third and fourth zones in the East there were old non-national empires and the patchwork of folk cultures and cultural diversities separating social strata and adjacent territories (Gellner, 1994a: 30). As a result, the straightforward, even simplistic, understandings of uniform, territorial nationalism derived in the West are something of a hindrance to understanding. Brubaker argues that in addition to 'national minorities' located within a single state, there is also 'nationalising' nationalism which is promoted on a territorial basis by the newly independent or reconfigured state, on the one hand, and on the other, the nationalism of 'external national homelands'. The key distinction (and conflict) is often between the latter two conceptions, that is, nationalising nationalism, and homeland nationalism. The former, most readily recognised by Westerners, derives from the expectation that residents within the territory of a state share its common identity of citizenship. The latter focuses on the shared ethnic identity (reflected most obviously in language, religion etc.) of peoples who are distributed across states. Hence, there will be (ethnic) Hungarians who are citizens of Romania, and vice versa. The Western assumption that people's 'national' identity is with the territorial state in which they live and with no other (except in a residual way) is of little help here.

In fact, there is likely to be a triadic confrontation between national minorities, nationalising states and external national homelands. National minorities are to be understood not as unitary groups but in terms of the field of 'differentiated and competitive positions or stances adopted by different organisations, parties, movements, or individual political entrepreneurs', each seeking 'to "represent" the minority to its own putative members, to the host state, or to the outside world, each seeking to monopolise the legitimate representation of the group' (Brubaker, 1996: 61). Brubaker prefers the term 'nationalising state' to 'nation-state' because it does not presuppose ethnic homogeneity, nor imply that it has reached its final shape. Once more, he sees it as a 'field' (a term he borrows from Bourdieu) consisting of differential and competing positions. Again, the 'external national homeland' is a dynamic political stance with shared associations and orientations rather than a distinct thing.

The value of these distinctions is that it captures much of the complexity and confusion of 'nationalist' conflicts. For example, this 'triadic nexus' (ibid.: 69) can be seen in operation in the break-up of Yugoslavia. Brubaker shows that the Croatian conflict was triadic rather than dyadic insofar as it involved an incipient national minority (Serbs in Croatia), an incipient nationalising state (Croatia), and an incipient external homeland (Serbia proper). What is then generated is a conflict of three overlapping and intensifying processes: 'the nationalisation of the Croatian incipient state . . . the increasing disaffection and mobilisation of Serbs in the ethnic borderlands of Croatia; and the development of a radical and belligerent "homeland" stance in the incipient Serbian state' (ibid.: 70).

While the conflict between the Croat and Serbian states was the most remarked upon aspect, it was construed by Western commentators as one of secession, when in fact it was much more complex than that, and involved the nationalising tendencies of the incipient Croat state (something, of course, which Western analysts could recognise and give their approval to. After all, what could be more reasonable than a state seeking 'sovereignty' over its territory on the Western model?). The Serb minority in Croatia, however, was neither behaving 'unreasonably' (although Tudjman was adept at implying this through his Western allies), nor was it the puppet of Milosevic's regime in Belgrade. After all, the homeland politics of 'greater Serbia' had a long historical pedigree, and brought its own reactions from Croatia, Slovenia and other neighbours which were part of an older pattern. In the context of the complexities generated by minority, nationalising and homeland nationalisms, it is little wonder that the political outcomes were so uncertain, and so poorly understood by the West whose perspectives on all this were forged in a much simpler and cruder form. This might not matter much if the military-political power of the West had not been mobilised in the Balkans in the way it was, based on the assumption that it was merely an unpleasant legacy of ethnic divisions which the West had long left behind (Woodward, 1995).

One of the important points in Brubaker's analysis (1996) is that nationalism should be seen as a form of remedial political action, rather than as the inevitable outcome of either ethnic forces or political dysfunction. He points out that when nationalism is treated as a form of politics, it usually focuses on polity-seeking movements which, after all, are the forms which the West has in its mental locker of history. His view is that far less attention has been paid to what he terms polity-based, nation-shaping nationalisms which seek to make complete or to realise nation-states, and that this dimension is of greater relevance to the new nationalisms of Eastern and Central Europe.

The states which emerged out of the remnants of the former empires of Eastern and Central Europe in the twentieth century were crucially nationalising states, which were inherently more diffuse than state-seeking nationalisms, and with less-than-clear political goals. Brubaker takes as an example inter-war Poland. Unlike its predecessors, the modern Polish state was defined as the state for and of the Polish nation characterised in linguistic and religious terms. This 'polonisation' of the territory presented problems of and for ethnic Germans, for example, as well as Jews. In other words, there was a clear distinction between the Polish nation and the citizenry of the state. It was not deemed necessary, unlike in the Western mind-set, to turn one into the other. Although there are specific and peculiar aspects of the Polish case, Brubaker draws out implications for new nationalising states insofar as the state is seen as the instrument for promoting the core nation, and that the state-owning core nation is distinct from the citizenry as a whole which is assembled within the territory. He concludes that there is little chance of the 'civic', territorial state-modelling based on Western notions of citizenship with ethnicity irrelevant to one's political rights. Nor is the alternative future likely whereby a multinational state is formed unless it is the outcome of a joining together of previously independent states (whether the proposed re-integration of Russia and Belarus announced in the spring of 1997 will have this effect remains to be seen).

Brubaker points out that the conflicts generated by these competing nationalisms are not new. For example, in the inter-war period, the clashes between the nationalising nationalism of Poland and Czechoslovakia, and the homeland nationalism ('*Deutschtum*') of Germany was one of the defining experiences of the twentieth century. Today, there are plenty of instances of similar possibilities, notably between the nationalising nationalism of Estonia and Latvia, and the homeland nationalism of Russia which has a potential appeal to the large Russian minorities in both Baltic states (30 per cent in Estonia, and 34 per cent in Latvia

(G. Smith, 1996)). We should of course avoid implying that common ethnicity has the same meaning and mobilising force. For example, in Latvia nearly two-fifths of Russian speakers supported independence, and in the 1991 referendum one-third of Russians voted 'yes' (compared with three-quarters of the total population, but nevertheless a significant minority of the population) (ibid.: 136). However, as Linz and Stepan (1996) point out, the processes of nation-building, state-building and democracy-building in Latvia and Estonia are complex and fraught with potential for conflict and authoritarianism.

There is no shortage of instances of this clash of nationalisms in late twentieth-century Eastern and Central Europe: the former Yugoslavia, Armenia and Azerbaijan, Romania, Slovakia and Hungary over their respective homeland and nationalising nationalisms, and so on. Irredentism, the reclaiming of a people and their territory 'lost' to its natural parent, is only one extreme version of homeland nationalism. Brubaker explains it thus:

> Nationalizing and homeland nationalisms are diametrically opposed and directly conflicting: nationalizing nationalisms (like that of interwar Poland) are directed 'inward' by states toward their own territories and citizenries, while homeland nationalisms . . . are directed 'outward' by neighboring states, across the boundaries of territory and citizenship, toward members of 'their own' ethnic nationality, that is toward persons who 'belong' (or can be claimed to belong) to the external national homeland by ethnonational affinity, although they reside in and are (ordinarily) citizens of other states.
>
> (Brubaker, 1996: 111)

Both forms of nationalism are oriented to the 'nation' as distinct from the citizenry of the state. They differ from each other insofar as in states which undertake nationalising nationalism, the core nation is smaller in size than the citizenry, whereas in homeland nationalism the nation is much broader than the citizenry, and much of it resides in other state jurisdictions. Brubaker points out that these are not mutually exclusive, for each type of nationalism may be found in the same state. His examples are as follows:

> Serbia is a nationalizing state *vis-à-vis* Albanians in Kosovo and an external national homeland *vis-à-vis* Serbs in Croatia and Bosnia-Hercegovina. Romania is a nationalizing state *vis-à-vis* Hungarians, a homeland *vis-à-vis* Romanians in Moldova. Russia today is a homeland for diaspora Russians, but also (potentially) a nationalizing state *vis-à-vis* non-Russian minorities in Russia. Interwar Germany was of course not only an external national homeland for transborder Germans, but a murderously nationalizing state *vis-à-vis* Jews.
>
> (Brubaker, 1996: 112, footnote 12)

In other words, the complexity emerges when the citizens of one state do not correspond with its 'nationals' who in turn are also present in numbers in another state of which they are citizens, and so on. What Brubaker provides is a much more systematic development of the simple civic/ethnic distinction, which in its usual conception attributes the former (good) to the West, and the latter (bad) to the East. As we have seen, it is considerably more complex than that. While the Western model assumes that citizens are nationals (hence, the (con)fusion of 'state' and 'nation' which bedevils much writing on nationalism), in Central and Eastern Europe the relationship is often different and more subtle, for there is far less congruence between nation and state.

The linking pin between East and West is Germany, as Brubaker shows in both of his studies (1992 and 1996). He points out that the tension between nation and state, between ethno-linguistic and political units, has deep roots in German history, reflected in the focus on the nation in the works of Herder. By the end of the nineteenth century, but especially under the Weimar Republic, a considerable civil society had developed outwith the German state with an apparatus of churches, associations, schools and clubs which helped to underpin '*Deutschtumspolitik*', that is, Germandom. This in turn became a major political issue when Germans became substantial minorities in newly nationalising states such as Czechoslovakia (most obviously in the Sudetenland), Hungary and the Baltic states, and helped to generate homeland nationalism in the 1930s, and provided fruitful conditions for the rise of Nazism. While there was a world of difference between the Weimar Republic and the Third Reich, the network of civil associations fostered by the former was a key resource for Hitler's greater Germany project.

Nationalism in Russia

The collapse of Soviet communism, Brubaker argues, also provides potential fertile ground for the development of homeland nationalism. He observes: 'the Soviet nationality regime with its distinctive and pervasive manner of institutionalising nationhood and nationality, has transmitted to successor states a set of deeply structured and powerfully conflicting expectations of belonging' (Brubaker, 1996: 54). The regime created and institutionalised a system of identifying and classifying national minorities. Similarly, political developments since 1989 suggest that there is potential for 'communist nationalism', a fusion of strong state and strong nation, what has been called 'red form, white content' (Lester, 1997: 44). The possibilities of a Red/Brown alliance have exercised commentators in the 1990s, fuelled by political developments in Russia. The leader of the Communist Party of the Russian Federation, Gennadii Zyuganov, has argued that Russian communism can only be defended by mobilising nationalism, perhaps by drawing on the proto-religious concept of '*obshchina*', community. It has been argued, for example, that Russian nationalism 'has always been designed to be used in highly conservative and reactionary ways to serve exclusively the interests of an all-powerful, absolutist state' (ibid.: 42).

What makes the fall of communism in the former Soviet Union doubly complex is not simply the possible alliance between nationalism and communism, between nation and (former) state, but what Brubaker calls 'conflicting expectations of belonging' (1996: 54). (We might also remind ourselves in passing that nationalism and communism were connected for much of the twentieth century in many liberation struggles, especially in the Third World.) In the first place, the institutionalisation of political identity in successor states gives them an expectation that they own the territories in a political as well as a cultural sense. Further, the codification of ethnic identity and difference which went on under Soviet rule encourages ethnic minorities to make a distinction between their nationality/ethnicity and their citizenship. Most obviously, Russian minorities in non-Russian states are deemed (and many deem themselves) to belong to the Russian 'external' state. We can see this most obviously in Estonia and Latvia where there are not only large Russian minorities, but a reaction by ethnic Estonians, for example, to make ethnicity (as measured by language) a condition of civil rights. This, says Brubaker, is likely to make 'the dynamic interplay between non-Russian successor states, Russian minorities, and the Russian state a locus of refractory, and potentially explosive, ethnonational conflict in coming years' (ibid.: 54).

It is important to remember, however, that this codification and institutionalisation of ethnicity does not imply that it will automatically generate conflict. It was essentially a 'sub-state' identity under Soviet communism, while there was also no attempt at creating a Russian 'nation-state' (ibid.: 28). In this respect, there is a danger in applying Western models of understanding, because in these model citizens and nationals usually mean the same thing or, where they do not, there is an in-built tension regarding the politicisation of national differences. In the British case, for example, the nation-state model which is followed generates stresses and strains because it cannot be reconciled with national differentiation. In the Soviet case, while Russians (like the English) were the majority people in the state, it did not define that state in *national* (i.e. Russian) terms. To underline the point, the Soviet Union was never designed or operated as a Russian nation-state in the way that the UK (ironically, also a state with no ethnic name in its title) largely operated as an English nation-state. As Anatoly Khazanov (1997) observed, six years after the break-up of the Soviet Union, Russia still lacks basic elements of state symbolism. Not only does it have two official names – the Russian Federation, and Russia – but there is no law regarding the state emblem and the new national anthem (originally written in praise of the Tsar and the Orthodox people). There is contestation over the national flag, and the Russian double-headed eagle was actually borrowed from Byzantium in the fifteenth century. Khazanov comments: 'The ambiguity of the basic elements of state symbolism reflects a lack of public consensus and is a symptom of the uncertainty felt by both society and the authorities in regard to the character of the Russian state and the Russian nation' (1997: 132). Here, once more, is the difficulty of applying a simple Western model of nationalism to a much more complex ethno-political set of circumstances in Eastern and Central Europe.

This complexity can be gauged by examining the ethnic structuring of the former Soviet Union. At the top were the fifteen Union Republics each with an ethnic name and a high degree of jurisdictional sovereignty, which made the transition to become the successor states of the Soviet Union. Cross-cutting these was a system of personal nationality or ethnicity categories which numbered over 100, with twenty-two having more than a million members (Brubaker, 1996: 31). This produced a complex mesh of political and ethnic identities which was institutionalised, and while national territorial jurisdictions often corresponded with (ethnic) nationalities (Ukrainians lived mainly in Ukraine, for example), there was no necessary congruence or hierarchy between the two levels. Political and ethnonational identities were not only available to people, but the state institutionalised the rights embedded in each. In Eastern Europe more generally, there remains no neat territorialisation nor nationalisation of identity, and while to Western eyes this looks to be a recipe for trouble, in many ways it recognises the complexities of political identities – territorial, ethno-cultural and personal – which are historically present in the whole region, and seeks to stabilise them.

The degree to which there is a lack of correspondence between territoriality and nationality can be gauged from the figures derived from the 1989 Soviet census cited by Brubaker (1996: 36). More than 73 million Soviet citizens (25 per cent of the population) lived outside 'their' national territories. These included: 17 per cent of Russians (that is, 25 million people) living outside the Russian republic; 12 million of them living in non-Russian national territories inside the Russian republic. Three-quarters of Tatars did not live in the Tatar republic, and one-third of Armenians lived outside Armenia. Brubaker comments that 'nations were to be seen but not heard', but the Soviet regime had no systematic policy of 'nation-destroying' (ibid.: 36–7). He later adds:

> The Soviet regime, then, deliberately constructed the republics as national polities 'belonging' to the nations whose names they bore. At the same time, it severely limited the domain in which the republics were autonomous. The regime institutionalised a sense of 'ownership' of the republics by ethnocultural nations, but limited the political consequences of that sense of ownership.
>
> (Brubaker, 1996: 46)

What was constructed was a complex and subtle way of handling the ethnic and political identities in a region in which the simple correspondence of nation and state was not feasible. For Western scholars to simplify that system into the equation 'we-civic/you-ethnic' is to fail to recognise that fact, and thereby to reduce the plausibility of their own theories of nationalism.

Where many of these Western theories break down in relation to Eastern Europe in particular is in their assumption that 'Russians' were the dominant and dominating, quasi-imperial group. Brubaker points out that it was the Soviet Union as a whole, and not the Russian Federation, which was the frame of and for

Russians. 'Union territory was "their" territory; union institutions were, in an important sense, "their" institutions. By contrast, Russians did not think of the territory or the institutions of the Russian republic as "their own"' (ibid.: 51). What this implies is that when the Soviet state collapsed, Russians in particular had an identity problem. The territorial frame in which they operated had disappeared. To say that they had the Russian 'homeland' is to misinterpret its significance, just as it is to imply that Russian nationalism is somehow like Serbian nationalism so that the political project is 'greater' Russia. To take an optimistic view, it is possible that ethnic Russians will not have the predicted problems adjusting to life in the Baltic states given that their relationship to the 'motherland' is not at all straightforward. While some Russian politicians like Zhirinovsky might see political capital in defending 'their' Russians in other republics, one might doubt whether it would be reciprocated by ethnic Russians in these republics. The evidence that around one-third of Russians in Estonia supported independence in the 1991 referendum (at a time when one might have expected anxieties to be at their height) gives reasonable grounds for hope.

A less optimistic interpretation appears to be taken by Brubaker, who compares post-Soviet Russia and Weimar Germany as regards 'homeland nationalism'. The loss of political and territorial power, the stranding of ethnic Russians in 'foreign' successor states, the mobilisation for home consumption of 'atrocities' against fellow-ethnics, would seem to be alarming similarities. However, he points out that unlike Weimar, homeland Russia with its associated nationalism is much more visible, and has become entrenched in Russian politics. Second, civil society homeland nationalism in Russia is much weaker. 'The core of civil society homeland nationalism in Weimar Germany – the dense and vigorous network of associations concerned with co-ethnics abroad – has no counterpart in Soviet successor states' (ibid.: 141). Third, there is something fundamentally problematic about what 'Russian' means. In all, there are five possibilities: '*russkie*', which means Russians by ethno-cultural nationality; '*rossiiane*', which refers to the territorial state of 'Rossiia'; '*russkoiazychnye*' or Russian-speakers; '*sootechestvenniki*' or compatriots, those who share a common fatherland; and finally, '*grazhdane*', or citizens. In other words, there is no single and straightforward appeal which can be made to all groups. While this 'shifting and ambiguous vocabulary of homeland claims enables Russia to play in multiple registers, and to advance multiple and only partly overlapping jurisdictional claims in the near abroad' (ibid.: 145), it is also true that it does not have the emotional and political power to connect them together in the way it happened in Weimar Germany. 'As a cultural idiom, Russian homeland nationalism has been much more uncertain, ambiguous, and fluctuating than its Weimar counterpart' (ibid.: 146). Russian nationalism has to be assembled in a *bricolage* from cultural scraps, and as such it is multivocal and opportunistic, playing 'on multiple registers and lacking consistency' (ibid.: 147). In this regard, the future is more promising than in pre-war Germany.

The fall of Yugoslavia

The conclusions about Russia might seem overly optimistic in the light of the violent episodes and wars which have broken out in Eastern and Central Europe since the fall of communism, notably in the former Yugoslavia. After all, the 'velvet divorce' between Slovakia and the Czech Republic implies that this is the (peaceful) exception. To take the Yugoslav example, we might ask why nationalism took a violent turn, but not in the former Czechoslovakia, and not (yet?) in the former Soviet Union, at least on the scale of the Balkans. One might have recourse to arguments of historicism, seeing it as 'inevitable' – violent or peaceful – but we do not get far with that. Nor is 'contingency' much good as an explanation, and many 'political' accounts run the risk of this, namely, that some politicians exploit ethnic/national differences for their own ends: but it was ever thus, and there is no shortage of politicians trying to do so in so-far peaceful territories. We have already mentioned Tim Judah's important point (1997) that what he calls the 'sweet and rotten smell of history' provided the Serbs with the cultural where-withal to explain their wars to themselves and anyone who will listen. The micro-politics of ethnicity is also crucial here. Sinisa Malesevic (1997) has analysed the ways national stereotypes were mobilised in political cartoons in the Serbian and Croatian war. Each side in its jokes used a similar repertoire of delegitimation: dehumanisation, outcasting, trait characterisation, political labelling, and group comparison. He concludes: 'group comparisons of main ethnic actors involved overlap with political labels since general depictions of Serbs as *Chetniks*, Croats as *Ustashas* and Bosnian Muslims as Islamic fundamentalists relate not only to their political activities and ideas but also to how they were compared with the groups considered to be the most undesirable in the cartoonist's society' (Malesevic, 1997: 24). By focusing on the everyday and banal, we can see how stereotypes are politically activated with devastating effect. What could be more natural than killing your next-door-neighbour who was considered less than human?

At the macro-level, Yugoslavia's problem (in contrast to that of the Soviet Union) seems to have been that ethnic/national divisions overwhelmed a weak state structure to the extent that too few of its citizens actually defined themselves as Yugoslavs: urban residents, the young, those from nationally mixed parentage, members of the Communist Party, and people from minority nationalities in their republic were most likely to define themselves as Yugoslavs, and they were swept aside by centrifugal forces (Sekulic *et al.*, 1994). The weakness of Yugoslavia was further undermined by the small percentage of the population who gave it as their official census identity: a mere 5.7 per cent in 1981. For many years people were forbidden to call themselves 'Yugoslavs' in the censuses because it referred to 'citizenship' not 'nationality'. They were allowed to call themselves 'undetermined' and hence 'Yugoslav' if they could show mixed marriages (Samary, 1995: 159–60). When the state itself was threatened by internal fission from the ethnic republics, the Federal Republic of Yugoslavia had neither demographic nor sociological strength on which to draw. The state simply began to wither on the vine.

A further irony is that 'civil societies' in the republics were strong, but corresponded much more with the national/ethnic dimensions, unlike the Soviet Union where territorial and ethnic pressures cross-cut each other to a much greater degree, and where civil society was very weak. This is a point taken up by Linz and Stepan who comment that in the USSR and Yugoslavia 'the landscape of civil society is very flat' (1992: 132). As a result, it was relatively easy for politicians to mobilise the hopes and grievances relating to ethnicity. In other words, what mattered in the former Yugoslavia was not so much 'ethnicity' *per se* as the *politics* of ethnicity. Terms like 'Serb', Croat' and so on have been constructed out of historical experiences in which religious, linguistic and political conjunctures stacked up in alignment. For instance, in Malcolm's words: 'To call someone a Serb today is to use a concept constructed in the 19th and 20th century out of a combination of religion, language, history and the person's own sense of identification' (Malcolm, 1994: 81).

In the context in which republics were deemed to be legitimate primarily in ethnic terms, Bosnia and Bosnians found themselves at a grave disadvantage. Malcolm points out: 'For more than century, Croats have written books claiming to prove that the Bosnians are "really" Croats; Serbs have argued equally unceasingly that they are all "really" Serbs' (ibid.: xxiii). In other words, the inhabitants of Bosnia were deemed not to be a 'real' nationality by the two dominant ethnic groups in Yugoslavia, the Serbs who numbered 36 per cent of the population of the Federal Republic, and the Croats who were 20 per cent (figures are from the 1981 census, the last reasonably accurate one before the outbreak of war).

The Serbs and the Croats both saw Bosnia as a non-nation, merely a fragment of the other two (hence plans to divide its territory between them), which had sold out or succumbed to pressure to convert to Islam under the Ottoman empire. Bosnia's problem was that it could not (and often did not want to) claim ethnic-religious uniformity. Muslims counted for 9 per cent of Yugoslavia in 1981, and even in Bosnia-Herzegovina itself, they counted for only 44 per cent (Serbs were 31 per cent, and Croats 17 per cent). The term 'Muslim' itself has two meanings in Serb-Croat (Samary, 1995: 160). With a capital M (Muslim) it refers to ethnicity; with a small m (muslim) it referred to practitioners of religion. Thus, only 17 per cent of the population of Bosnia-Hercegovina was 'muslim', but 44 per cent was 'Muslim'. In other words, the secular and pluralistic nature of the republic stood Bosnia in very bad stead. Further, there was a clear difference between a '*Bosnjak*', someone from the Muslim ethnic-national community, and a '*Bosanac*', a citizen of Bosnia in general (ibid.: 162). This three-way split between Bosnian 'Muslims', Bosnian 'muslims', and Bosnian 'citizens' was a severe disadvantage when faced with enemies who aligned ethnicity, religion and citizenship in a much more potent and threatening way.

Conclusion

Eastern and Central Europe have long held a fascination for Western scholars of nationalism. Even before the fall of communism in the late 1980s it was recognised that they did things differently there. Ernest Gellner spent the last part of his life studying nationalism in his homeland, and recognised, most notably in his time-zone theory, that Western and Eastern nationalism had quite different features. The zone (III) of Central Europe he saw as historically lacking well-defined and well-sustained high cultures, but instead a patchwork of folk cultures which did not neatly map onto political boundaries. The more easterly zone (IV) which corresponded with the old Tsarist empire was defined by its capture by Soviet communism after 1917 which kept nationalism at bay, destroyed what existed of civil society, and prevented the identification of people with high culture. Gellner's analysis of nationalism has something of the 'deep-freeze' character about it, and his primary interest is in how it was that nationalism never arose in a Western form. However, Gellner's theory also focuses on the East–West split, even though he offers us a continuum (from zone I to IV) rather than a dichotomy.

What Brubaker's account gives us is a much more rounded understanding of 'new nationalisms', to use Hroch's phrase, in Central and Eastern Europe. By injecting a triadic configuration of 'national minority', 'nationalising state' and 'external national homeland', he is able to present a more complex picture, and one which escapes from the value-judgmental civic/ethnic distinction which represent the orthodoxy. We are thus able to avoid the 'why can't they be more like us?' response. We now know that not only do Eastern and Central Europe have a different tradition of state- and nation-building, but crucially there is a much more complex lack of correspondence between political and ethnic identities. Brubaker's distinction between 'nationalising nationalism' and 'homeland nationalism' gives us the key to unlock these complexities. If there is a criticism to be made of his work, it is that there is a tendency to take ethnic distinctions for granted, to read them off the official registers with the implication that they were sociologically rather than simply institutionally real.

To take an example, given the variety of ways in which one can be 'Russian', we now need to know the conditions under which claims to these identities are made and how they are negotiated. For instance, to what extent do 'Russians' in Estonia define themselves as such, and in what senses, *vis-à-vis*, for example, being 'Estonian' (which, of course, also requires to be decoded in different contexts)? Much more needs to be done, but there can be little doubt that Brubaker's stricture that we need a more nuanced, differentiated approach to the varied and multiform conditions under which nationalisms are generated and mobilised holds true not simply for Eastern and Central Europe. And why stop there? Indeed, might not his analysis be applied to situations in the West?

Northern Ireland, for example, is usually a case which analysts of nationalism avoid, in large part because it does not conform to the standard case of separatist or autonomist nationalism (as in Scotland, and Wales, for example). Yet it is a good example of inverted homeland nationalism. The Protestant-Unionist community makes a claim to political identity (being British) which is negatively or at best only lukewarmly received by the British 'homeland'. In similar manner but to a different degree, neither do Northern Irish Catholics have their desire to (re)join the Irish Republic requited (the Republic has always drawn the line at sending its troops across the border to defend nationalists, even when, in the 1970s, there was mass conflict). We have then two instances of political communities which do not have their identities confirmed by the larger homelands to which they aspire. The general lesson might be that we cannot afford to draw circles around nationalism in the 'West' and 'East' as if they require quite different explanations. In the final chapter, we will take more general stock of the different ways in which nationalism manifests itself, and ask whether we need new tools of analysis and understanding for a new millennium.

Annexe: a chronology of the fall of communism

March 1985	Gorbachev becomes Soviet leader, general-secretary of Communist Party
May 1988	Janos Kadar, Hungary's long-standing Communist leader, is toppled
February 1989	Hungary and Austria symbolically cut Iron Curtain
June 1989	'Free' elections in Soviet bloc: Solidarity triumphs in Poland winning 161 of the 162 seats it is allowed to contest; Hungary's ex-premier Imry Nagy, killed after 1956 Uprising, is reburied
August 1989	Mazowiecki, first non-Communist premier, is appointed in Poland; East Germans flee west through Czechoslovakia and Hungary
September 1989	Hungary opens border with Austria to allow through East Germans going west; Berlin Wall rendered meaningless
October 1989	Gorbachev presides at forty years celebration/funeral of GDR whose citizens continue to protest
November 1989	500,000 people protest in East Berlin; Berlin Wall is opened by GDR; Zhivkov, Bulgarian leader of thirty-five years, is toppled in a coup; Student demonstration in Prague is broken up by police, but the ten-day 'Velvet Revolution' is launched; Czechoslovak Communist leadership resigns
December 1989	Gorbachev and Bush declare Cold War at an end;

Opposition-dominated coalition government in Prague;

Religious protests in Timisoara, Romania, trigger revolution;

Ceausescu tries to rally support in Bucharest, fails, and is executed;

Vaclav Havel is elected president of Czechoslovakia

January 1990   Poland launches pioneering dash from communism to capitalism;

Stalin's statue is toppled in Albania

March 1990   State of emergency in Yugoslav republic of Kosovo;

East German elections – victory for CDU candidates;

Hungary's first free elections are won by centre-right

May 1990   Romania's free elections won by communist-led National Salvation Front

June 1990   Czechoslovakia's free elections won by Havel's Civic Forum Movement;

Bulgaria's free elections won by communists – as 'socialists'

July 1990   Germany's monetary union

March 1991   Albania's communists win free elections

June 1991   Slovenia and Croatia declare independence; Yugoslav army mobilised

December 1991   Germany recognises Slovenian and Croatian independence

April 1992   Siege of Sarajevo begins

May 1992   Milosevic's Socialist Party wins elections in Serbia

June 1992   Klaus and Meciar win election victories in Czech Republic and Slovakia respectively, and 'velvet divorce' begins

August 1992   Tudjman wins first elections in Croatia

January 1993   Czech Republic and Slovakia born again as independent states

September 1993   Poland's former communists return to power in election

9

NATIONALISM AND ITS FUTURES

The approaching millennium offers us an opportunity to take stock of nationalism and the nation-state. Despite (or maybe because of) the momentous events of this century, the world of 2000 looks in many ways remarkably similar to that of 1900. The 'nation-state' remains the basic unit of political currency in the modern world (the quotation marks around the term indicate its problematic nature). The supra-national ideologies of communism and fascism (albeit that each made rhetorical use of national symbolism) came and went. Liberalism proper had predicted the emergence of universal individualism, but as Ernest Gellner showed, came to settle for a national, modularised version of that doctrine. In Eastern Europe since 1989 states are reborn using the apparatus and ideologies of nationalism. Empires have come and gone. When the century opened, British pink-red coloured the world's maps, but the war with the Boers which ushered in the century was early writing on the wall. By mid-century and after two world wars, much of the British empire was in ruins, and only graceful rhetoric (Harold Macmillan's winds of change blowing through Africa) covered its retreat from most of the globe.

The after-shock of decolonialisation was to take longer, as the waves of political change which swept through Rwanda, Burundi and the former Zaire made plain. Whatever ultimate political settlement there is in Central Africa, it is likely to take the form of something recognisable as 'nation-states'. In the East, the 'nation-state' seemed more secure than it had been for much of the century. While the post-war state 'barely exists in the Japanese consciousness' (Tamamoto, 1995), there is a strong but implicit sense of national identity upon which the economic miracle has been based. The emergence of other 'Asian tigers' in the second half of the twentieth century ushered in a strong version of economic nationalism with aggressive pursuit of markets abroad and rigid social discipline at home. Even the survival of the world's only significant communist regime in China reinforced that point. The emergence of nationalism in Taiwan, despite its ethnic similarity with the 'mainland', seemed to confirm this. No amount of the late twentieth-century equivalent of sabre-rattling across the East China Sea made it likely that shared ethnicity was sufficient to unite the Republic of China with the People's Republic, despite the experience of Hong Kong in 1997.

If anything, the proliferation of 'nation-states' confirms the point. Few such states have ceased to exist, and where they do, it is either the result of fission (as in the Czech and Slovak cases) or of fusion (the unification of Germany was clearly driven by nationalism on both sides of the Oder-Neisse). Such has been the proliferation, that statelets have been born, or at least have found a new economic niche. The likes of Andorra, Liechtenstein and the Cayman Islands may be little more than *post-restante* addresses for dubious capital flows, but they signify that viability in terms of geography or demography is no longer a condition of the nation-state (Bauman, 1992). Instead, in Bauman's phrase, nationalism has become fissiparous.

Critics of this position, and readers of this book so far, might raise an eyebrow. What, they will ask, of supra-national organisations like the European Union, the International Monetary Fund, the World Bank? Do these not indicate that the conventional 'nation-state' is no longer in control of its own economic destiny, that it has had its fiscal day? Is the 'nation-state' not in retreat? And what is the 'nation-state' these days anyway? Has the author not spent eight chapters arguing that nations and states are different orders of things – that one can have nations without states, and states which are evidently not nations? We recall Walker Connor's observation (1990) that less than 10 per cent of existing states are actually nation-states, that is, ones in which there is even a modest degree of cultural and ethnic homogeneity.

One can take issue with the arithmetic, but not the broad force of the logic. There has long been a disjunction between the emergence of the modern state (as early as the fifteenth century), of nationalism as a political ideology (in the late eighteenth century) and the reality of the nation-state in the second half of the twentieth century. The relation between nation and state has, of course, long been unstable. Linz and Stepan (1996) point out that of the eight new states formed in Europe after the First World War, only three, in their view, were stable democracies. We might even take issue with this conclusion. Czechoslovakia has since disappeared; Ireland provides classic evidence of the difference between the Irish nation (at least the whole island, and substantial numbers abroad) and the Irish state (the twenty-six counties). This leaves only Finland as the solitary success story. In general, we appear to have a language of the nation-state, but not much of a reality. Even sceptics concerning the dissolution of the nation-state like John Dunn argue that 'it is unlikely that there is single nation state in the world at present, and moderately unlikely that any such state has ever existed' (1995: 3).

In like manner, the ideology of nationalism – which, put simply, claims that all 'peoples' should have a state of their own – has waxed as other political ideologies like socialism have clearly waned to the point of extinction. John Hall comments: 'Nationalism is the world historical force of the 20th century, however surprising that might be to the thinkers of the 18th century. Its only rival is socialism' (Hall, 1985: 217). Critics of nationalism such as Eric Hobsbawm may not much like this turn of events, but it is undoubtedly true. His way of handling this is to argue that, like the owl of Minerva, nationalism has merely emerged at the dusk of the nation-state (Hobsbawm, 1990). (Ernest Gellner characteristically referred to Minerva's owl as an 'overrated bit of poultry' (Minogue, 1996: 124).) The implication is that it is a form of false consciousness which fails to recognise the fading reality of the classical nation-state. Why precisely people should be so thoroughly if belatedly fooled is not explained to us.

We can, though, begin to glimpse that there is an important conundrum to be tackled, and if possible, answered. Why should nationalism emerge at the point in history when the 'nation-state' is actually losing its power? That would be to put the Hobsbawm question in a slightly different way. To what extent is nationalism actually the gravedigger of the nation-state? That is, has it helped to erode and corrode its power and influence to such an extent that there is precious little to inherit, never mind the earth?

This chapter seeks to bring the threads of the argument together. First, it will review the ongoing debate about the future of the 'nation-state' which ranges from the view that its days are numbered as an economic, political and cultural unit on the one hand, to the argument that, in Michael Mann's words (1993), it is diversifying, developing but certainly not dying. The second task will be to ask why nationalism in its many forms has such a lease of life in the late twentieth century. It is patently not enough to imply that people are so easily fooled by its rhetorical power that they do not notice that its desired outcome, the nation-state, is disappearing: there must be more to it than that. Finally, we will examine the capacity of nationalism to transform itself into so many variants and mutations, to the extent that one way out of the puzzle for some is to argue that it is not really nationalism at all, but regionalism, territorialism, localism and so on. Simply denying the validity of the term used by activists themselves is not a very satisfactory way out of the maze.

Some would argue that nationalism is only such when it is red in tooth and claw, when it is 'ethnic', and devoted to killing people, or not averse to doing so if the opportunity came up. Steve Bruce has put this well when he pointed out that nationalism must evoke powerful emotions; it must 'be something to get out of bed for'. My own response is that most of us get out of bed for the alarm clock, in other words, because it is a call to the day's routine to which we have made some distant, now inherent and ill-remembered commitment. It is precisely this routinisation (recall Max Weber's famous aphorism that the early Protestant *wanted* to be a '*berufsmensch*', but we *have* to be (Poggi, 1983: 87)) which is the call to arms. Ernest Renan's 'daily plebiscite' nicely captures this implicit reinforcement of our national identity. The more implicit and embedded it is, the more powerful it can be. That is why what is called 'civic' nationalism is a much more powerful mobiliser in the long term than its 'ethnic' variant (assuming we want to make the distinction). It is its capacity to routinise, the feeling that we have no alternative, indeed, we want to be because that's who we are, that matters. Recall the resentful comment by the Croat writer Slavenka Drakulic who recognised the forced and narrow quality of being 'Croat' in the way that forefronted ethnicity in an unwanted manner (Brubaker, 1996: 20, footnote 17).

The second assumption we need to make clear is that no single theory of nationalism is possible. That is, no one set of analytical tools will account for all, or even the main, variants of nationalism whether it is 'classical' nineteenth-century state-building, liberation nationalism in the Third World, neo-nationalism in the West, or post-communist nationalism in Central and Eastern Europe. This might seem like a cop-out, as if we simply treat them as exotic species of the same plant but don't know what the common genus is. It is a defence to say that social science is precisely like that. We would not, after all, expect there to be a common theory of social class, arrived at if only everyone put their heads together and promised to agree on how key terms should be defined. We accept that definitions and explanations are inextricably bound up together, that there is no sociological equivalent of atoms and molecules. Further, the variants which nationalism produces reflect the richness and mutability of the phenomenon, not the inability of theorists to recognise it for what it is. We can, of course, recognise the basic assumptions and approaches of different writers. Those who prefer to see nationalism as much older than industrialisation (no-one wishes to be labelled a 'primordialist' these days) will look for common elements in different variants, just as those who prefer political explanations can range across the different historical experiences.

The sustained study of nationalism is barely thirty years old. Much of the mid-twentieth-century writing was either historical or premised upon modernisation theory, that societies would sooner or later converge into state-nation machines. While Hans Kohn made his mark in the 1940s with his distinction between 'political' and 'cultural' forms of nationalism which has both enlightened and bedevilled its study subsequently ('Eastern' and 'Western' forms of nationalism are treated as reactionary and progressive appropriately), it was Ernest Gellner in the 1960s who put the study of nationalism onto the map and into the textbooks of the social and political sciences. Tom Nairn has made the important point that personal biography and life experience have been a major determinant of what and how nationalism gets studied. Gellner's focus on processes of industrialisation *vis-à-vis* the rise of nationalism is plainly related to interest in his own Central European experience, as is his relative neglect of Western neo-nationalism in the late twentieth century. Gellner was a person of his history as well as his geography. We can expect new advances in the sociology of nationalism to be made by others operating with different accounts of time and place. Inevitably, but not regrettably, the focus here will be moulded by the Scottish, British and European experiences. We are what our world makes us.

Students of nationalism are used to the riposte that it is not worth studying. Yael Tamir begins her book on *Liberal Nationalism* with an account of writing her Ph.D. at Oxford. 'When I embarked on this project, nationalism seemed almost an anachronistic topic. During my years in Oxford, I exhausted a stockpile of phrases in answer to the comment, "How interesting!" (Oxfordese for "how weird!") – usually uttered after I reported I was writing a thesis on nationalism' (Tamir, 1993: ix). Nationalism has long carried the assumption that those who study it must be secret or not-so-secret nationalists themselves. There is always a danger in social science that we are attracted to what we find interesting, and succumb to its charms. Hobsbawm was only partly correct, however, when he commented that leaving the study of nationalism to nationalists was like relying on rail enthusiasts for a history of the railways. To extend his analogy, it would be equally unreliable to depend on the road transport lobby also, just as it would be to rely simply on sceptical-to-hostile analysts of nationalism.

Nationalism shows no signs of dying. On the contrary, an elegy is premature as nationalism takes on new forms and meets new needs in the late twentieth century. There is no shortage of putative gravediggers: industrialisation, post-industrialisation, modernity, postmodernity, globalisation, technology and so on. We have always been susceptible to the simple account. Treanor comments: 'It is said that Internet will dissolve nations. Much the same thing was said about satellite television, air travel, radios, the telegraph and railways' (1997, paragraph 4.1). He points out that globalisation (implied by these technologies in turn) does not erode nationalism, because nationalism is 100 per cent global. It is an integral part of the world order. Being both global and local is a perfectly logical paradox. As Benedict Anderson points out, nationality is a *universal* socio-cultural concept, while being irremediably *particular* in its manifestations (Anderson, 1996a: 5). The general economic, cultural and political trends to which we give the catch-all term 'globalisation' show no signs of ridding the world of nationalism. Virtually all pan-nationalist ideologies, political or religious, have to work within its parameters, have to be 'nationalised' to stand any chance of success. The post-communist Western panic about Islamic fundamentalism is likely to remain little more than that because Islam, like other politicised religions such as Christianity before it, has to work within national and nationalist parameters.

Nationalism and the nation-state

To say that we live in a nationalist world is not to imply that nothing changes. Benedict Anderson is surely correct when he says that there is undoubtedly a crisis of the hyphen, of the 'nation-state'. Whether or not this has happened, and if so, the degree to which it has, is the subject of a lively debate which we will now review. We can set its parameters by these statements from David Beetham and Michael Mann:

> Just as the sovereign nation-state developed because it was the political formation that corresponded most appropriately to the historical forces at work in the past centuries in Europe, so it is becoming increasingly inappropriate in the face of forces at work in the contemporary world.
>
> (Beetham, 1984: 221)

> The nation is . . . not in any general decline, anywhere. In some ways it is still maturing. However, even if it were declining in the face of supranational forces . . . it is still gaining at the expense of the local, regional, and especially the private forces. The modern nation-state remains a uniquely intense conception of sovereignty.
>
> (Mann, 1993a: 118)

Our task here is not to decide who, if either, is correct, but to use the debate to examine the ways in which the nation-state is changing, and why. We are using the term 'nation-state' here in its political rather than its sociological sense. We are assuming that the state is not simply a political entity but requires the active allegiance of the citizenry so that it derives its legitimacy from that body.

First, let us look at the argument that the nation-state has had its day. We might organise this broad theme into its economic, political, military and cultural components. These break into two sets of reasons: those accounting for its rise, and those for its fall. The economic rationale for the rise of the nation-state is broadly that those states were successful in which a free market was established with a unified system of law, taxation and administration. Sociologists in particular will be acquainted with Max Weber's argument that only in the West did autonomous cities emerge which provided the cultural, economic and political conditions in which capitalism flourished in the early modern period. '*Stadt luft macht frei*' – literally, city air makes free – was its obvious expression. Weber saw the emergence of the nation-state and that of national capitalism as intertwined developments. He commented: 'Out of the alliance of the state with capital, dictated by necessity, arose the national citizen class, the bourgeoisie in the modern sense of the word. Hence, it is the closed national state which afforded capitalism its chance for development' (Weber, 1966: 249). Thus the 'national economy' became a vital part of the lexicon of the modern state. It also provided the institutional means for delivering income taxation and redistribution summed up in the term 'welfare state' in the twentieth century. Without this capacity to effect economic policy within its boundaries, the state would have little economic rationale.

The decline in this economic state of affairs derives from obvious sources. The idea of a single, national economic market has grown redundant, for capital is mobile and globally oriented. While transnational corporations still require the national state to provide and train the labour-force, infrastructure and so on, their capacity to control economic relations within its frontiers is limited. In particular, Beetham argues, the multinational corporation 'is able to optimise conditions for its operation on a world scale, without reference to the interests of particular national economies' (1984: 212). Countries are relatively powerless in the face of these multinational corporations, hence the well-known and accurate assertion that many multinationals like Ford, Exxon and ICI are worth more than most individual states. Those who argue that the national state has largely lost its economic *raison d'être* point to the growing importance of international trading and currency speculation since the 1970s, and the influence of supra-state economic organisations like the World Bank, and the International Monetary Fund (IMF). They argue that it is no defence to say that capitalism has always been global (at least from the sixteenth century), but that in the third quarter of the twentieth century its ability to shift resources (notably capital by electronic means) has increased qualitatively as well as quantitatively.

In like manner, the argument goes, the national state is losing its political *raison d'être*. Broadly, from the mid-nineteenth to the mid-twentieth centuries it was the means for incorporating its population as 'citizens' into the decision-making process, most obviously by extending the franchise. People became citizens precisely because the state needed them to be, and to give political legitimacy to its activities, notably by waging all-out war against its enemies. Without this bonding of people to state, it could not have achieved this. This was, of course, a two-way process, for the bureaucracies of the state were the means whereby it delivered economic and social welfare, thereby reinforcing the political identity of citizenship. This was most obviously carried furthest in republican states where the concept of citizen was most thorough-going, but no modern state could escape the need to bind its population to it.

The argument that this state of affairs is being eroded, even lost, can be summed up by the phrase, the 'internationalisation of the state'. Its competence, authority and autonomy, even its form, are being lost. In other words, 'the state appears on the international stage as a fragmented coalition of bureaucratic agencies each pursuing its own agenda with minimal central direction and control' (McGrew, 1992: 89). It may claim to have *de jure* sovereignty, but diminishing *de facto* autonomy. After all, the Second World War ushered in the concept of the superpower, within which the sovereignty of national states was subordinated to their place within the hierarchy of the superpower complex.

The national state is also challenged from above and below: by both supra-state forms of organisation, and sub-state demands for greater political autonomy, even for independence. In West European terms, for example, there is pressure on the national state from above (e.g. in terms of the British state, from the European Union) and from below, from nations such as Scotland and Wales. Taken to its extreme, this view sees the national state as 'at best immobilised and at worst obsolete' (ibid.: 92).

In a related dimension, the military competence of the state has also been subject to the changing fortunes. For example, and in a very fundamental way, the *raison d'être* of the state is its *raison d'état*. If it is unable to defend its territory and its citizens, then it can be said to have ceased to exist. The rough rule of thumb in the world of diplomacy is that recognition can only be afforded if the state can defend itself properly. In other words, control of the means of violence is *par excellence* the business of the state (Beetham, 1984: 213), both in terms of external predators and in terms of internal order. Hence, the national state is required to defend its borders and to protect its citizens from each other and from external aggressors. Those states have survived and prospered which are the product of successful warfare and internal conquest and pacification. When either or both of these conditions are not met, then the state goes into rapid decline, in part because neighbouring states withdraw their recognition. War is both a means of protecting the borders and of mobilising the population to the point at which '*dulce et decorum est pro patria mori*'.

In the twentieth century, we entered a system of world wars. By and large these days, wars are global, not national. Even in those which take on the appearance of 'limited' war (as in the Gulf in the early 1990s, for example), the global ramifications are obvious, otherwise they would often not take place. The world has shrunk in both time and space, and wars have immediate repercussions on trade and resources (oil would be an obvious example, but the shortage of any commodity would show up instantly on global trading screens). At a technical level, war is increasingly total and destructive in its power, most obviously in its nuclear capacity. This in particular has put an end to the national state's capacity to guarantee the security and health of its citizens. Nuclear fall-out, whether the result of military or civilian action (as in Chernobyl), is no respector of national frontiers. Sovereign national states find themselves caught up in an arms race as the result of continuously changing technology and as these means become more and more expensive to own and operate ('virtual' war can be waged on computer screens to show the desired outcome to recalcitrant foes). The irony is that the more states try to control the means of their own destruction, the more they are vulnerable to others.

The final dimension to be considered is the cultural one. In a very fundamental and obvious way, the modern state has to become the 'nation', to capture the legitimacy conferred by its capacity to speak for a distinctive culture, and to defend and promote it. On the one hand, the state needs the nation to confer upon it the authority to act on its behalf, while on the other, the nation needs the political system to defend and extend its cultural influence. These arguments will be familiar by now to readers of this book. While peoples in a territory under the jurisdiction of the state may be diverse in linguistic, religious and ethnic terms, the modern state sought to select and promote one language, one religion and one ethnic group (usually the most numerous) as its 'national' base.

It is plain that in the late twentieth century there is no simple coincidence of nation and state any more – hence the crisis of the hyphen in nation-state. States are recognised as culturally homogeneous, and are challenged on cultural grounds by groups marked out by cultural identifiers who are or believe themselves to be disadvantaged or excluded from power. We now talk of 'stateless nations' (nations which do not have formal states) and 'nationless states' (territories which are culturally heterogeneous). It is no strong defence to say that 'nation-states' have rarely been such. The belief that 'proper' states were just that has always been a matter of political aspiration rather than sociological reality. It is only in the last decade or so that scholars are willing to recognise this fact, and to chart, as Brubaker has done to telling effect, the different routes whereby nations become states and states nations (Brubaker, 1992). The reasons for this de-alignment are complex and varied, but relate in part to broader cultural influences sweeping across the world at increasing rates, which do not of and in themselves create cultural homogeneity, but which destabilise older ways of doing things, and offer new forms of explaining things and provide different agendas for action.

In short, the 'nation-state' has undergone a degree of economic, political, military and cultural change which allows the possibility of arguing that it in effect no longer exists, that it is being dissolved, and by those very forces which brought it into existence in the first place. In Daniel Bell's pithy words, the nation-state 'is too small for the big problems of life, and too big for the small problems of life' (quoted in McGrew, 1992: 87). The various processes in the modern world do not come naturally to rest on the platform offered by the national state. Some operate at a lower level, while others are global in their source and impact. As David Held put it: 'any conception of sovereignty which assumes that it is an indivisible, illimitable, exclusive and perpetual form of public power – embodied within an individual state – is defunct' (Held, 1988).

Critics of this approach take issue with the characterisation of the nation-state and its origins, arguing that these were never as straightforward as were made out. Their view is that something of a 'straw-man' has been constructed in order to show that current reality is no longer like that. Their riposte is to say that it was never like that to start with, and the 'nation-state' was simply a convenient ideal-type to allow us to get to grips with the complex and messy reality in which states found themselves. There is also danger in throwing babies out with the bath water, for states, through the monopoly of the means of violence and attention to the balance of power, remain the critical agents in maintaining global order. To take the issue of military power, the fact that it is infrequently used may well be a feature of the resilience and influence of nation-states, rather than their weakness. Similarly, we should not mistake international co-operation for the weakness of states, because it permits them to pursue national interests and to achieve more effective control over what they claim to be the national destiny. In McGrew's words: 'to suggest that globalisation necessarily undermines state autonomy is . . . to ignore the ways in which states empower themselves against the vagaries of global forces through collective action' (1992: 93). There is also a need to distinguish between inter-connectedness (the condition of mutual vulnerability) and inter-dependence (the condition of assymetrical vulnerability), so that the world may be more inter-connected but less inter-dependent than earlier in the century.

The counter-argument against the dissolution of the 'nation-state' is put most forcibly by Michael Mann (1993a). His general thesis is that the nation-state is not dying, but changing and developing. Focusing largely on Western Europe, he argues that the weakening of the nation-state is slight, *ad hoc*, uneven and unique to the West, while across the world the nation-state is still maturing. In his later writing, he acknowledges that 'for much of the world a true nation-state remains more aspiration for the future than present reality' (1997: 477). His justification for using the term nation-state is that most states base their legitimacy on the nation as a cultural concept. Mann's general point is that the modern state is uniquely placed to maintain internal order, defend against foreign aggression, supply communication infrastructures, and effect economic redistribution. To return to an earlier argument in this book (chapter 5), Mann (1984) points to the 'infrastructural' power of the modern state which has much greater authority and reach than any 'despotic' system which made more noise but effected less. The national state remains the key site for political democracy, and is the guarantor of social citizenship rights for the mass of the population.

While it is true that in the last twenty-five years neo-liberal ideologies and transnational forces have diminished some national state powers, their effects have only been at the margin so that the state increasingly regulates the most intimate private spheres of life and the family (such as relations between men and women, family violence, care of children, moral and personal habits) all once thought 'private' and well beyond the remit of the public state. Mann takes issue with the easy association of state, nation and society, and argues that 'society' has never been merely national, but has transcended territory. Further, in its early industrial phase, the capitalist economy was rarely constrained by national boundaries and was especially transnational. In terms of the key functions of the modern state – military, communications, democracy, citizenship and macro-economic planning – Mann argues that there is no reason why these should be located in the same political agency (the national state) when for most of history they were not. The extension of transnationalism in both economic and cultural terms does not undermine states but offers them new geo-political roles. Capitalism, for example, still relies on continuous negotiations between sovereign states in a variety of *ad hoc* agencies. Mann concludes: 'the nation-state is not hegemonic, nor is it obsolete, either as a reality or as an ideal' (1993a: 139).

Of the supposed threats to the nation-state, Mann (1997) argues that most northern states are now less committed to war than at any point in their histories, and the consequence is the absence of serious hard geo-politics within Europe. The rest of the world, however, remains more susceptible. In general terms, he concludes, the patterns are too varied to permit us to argue in a simple way that the nation-state and its system are strengthening or weakening. However, what he calls the 'modest nation-states' of the north have undergone transformation as a result of the European Union. 'Thus Europe has been politically and economically transformed, with a substantial decline in the particularistic autonomy and sovereignty of its nation-states' (Mann, 1997: 487).

Europe and the nation-state

A key battleground for combatants arguing for the dissolution on the one hand, and for the rejuvenation of the 'nation-state' on the other is the development of the European Community/European Union (EC/EU). Mann argues that the nation-state was not seriously threatened by the development of the EC/EU until the 1980s at which point three sets of forces came into play: the development of Community Law, especially on issues of trade liberalisation, product integration and standardisation; the single market (Single European Act) since 1986; and the European Monetary System moving towards a single European currency by 1999. However, he points out, the EC/EU is an economic giant, a political dwarf, and a military worm. In other words, it has considerable economic strength, a degree of cross-national political authority, and no military facility to speak of. The most one can say is that sovereignty is shared between the EC/EU and the national states, and that there is little likelihood of it heading towards a 'federal' Europe in the form of a single state.

An important contributor to this debate on the side of the 'statists' is Alan

Milward whose book, *The European Rescue of the Nation-State* tackles head-on the view that there is a zero-sum competition between European integration and the sovereignty of the national state, that 'it implies that the economies, societies and administrations of these national entities become gradually merged into a larger identity' (Milward, 1992: 2). There is, says Milward, no antithesis because the evolution of the European Community has been an integral part of the re-assertion of the nation-state as an organisational concept, and that without this process of integration, the Western European nation-states would have been struggling to retain the support and allegiance of their citizens. Far from there being even a trade-off of power to the detriment of the national level, 'the EC has been its buttress, an indispensable part of the nation-state's post-war construction. Without it, the nation-state could not have offered to its citizens the same measure of security and prosperity which it has provided and which has justified its survival' (ibid.: 3).

Not only did the European nation-states themselves actively create the suprastate organisation in the post-war period, they did so in order to sustain their own legitimacy. They themselves were unable to provide on their own the standard of living which their populations demanded, and they saw in integration a way of formalising, regulating and limiting their own freedom of action in return for central and concerted action. Milward argues that the rapid increase in the material standard of living between 1945 and 1968 was twice the rate of increase in the 1922–37 period. The new arrangements also allowed the pursuit of a programme of reconstruction in agriculture, coal, iron and steel, and the promotion of an economic project of high welfare and high employment throughout the Community. Not all of this was progressive, and Milward likens the Common Agricultural Policy (CAP) to 'some clumsy prehistoric mastodon' (1992: 317). This, however, helps him to prove his point as it indicates that the Europeanisation of agricultural protection was the outcome of the project to rescue the nation-state rather than a by-product of pursuing economic efficiency which the CAP is manifestly at odds with.

The proof of the European project's success is that the one major European power which stood outside the 'rescue' – the UK – is the one state whose relative power has declined over the period, and whose prosperity has grown more slowly. He argues that its failure to join is directly connected to this loss of influence and power.

> In refusing to join, British governments were weakening the nation more than defending its sovereignty. They were left to carry their own burdens of welfare and agricultural policy and the consequences for manufacturing industry were immediate. Economically and politically, Britain's role became increasingly peripheral, and the benefits from not having joined the communities were reduced to no more than the preservation of that same illusion of independence which led to the mistake [not to join] in the first place.
>
> (Milward, 1992: 433)

One might add that the UK was also the exception in trying to hold on to all power at the centre. Its refusal to 'give up' sovereignty to the EC/EU was matched by its refusal to devolve power to the nations and regions of the UK, which, only with the swingeing defeat of the Conservative government in 1997, brought to an end a zero-sum state nationalism which Mrs Thatcher had created in the late 1970s. This also confirmed the view that there are no more vociferous nationalists other than those who would deny it to others. Milward argues that both 'federalism' and 'national sovereignty' are bogeymen. He concludes: 'The argument that the Europeanisation of policy necessarily usurps national democratic control treats the abstract concept of national sovereignty as though it were a real form of political machinery. The states will make further surrenders of sovereignty if, but only if, they have to in the attempt to survive' (ibid.: 446).

By this stage in our argument it should be clear that the debate concerning the dissolution or development of the 'nation-state' is largely about how the modern, Western-style state will evolve. It is hard to find any writer who is willing to argue on the basis that the crisis, if there is one, concerns the 'nation-state' in the strong sense, that is, the fusion of cultural and political communities. In other words, this is a putative crisis of liberal capitalist states which have come to acquire the epithet 'nation'. John Dunn, cited previously in this chapter as someone who does not believe that nation-states have ever existed as a norm, argues that nation states 'are altogether scruffier than this: medleys of birth [his definition of 'nation'], mutual choice, provisional instrumental exploitation approximately within the law, and vigorous manipulative penetration from well outside it [his definition of the state]' (1995: 8). If there is a crisis, says Dunn, it is because there has been a fading in the normative appeals of the idea of the nation-state, together with a fall in the efficacy in its political action, its capacity to deliver services to its population in the context of economic liberalisation, ecological degradation and problems in securing effective and trustworthy international co-operation. There is, he concludes, no crisis of the nation-state today, but there may well be one tomorrow.

What, one might ask, does this have to do with nationalism? If most writers, like Dunn, are concerned with the political part of the equation (the state) and only tangentially with the cultural part (the nation), what implications if any does this have for nationalism? The answer is that few writers treat the two aspects as co-equal parts, and they should. This is because, taking our lead from Gellner, we have to see nationalism as endemic to the modern state rather than some optional extra. The 'realist' school to which the likes of Dunn belong downgrades cultural matters to the role of bit-players in a political drama whose main characters may (or usually may not) involve the 'minor' characters. The key, however, resides in the ideological capacity of the modern liberal state to mobilise its citizenry when it matters. William Wallace offers this comment on the West European nation state whose key was the linking of political community (the nation) with state power:

> The nation as a political and social community is disconnecting from the state as provider of security and welfare. Both nation and state have lost

coherence, as borders have become more permeable, national myths harder to maintain, ethnic diversity more evident, personal prosperity more dependent on local or transnational factors than on national protection.

(Wallace, 1995: 75)

What has happened in Western Europe in particular, says Wallace, is that the territorial congruence of state, society and nation has grown apart under the pressure to separate on the one hand the forces of production and services no longer tied to 'national' territories, and on the other, political and cultural loyalties around which identity-politics increasingly muster. Although he does not draw this conclusion, we can take the argument further forward by focusing on the national dimension. Critics such as Mann, Milward and Dunn who take the view that the nation-state is neither dead nor dying, largely do so by arguing that the economic and political functions of the 'nation-state' remain largely in its hands. If we share their view that the death of the nation-state has been greatly exaggerated, we cannot conclude with this school of political realism that nationalism is misguided, largely irrelevant, or at best an ideological device for mobilising for ulterior purposes. We have to take nationalism much more seriously than that.

Why nationalism?

We return to Ernest Gellner's major contribution to the study of nationalism which was to show how essential it is to the workings of modern societies. It is the ideological cement which binds people to the state and to civil society. If that cement weakens and loses its binding force then the state is in trouble. To him we owe the view that, in Brendan O'Leary's words: 'nationalism is the major form in which democratic consciousness expresses itself in the modern world. It will be to Ernest Gellner's eternal credit that this thought helps us understand why that is so, and why it must be so' (O'Leary, 1996: 111). (Characteristically, Gellner thought there was too much nationalist sentiment in this plaudit, and replied: 'My trouble with this is not that I do not wish nations to be free, but that I do not believe nations exist universally, as a kind of basic component of social furniture' (Gellner, 1996e: 637).)

Gellner also showed us how nationalism, or rather its personal metamorphosis, national identity, was largely implicit, taken-for-granted: in his phrase, 'every man is a clerc', by which he meant that in modern societies everyone participated in the day-to-day reinforcement of national identity through the routine tasks of reading and writing. The power of nationalism lies in this daily plebiscite (Renan, 1882), this personalisation of the nation in everyday life (A.P. Cohen, 1994). This implicitness lies at the root of its neglect, especially where it is associated with the core of power. 'I am patriotic; you are nationalistic' is the claim of the centre over the periphery. It is hard, and ultimately unsuccessful, to mobilise an explicit sense of nationalism against one threat (the European Union) while rejecting as illegitimate

181

another set of nationalist demands from within the existing state (from Scotland and Wales).

To focus on these instances is to give a Euro-centric, even British-centric, aspect to these things. This is in many ways inevitable, for we begin with the contradictions closest to home. The lessons are, however, much wider than that. Nationalism is not simply one of the most pervasive political forces of the twentieth century, it is also one of the most flexible. It is pressed into the service of central states, as well as peripheries which wish to invent or recreate political autonomy. Nationalism lends itself to ideologies of the right as well as the left. It provides a sense of historical continuity; it is a flexible ideology which is Janus-faced, looking backwards to create the future.

Alberto Melucci (1989) has argued that social movements, including nationalism, expose problems relating to the structure of modern complex societies, while at the same time being firmly rooted in history. Both the modern and historic dimensions are vital. If we treat social movements as simply historical by-products (an obvious risk when dealing with nationalist movements which can too readily be dismissed as some 'ethnic' hangover from a bygone age), then we risk ignoring the issues of contemporary structural transformation which they manifest. And if we handle them simply as highlighting structural contradictions in the present-day, we risk ignoring their origins in 'national questions'. Nationalist movements are especially complex in this regard. Melucci comments:

> The ethno-national question must be seen . . . as containing a plurality of meanings that cannot be reduced to a single core. It contains ethnic identity, which is a *weapon of revenge* against centuries of discrimination and new forms of exploitation; it serves as an instrument for applying *pressure in the political market*; and it is a response to *needs for personal and collective identity* in highly complex societies.
>
> (Melucci, 1989: 90)

We might translate these three aspects of nationalism as the sociological ('a weapon of revenge'), political ('an instrument . . . in the political market place') and psychological functions ('needs for personal and collective identity'). These make nationalism a particularly potent ideology in the late twentieth century especially at a time when conventional state structures premised on their sovereignty over cultural, economic and political aspects seem to be on the wane. Nationalist movements can, then, encapsulate cultural defence, the pursuit of political resources from the centre, as well as being vehicles for social identity in rapidly changing societies. It will not be possible to reduce any nationalism automatically to one of these, but the rapidly increasing rate of social change makes it more rather than less likely as a potent vehicle of social protest.

As the twentieth century draws to a close, so the issue of national identities becomes more salient. In the modern world, we have become used to conflicts over forms of political identity. We can find examples of disputed identities in many

Western countries. The peoples of Quebec, Catalunya and Euskadi (the Basque Country), Scotland and Wales are among the most obvious groupings who, to a greater or lesser extent, dispute the political identities conferred on them by the states to which they belong. In many respects this is a remarkable feature, because for most of the century, indeed for most of the period we now call 'modern', it seemed as if the problem of national identity had been solved once and for all.

The rise of nationalism is one reflection of a new form of identity-politics. Issues of nationality and identity forefront the 'personal' dimension, and open up the taken-for-granted assumption of malestream politics. The quest for new forms of autonomy lends itself to challenges from groups relatively excluded from the political process, notably women, in such a way that demands for national and gender power interlock. Similarly, the quest for national identity is a highly personal one. In Anthony Cohen's words: 'Individuals "own" the nation; the nation conducts itself as a collective individual' (1994: 157). We are perhaps presented with a new and ironic meaning of the phrase: '*l'état, c'est moi*'. The power of nationalism in the modern world lies in its capacity to reconfigure personal identities and loyalties in a way more in tune with the social, cultural and political realities of the late twentieth century. Conventional nationalism stresses the cultural similarities of its members, and implies that political boundaries should be coterminous with cultural ones. Tamir (1993) observes that this 'thick' nationalism approach assumes that individuals are thereby locked into their cultural identity, and that it will be the paramount form of identity. On the other hand, a more pluralistic, or 'thin', approach does not imply that ethnic identity will have priority over other forms of social identity including those of gender and social class. In Edward Said's words: 'No one today is purely one thing. Labels like Indian, or woman, or Muslim, or American are no more than starting points, which if followed into actual experience for only a moment are quickly left behind' (1993: 407). It is this connection between nationalism and identity which helps to place it in an modern (even postmodern) frame. It is a response to the problem of who we wish to become.

This quest for identity-politics does not necessarily imply that independent statehood will automatically follow. In Western politics in particular, there is an ongoing debate about the degree of autonomy required in the interlinked modern world. The issue is more likely to be expressed in terms of degrees of autonomy rather than its presence or absence. Hence, there are similarities between Scotland, Catalunya and Quebec, to take our examples, with regard to negotiated autonomy in the context of existing state and supra-state levels of power. A concomitant language has evolved which speaks of 'Home Rule', 'Autonomy' and 'Sovereignty-Association' respectively. We should not, of course, assume that nationalism automatically leads to statehood. Indeed, setting up a separate state is probably the exception rather than the rule for most self-defined nations. There are, too, many examples in history of states coming into existence almost by accident, which are then given a nationalist gloss as if the outcome was inevitable. The break-up of the Austro-Hungarian empire did not result from nationalist pressure alone, but from wider geo-political forces culminating in the First World War. Social democrats like Otto Bauer and liberals like Max Weber recognised that separating state structures from national identities was not only possible but desirable. Closer to home, Irish independence came about almost by happenstance rather than as the result of a grand nationalist design on the part of the people (Lyons, 1979). Similarly, if Scotland, Wales, Catalunya and Quebec become formally independent, then this will perhaps be less the inevitable result of the quest for self-determination, and more the outcome of serendipity.

Well, the critic might reply to that, this is because these are not 'real' nationalisms at all. Real nationalisms involve ethnic cleansing, killing people or burning them out of their houses in the name of the tribe. This would be to miss the point, and to forget Melucci's stricture that there is a lot more to it than that, to reduce nationalism merely to a weapon of revenge. The common thread which runs through all nationalisms is the increasing disjuncture between culture and politics, the lack of fit between the levels of responsibility and identity, the problem of sovereignty. Let us return to the example of Europe to make the point. If we adopt the older understanding of these things, nicely expressed for us by David Beetham, 'exclusive jurisdiction internally, and independence externally–these are summed up together in the idea of sovereignty' (1984: 208), then we can see that it is an idea that originates in an earlier age. The eighteenth-century Enlightenment gave birth to the idea of the 'nation-state' in which political, cultural and economic power coincided, or at least were meant to. The political world was deemed to be made up of sovereign entities speaking and acting on behalf of culturally homogeneous and politically sovereign people. The fact that in reality few countries were like that was neither here nor there. The template on offer was the 'nation-state'. So powerful was this idea that even when we know better we treat the 'nation' as a synonym for 'state'.

We would be mistaken if we expected 'European' to become a competing political identity with either national or state ones, at least in their current form (Schlesinger, 1992). Why cannot the European Union become an 'imagined community', a nation like any other? First, the conventional cultural identifiers like language and religion do not line up. You cannot make a national brick without a modicum of cultural straw of this sort. In Schlesinger's words, 'there is no predominant cultural nation that can become the core of the would-be state's nation and hegemonise Euro-culture' (1991: 17). Second, we know that nationalism grows best in a medium in which there is an Other – an enemy against which we can measure and develop our own identity. But who, if anyone, is to be that Other? In the shorter term immigrants and foreigners who breach Europe's 'thick' boundaries would seem to be candidates (that is, 'people' rather than 'a People'). The rise of racist movements and parties across the Union is testimony to that. In the longer term, other continents like Asia and America have some potential as Others, but the mechanisms for bringing this about are less clear. Third, we have to consider a radically different environment for the European state (if that is what develops) from the one in which 'nation-states' emerged in the last two centuries.

New state structures emerge into a world framed by 'globalisation' and the impact of a world economy. In Cable's words: 'national governments face the difficult task of retaining and asserting enough sense of the shared nationhood to maintain their underlying legitimacy while adjusting to a world in which the role of government in national states is becoming increasingly circumscribed' (1995: 50). The correspondence of the nation with the state, the cultural with the political, was always more of an aspiration rather than a reality, but in the social conditions of globalisation in the late twentieth century, the age of the nation-state, even as a dream, seems past its best.

What kind of Europe is on the agenda? It is significant that 'Europe' is as much defined by the plurality of expectations people have of it as by its reality. In a British context, 'Europe' has become a shorthand for quite diverse processes. To Scottish (and Welsh) nationalists, it is a means for bypassing the British state so as to usher in a new political system more sympathetic to small nations. For many on the Liberal and Labour Left, it provides a viable political project towards federalising both Britain and Europe and towards developing the social-democratic project which Conservative governments since 1979 sought to bring to an end. For the radical Right, it offers enlarged economic markets without the hindrance of political regulation. And, of course, for the Conservative Right, it represents the major threat to 'national' sovereignty for at least 500 years. We might conclude that much of Europe, whether negative or positive, lies in the eye of the beholder. As Gerard Delanty points out; 'Europeanism is not a fixed set of ideas and ideals which can be unilaterally aspired to as an alternative to national chauvinism and xenophobia. It is a strategy of discourse and is constituted by constantly shifting terms of reference' (1995: 143).

There is little doubt, furthermore, that 'Europe' does not have the wherewithal to become a nation-state. It is far more likely to develop as '*demos*' than as '*ethnos*', as a political rather than a cultural system, much, ironically, as 'Britain' did in the eighteenth century but, one hopes, without the pretensions to be a nation as well as a state. Philip Schlesinger (1997) has shown how the audio-visual media are so dominated by global industrial competition that building a common political culture in Europe in this way is a tall order. The best plan for the European Union would seem to be to work with rather than against the grain of postmodern, even in a sense, post-nationalist times. In this context, we are seeing the reconceptualisation of notions of identity and of citizenship. In both cases, the 'national' level focused on existing states becomes less salient. As Meehan (1993) points out in a discussion of citizenship and the European Community, legal status and the content of citizenship rights are not determined by conventional nationality alone. Instead, a new kind of multiple citizenship appears to be developing which recognises different identities and interests operating at various levels, local, regional, national, and transnational.

Europeanness, if it develops beyond an embryonic stage, has to work as a complement of, rather than a competitor to, rapidly changing state structures. Similarly, 'to suppose that the Europe of European unity refers to a cosmopolitan ideal beyond the particularism of the nation-state is, quite simply, an act of delusion' (Delanty, 1995: 157). Its future seems to lie in its association with democracy, pluralism and the rule of law, as a means of redressing the democratic deficit at the regional, national and supranational levels. There seems to be little future in a Europe which translates its Europeanness as a restrictive, ethnically defined and exclusivist identity rather than one which is pluralist, territorial and inclusivist. This is a message not simply for Europe but for national identity in the modern world. Some writers, such as Habermas (1996a), argue that we should be aiming for what he calls 'constitutional patriotism' as a device to protect civil society and democratic institutions from nationalistic passions. However, Dominique Schnapper asks: 'Would a purely civic society, founded on abstract principles, have the strength to control passions born from allegiance to ethnic and religious groups?' (1997: 211).

Issues of political identity have circulated around debates on sovereignty, especially *vis-à-vis* Scotland, the UK and the European Union. Defenders of the constitutional *status quo* have laid stress on the indivisibility of sovereignty despite the fact that the relationship between the UK and the European Union over the last twenty years has called it into question. New attempts have been made to redefine sovereignty, and to shift it away from absolute and unitary definitions. In Neil MacCormick's words:

> Neither politically nor legally is any member state in possession of ultimate power over its own internal affairs; politically, the Community affects vital interests, and hence exercises political power on some matters over member states; legally, Community legislation binds member state and overrides internal state-law within the respective criteria of validity.
>
> (MacCormick, 1995: 9–10)

The juxtaposition here is between viewing sovereignty as property which is given up when another gains it, or viewing it more like virginity, when it can be lost without another gaining it. MacCormick is arguing that the days for 'monolithic democracy' – that is, crude majoritarian politics – are over. In addition, 'The demise of sovereignty in its classical sense truly opens opportunities for subsidiarity and democracy as essential mutual complements. It suggest a radical hostility to any merely monolithic democracy.' The European Union seems to offer the possibility of new forms of citizenship rights based on 'demos' – civil rights – rather than deriving from 'ethnos' – cultural specificities (Meehan, 1993). In essence, we can transcend the state without dissolving the nation (MacCormick, 1995).

Here we confront the old duality of 'civic' versus 'ethnic' nationalisms which has been such a help but is increasingly a hindrance to our understanding of nationalism in the late twentieth century. What new work by MacCormick and Tamir on liberal nationalism does is to erode the old habit of implying that nationalism can only be in essence ethnic because it is so at odds with liberalism and its conception of the individual. MacCormick argues that liberalism and nationalism are not mutually exclusive because the latter is actually based on 'contextual individualism', the sense that fundamentally our individuality can only derive from our social identity, that our individuality and sociability are two sides of the same coin. It has no other standing, moral or methodological. Tamir agrees: 'We readily accept that life-plans, religious beliefs, and social roles are objects of reflection and choice, yet constitutive of our identity. Cultural and national affiliations fall under the same category, of being both chosen and constitutive' (1993: 33).

The problem for ethnic forms of nationalism is that they cannot be freely chosen. They imply that you are either a Scot, Welsh, a Croat, a Hutu, or you are not. You cannot opt out because ethnicity is conveyed at birth; it is something you have no control over. To reduce national identity to a matter of birth and hence to 'ethnicity' in a non-Barthian sense as Dunn does (1995: 3) is to miss the point. Multiplicities of identity are the norm. When the English Conservative politician, Norman Tebbit, sought to apply his 'cricket test' – if you live in England, you should support the national team, even if it is playing your country of origin – he failed to acknowledge this point. People have many and complex allegiances. Neil MacCormick's argument that both ethnic-nationalist absolutism and civic-state absolutism are untenable is well-taken (MacCormick, 1996). Both diminish active, personal choice, and hence are fundamentally illiberal, and in the modern world unworkable. It follows that new conceptions of statehood and citizenship are required based on shared or limited sovereignty. He argues that the European Union offers the possibility of a new form of legal and political order based on a politics 'beyond the sovereign state', and leaving behind the absolutism of the nation-state, as well as unitary understandings of state sovereignty. This theme is echoed in the writings of the political philosopher David Miller who offers a positive and liberal defence of nationalism as opposed to what he calls 'multicultural cosmopolitanism' (1995). He argues that national communities are not the result of a set of common attributes, but are constituted by personal belief and attestation (Renan's 'daily plebiscite' again). The distinctively modern feature of nationalism is the belief that people are capable of acting collectively, and of conferring authority on political institutions as an expression of this act.

Where does this leave us? Certainly a long, long way from the old, comprehensive definition of national identity summed up in this view by the Irish nationalist Patrick Pearse in 1916:

> Independence one must understand to include spiritual and intellectual independence as well as political independence; or rather, true political independence requires spiritual and intellectual independence as its basis, or it tends to become unstable, a thing resting merely on the interests which change in time and circumstance.
>
> (quoted in Lyons, 1979: 570)

This is not in the spirit of the conditions of the late twentieth century. It is a better thing for that.

BIBLIOGRAPHY

Afshar, H. (1989) 'Behind the veil: the public and private faces of Khomeini's policies on Iranian women', in B. Agarwal (ed.) *Structures of Patriarchy: The State, The Community and The Household*, London: Zed Books.

Alter, P. (1991) *Nationalism*, London: Edward Arnold.

Anderson, B. (1983) *Imagined Communities: Reflections on the Origin and Spread of Nationalism*, London: Verso.

Anderson, B. (1996a) *Imagined Communities: Reflections on the Origin and Spread of Nationalism*, revised edition, London: Verso.

Anderson, B. (1996b) 'Introduction', in G. Balakrishnan (ed.) *Mapping the Nation*, London: Verso.

Anderson, P. (1992) *A Zone of Engagement*, London: Verso.

Anderson, R.D. (1995) *Education and the Scottish People, 1750–1918*, Oxford: Clarendon Press.

Armstrong, J. (1982) *Nations before Nationalism*, Chapel Hill: University of North Carolina Press.

Ascherson, N. (1988) *Games with Shadows*, London: Hutchinson Radius.

Ash, M. (1980) *The Strange Death of Scottish History*, Edinburgh: The Ramsay Head Press.

Balakrishnan, G. (ed.) (1996) *Mapping the Nation*, London: Verso.

Balcells, A. (1996) *Catalan Nationalism: Past and Present*, London: Macmillan.

Banton, M. (1983) *Racial and Ethnic Competition*, Cambridge: Cambridge University Press.

Banton, M. (1994) 'Modelling ethnic and national relations', *Ethnic and Racial Studies*, 17 (1).

Barth, F. (1981) 'Ethnic groups and boundaries', in *Process and Form in Social Life: Selected Essays of Fredrik Barth: Vol. 1*, London: Routledge & Kegan Paul.

Bartlett, R. (1993) *The Making of Europe: Conquest, Colonisation and Cultural Change, 950–1350*, London: Allen Lane.

Basu, A. (1996) 'Mass movement or elite conspiracy? The puzzle of Hindu nationalism', in D. Ludden (ed.) *Contesting the Nation: Religion, Community and the Politics of Democracy in India*, Philadelphia: University of Pennsylvania Press.

Basu, T. *et al.* (1993) *Khaki Shorts and Saffron Flags: A Critique of the Hindu Right*, New Delhi: Orient Longman.

Bauman, Z. (1992) 'Soil, blood and identity', *Sociological Review*, 40 (4).

Bauman, Z. (1996) 'From pilgrim to tourist: – or a short history of identity', in S. Hall and P. DuGay (eds) *Questions of Cultural Identity*, London: Sage.

Beetham, D. (1984) 'The future of the nation state?', in G. McLennan, D. Held and S. Hall (eds) *The Idea of the Modern State*, Milton Keynes: Open University Press.

Beetham, D. (1985) *Max Weber and the Theory of Modern Politics*, Cambridge: Polity Press.

Bell, D. (1976) *The Coming of Post-Industrial Society*, Harmondsworth: Penguin.

Beveridge, C. and Turnbull, R. (1989) *The Eclipse of Scottish Culture: Inferiorism and the Intellectuals*, Edinburgh: Polygon.

Bhabha, H. (ed.) (1990) *Nation and Narration*, London: Routledge.

Billig, M. (1995) *Banal Nationalism*, London: Sage.

Bourdieu, P. (1984) *Distinction: a Social Critique of the Judgement of Taste*, London: Routledge & Kegan Paul.

Brah, A. (1993) 'Re-framing Europe: en-gendered racisms, ethnicities and nationalisms in contemporary western Europe', *Feminist Review*, 45.

Brah, A. (1994) 'Time, place and others: discourses of race, nation and ethnicity', *Sociology*, 28 (3).

Brass, P. (1990) *The Politics of India since Independence*, Cambridge: Cambridge University Press.

Bremmer, I. (ed.) (1993) *Nation and Politics in the Soviet Successor States*, Cambridge: Cambridge University Press.

Breuilly, J. (1993) *Nationalism and the State*, Manchester: Manchester University Press (first edition, 1982).

Breuilly, J. (1996) 'Approaches to nationalism', in G. Balakrishnan (ed.) *Mapping the Nation*, London: Verso.

Brody, H. (1988) *Maps and Dreams: Indians and the British Columbia Frontier*, Vancouver: Douglas & McIntyre.

Brown, A., McCrone, D. and Paterson, L. (1996) *Politics and Society in Scotland*, London: Macmillan.

Brubaker, R. (1992) *Citizenship and Nationhood in France and Germany*, Cambridge, MA: Harvard University Press.

Brubaker, R. (1996) *Nationalism Reframed: Nationhood and the National Question in the New Europe*, Cambridge: Cambridge University Press.

Bruce, S. (1993) 'A failure of the imagination: ethnicity and nationalism in Scotland's history', *Scotia*, XVII.

Bruce, S. and Yearley, S. (1989) 'The social construction of tradition: the restoration portraits and the kings of Scotland', in D. McCrone, S. Kendrick and P. Straw (eds) *The Making of Scotland: Nation, Culture and Social Change*, Edinburgh: Edinburgh University Press.

Bryant, C. (1993) 'Social self-organisation, civility and sociology: a comment on Kumar's "civil society"', *British Journal of Sociology*, 44 (3).

Bryant, C. and Mokrzycki, E. (1994) *The New Great Transformation? Change and Continuity in East-Central Europe*, London: Routledge.

Cable, V. (1995) 'The diminished nation-state: a study in the loss of economic power', *Daedalus*, 124 (2).

Cashmore, E. (1989) *United Kingdom? Class, Race and Gender since the War*, London: Unwin Hyman.

Chapman, M. (1978) *The Gaelic Vision of Scottish Culture*, London: Croom Helm.

Chapman, M. (1992) *The Celts: The Construction of a Myth*, London: Macmillan.

Chatterjee, P. (1986) *Nationalist Thought and the Colonial World: A Derivative Discourse*, London: Zed.

Chatterjee, P. (1993) *The Nation and its Fragments: Colonial and Post-Colonial Histories*, Princeton: Princeton University Press.

Chatterjee, P. (1996) 'Whose imagined community?', in G. Balakrishnan (ed.) *Mapping the Nation*, London: Verso.

Cobban, A. (1944) *National Self-Determination*, Oxford: Oxford University Press; extract reprinted in J. Hutchinson and A.D. Smith (eds) (1994) *Nationalism*, Oxford: Oxford University Press.

Cohen, A.P. (1993) 'Culture as identity', *New Literary History*, 24 (1).

Cohen, A.P. (1994) *Self Consciousness: An Alternative Anthropology of Identity*, London: Routledge.

Cohen, A.P. (1996) 'Personal nationalism: a Scottish view of some rites, rights and wrongs', *American Ethnologist*, 23 (4).

Cohen, A.P. (1997) 'Nationalism and social identity: who owns the interests of Scotland?', *Scottish Affairs*, 18.

Cohen, R. (1994) *Frontiers of Identity: The British and Others* London: Longman.

Colley, L. (1992) *Britons: Forging the Nation, 1707–1837*, New Haven: Yale University Press.

Connor, W. (1990) 'When is a nation?', *Ethnic and Racial Studies*, 13 (1).

Connor, W. (1994) *Ethnonationalism: The Quest for Understanding*, Princeton: Princeton University Press.

Conversi, D. (1990) 'Language or race? the choice of core values in the development of Catalan and Basque nationalisms', *Ethnic and Racial Studies*, 13 (1).

Craig, C. (1987) *The History of Scottish Literature, Volume 4, Twentieth Century*, Aberdeen: Aberdeen University Press.

Crick, B. (1989) 'An Englishman considers his passport', in N. Evans (ed.) *National Identity in the British Isles*, Coleg Harlech occasional papers in Welsh studies, no. 3.

Crick, B. (1993) 'Essay on Britishness', *Scottish Affairs*, 2.

Crick, B. (1995) 'The sense of identity of the indigenous British', *New Community*, 21 (2).

Delaney, C. (1991) *The Seed and the Soil: Gender and Cosmology in a Turkish Village Society*, Berkeley: University of California Press.

Delanty, G. (1995) *Inventing Europe: Idea, Identity, Reality*, London: Macmillan.

Delanty, G. (1996) 'Beyond the nation-state: national identity and citizenship in a multicultural society – a response to Rex', *Sociological Research Online*, 1 (3).

Deutsch, K. (1953) *Nationalism and Social Communication*, London: Chapman and Hall.

Dodd, P. (1986) 'Englishness and the national culture', in R. Colls and P. Dodd (eds) *Englishness: Politics and Culture, 1880–1920*, London: Croom Helm.

Douglass, W. (1985) *Basque Politics: A Case Study of Ethnic Nationalism*, University of Nevada.

Dunn, J. (1995) 'Introduction: Crisis of the nation state?', in J. Dunn (ed.) *Contemporary Crisis of the Nation State?*, Oxford: Blackwell.

Eco, U. (1987) *Travels in Hyper-Reality*, London: Pan.

Eley, G. and Suny, R.G. (1996) 'Introduction: from the moment of social history to the work of cultural representation', in G. Eley and R.G. Suny (eds) *Becoming National*, Oxford: Oxford University Press.

Eriksen, T.H. (1993a) *Ethnicity and Nationalism: Anthropological Perspectives*, London: Pluto Press.

Eriksen, T.H. (1993b) 'Formal and informal nationalism', *Ethnic and Racial Studies*, 16 (1).

Fanon, F. (1967) *The Wretched of the Earth*, Harmondsworth: Penguin.

Fidler, R. (1991) *Canada Adieu? Quebec Debates its Future*, Oolichan Books.

Forsythe, D. (1989) 'German identity and the problem of history', in E. Tonkin, M. Chapman and M. McDonald (eds) *History and Ethnicity*, London: Routledge.

Foucault, M. (1980) *Power/Knowledge*, Brighton: Harvester.

Frank, A.G. (1971) *Capitalism and Underdevelopment in Latin America*, Harmondsworth: Penguin.

Fukuyama, F. (1989) 'The end of history?', *The National Interest*, Summer.

Gadoffre, G. (1951) 'French national images and the problem of national stereotypes', *International Social Sciences Bulletin*, 3.

Garton-Ash, T. (1990) *We the People: The Revolution of '89 Witnessed in Warsaw, Budapest, Berlin & Prague*, Harmondsworth: Penguin.

Gellner, E. (1959) *Words and Things*, London: Gollanz.

Gellner, E. (1964) 'Nationalism', in *Thought and Change*, London: Weidenfeld & Nicolson.

Gellner, E. (1973) 'Scale and nation', in *Philosophy of the Social Sciences*, 3.

Gellner, E. (1978) 'Nationalism, or the new confessions of a justified Edinburgh sinner', in *Political Quarterly*, 49 (1).

Gellner, E. (1981) 'Nationalism', in *Theory and Society*, 10 (6).

Gellner, E. (1983) *Nations and Nationalism*, Oxford: Blackwell.

Gellner, E. (1994a) *Encounters with Nationalism*, Oxford: Blackwell.

Gellner, E. (1994b) *Conditions of Liberty: Civil Society and its Rivals*, London: Hamish Hamilton.

Gellner, E. (1995) 'Nationalism observed', unpublished paper for seminar entitled 'Our current sense of history', Prague, December (posthumous).

Gellner, E. (1996a) 'The coming of nationalism and its interpretation: the myths of nation and class', in G. Balakrishnan (ed.) *Mapping the Nation*, London: Verso.

Gellner, E. (1996b) 'The rest of history', in *Prospect*, May.

Gellner, E. (1996c) 'Reply: do nations have navels?', in *Nations and Nationalism*, 2 (3).

Gellner, E. (1996d) interview, in *Scottish Affairs*, 16.

Gellner, E. (1996e) 'Reply to critics', in J.A. Hall, and I. Jarvie (eds) *The Social Philosophy of Ernest Gellner*, Amsterdam: Rodopi.

Gellner, E. (1997) *Nationalism*, London: Weidenfeld & Nicolson.

Giddens, A. (1981) *A Contemporary Critique of Historical Materialism, Vol. I: Power, Property and the State*, London: Macmillan.

Giddens, A. (1985) *A Contemporary Critique of Historical Materialism, Vol. II: The Nation-State and Violence*, London: Polity Press.

Giddens, A. (1991) *Modernity and Self-Identity*, London: Polity Press.

Gilroy, P. (1987) *There Ain't No Black in the Union Jack*, London: Hutchinson.

Giner, S. (1995) 'Civil society and its future', in J. Hall (ed.) *Civil Society*, London: Polity Press.

Glenny, M. (1990) *The Rebirth of History: Eastern Europe in the Age of Democracy*, Harmondsworth: Penguin.

Glenny, M. (1992) *The Fall of Yugoslavia: The Third Balkan War*, Harmondsworth: Penguin.

Goffman, E. (1973) *The Presentation of Self in Everyday Life*, New York: Overview Press.

Goulbourne, H. (1991) *Ethnicity and Nationalism in Post-Imperial Britain*, Cambridge: Polity Press.

Guibernau, M. (1996) *Nationalisms: The Nation State and Nationalism in the Twentieth Century*, Cambridge: Polity Press.

Guibernau, M. (1997) 'Images of Catalonia', in *Nations and Nationalism*, 3 (1).

Greenfeld, L. (1992) *Nationalism: Five Roads to Modernity*, Cambridge, MA: Harvard University Press.

Habermas, J. (1996a) 'The European nation-state – its achievements and limits', in G. Balakrishnan (ed.) *Mapping the Nation*, London: Verso

Habermas, J. (1996b) 'National unification and popular sovereignty', *New Left Review*, 219.

Hall, J. (1985) *Powers and Liberties: The Causes and Consequences of the Rise of the West*, Oxford: Blackwell.

Hall, J. (1993) 'Nationalisms: classified and explained', *Daedalus*, 122 (3).

Hall, J. (1995) 'In search of civil society', in J. Hall (ed.) *Civil Society*, London: Polity Press.

Hall, J. (1996) 'Obituary: Ernest Gellner (1925–1995)', *British Journal of Sociology*, 47 (1).

Hall, S. (1984) 'The state in question', in G. McLennan, D. Held and S. Hall (eds) *The Idea of the Modern State*, Milton Keynes: Open University Press.

Hall, S. (1990) 'Cultural identity and diaspora', in J. Rutherford (ed.) *Identity: Community, Culture and Difference*, London: Lawrence & Wishart.

Hall, S. (1992) 'The question of cultural identity', in S. Hall *et al.* (eds) *Modernity and Its Futures*, Cambridge: Polity Press.

Hall, S. (1996a) 'Introduction: who needs identity?', in S. Hall and P. DuGay (eds) *Questions of Cultural Identity*, London: Sage.

Hall, S. (1996b) 'Ethnicity: identity and difference', in G. Eley and R.G. Suny (eds) *Becoming National*, Oxford: Oxford University Press.

Hall, S. (1996c) 'The new ethnicities', in J. Hutchinson and A.D. Smith (eds) *Ethnicity*, Oxford: Oxford University Press.

Handler, R. (1988) *Nationalism and the Politics of Culture in Quebec*, University of Wisconsin Press.

Harvie, C. (1981) *No Gods and Precious Few Heroes*, London: Edward Arnold.

Haseler, S. (1996) *The English Tribe: Identity, Nation and Europe*, London: Macmillan.

Hayes, C. (1948) *The Historical Evolution of Modern Nationalism*, New York: Macmillan.

Hayes, C. (1960) *Nationalism: A Religion*, New York: Macmillan.

Hechter, M. (1975) *Internal Colonialism: The Celtic Fringe in British National Development, 1536–1966*, London: Routledge & Kegan Paul.

Held, D. (1988) 'Farewell to the nation state', *Marxism Today*, December.

Held, D. (1990) 'The decline of the nation state', in S. Hall and M. Jacques (eds) *New Times: The Changing Face of Politics in the 1990s*, London: Lawrence & Wishart.

Held, D. (1992) 'The development of the modern state', in S. Hall and B. Gieben (eds) *Formations of Modernity*, London: Polity Press.

Hennessy, P. (1993) *Never Again: Britain, 1945–51*, London: Vintage.

Herzfeld, M. (1992) *The Social Production of Indifference: Exploring the Symbolic Roots of Western Bureaucracy*, Oxford: Berg.

Hirschman, A.O. (1970) *Exit, Voice, and Loyalty : Responses to Decline in Firms, Organizations, and States*, Cambridge, MA: Harvard University Press.

Hobsbawm, E.J. (1969) *Industry and Empire*, Harmondsworth: Penguin.

Hobsbawm, E.J. (1986) 'Mass-producing traditions: Europe, 1870–1914', in E.J. Hobsbawm and T. Ranger (eds) *The Invention of Tradition*, Cambridge: Cambridge University Press.

Hobsbawm, E.J. (1990) *Nations and Nationalism since 1780: Programme, Myth and Reality*, Cambridge: Cambridge University Press.

Hobsbawm, E.J. (1994) *The Age of Extremes: The Short Twentieth Century, 1914–1991*, London: Michael Joseph.

Holy, L. (1996) *The Little Czech and the Great Czech Nation*, Cambridge: Cambridge University Press.

Hroch, M. (1985) *Social Preconditions of National Revival in Europe*, Cambridge: Cambridge University Press.

Hroch. M. (1993) 'From national movement to the fully-formed nation', *New Left Review*, 198.

Hroch, M. (1996) 'Nationalism and national movements: comparing the past and present of Central and Eastern Europe', *Nations and Nationalism*, 2 (1).

Hutchinson, J. (1994) *Modern Nationalism*, London: Fontana.

Hutchinson, J. and Smith, A.D. (eds) (1994) *Nationalism*, Oxford: Oxford University Press.

Hutchinson, J. and Smith, A.D. (eds) (1996) *Ethnicity* Oxford: Oxford University Press.

Ignatieff, M. (1994) *Blood and Belonging*, London: Vintage.

Irumada, Nobuo (1997) 'Re-interpreting national history and local-regionalism in Japan', paper presented to International Conference on Comparative Regional Studies, September 1997, Sendai, Japan.

Jayawardena, K. (1986) *Feminism and Nationalism in the Third World*, London: Zed Books.

Jeffery, P. (1998) 'Agency, activism and agendas', in P. Jeffery and A. Basu (eds) *Appropriating Gender: Women's Activism and Politicized Religion in South Asia*, New York: Routledge, and New Delhi: Kali for Women.

Jones, A. (1994) 'Gender and ethnic conflict in ex-Yugoslavia', *Ethnic and Racial Studies*, 17.

Judah, T. (1997) 'The Serbs: the sweet and rotten smell of history', *Daedalus*, 126 (3).

Juteau, D. (1996) 'Theorising ethnicity and ethnic communalisations at the margins: from Quebec to the world system', *Nations and Nationalism*, 2 (1).

Kamenka, E. (ed.) (1976) *Nationalism: The Nature and Evolution of an Idea*, London: Edward Arnold.

Keating, M. (1988) *State and Regional Nationalism*, Brighton: Wheatsheaf.

Keating, M. (1996) *Nations Against the State: The New Politics of Nationalism in Quebec, Catalonia and Scotland*, London: Macmillan.

Kedourie, E. (1960) *Nationalism*, London: Hutchinson.

Kellas, J. (1991) *The Politics of Nationalism and Identity*, London: Macmillan.

Khazanov, A.M. (1997) 'Ethnic nationalism in the Russian Federation', *Daedalus*, 126 (3).

Kidd, C. (1993), *Subverting Scotland's Past: Scottish Whig Historians and the Creation of an Anglo-Scottish Identity, 1689–c.1830*, Cambridge: Cambridge University Press.

Kohn, H. (1945) *The Idea of Nationalism: A Study of its Origins and Background*, London: Macmillan; extract reprinted as 'Western and Eastern nationalisms', in J. Hutchinson and A.D. Smith (eds) (1994) *Nationalism*, Oxford: Oxford University Press.

Kramer, M. (1993) 'Arab nationalism: mistaken identity', *Daedalus*, 122 (3).

Krejci, J. and Velimsky, V. (1981) *Ethnic and Political Nations in Europe*, London: Croom Helm.

Kumar, K. (1993) 'Civil society: an inquiry into the usefulness of an historical term', *British Journal of Sociology*, 44 (3).

Lacroix, J-G. (1996) 'The reproduction of Quebec national identity in the post-referendum context', *Scottish Affairs*, 17.

Laitin, D. (1992) *Language Repertoires and State Construction in Africa*, Cambridge: Cambridge University Press.

Latawski, P. (ed.) (1995) *Contemporary Nationalism in East Central Europe*, London: Macmillan.

Lee, C.H. (1995) *Scotland and the United Kingdom: The Economy and the Union in the Twentieth Century*, Manchester: Manchester University Press.

Lester, J. (1997) 'Overdosing on nationalism: Gennadii Zyuganov and the Communist Party of the Russian Federation', *New Left Review*, 221.

Levi-Faur, D. (1997) 'Friedrich List and the political economy of the nation-state', *Review of International Political Economy*, 4 (1).

Lieven, A. (1993) *The Baltic Revolution: Estonia, Latvia, Lithuania and the Path to Independence*, London: Yale University Press.

Linz, J. (1985) 'From primordialism to nationalism', in E. Tiryakian and R. Rogowski (eds) *New Nationalisms of the Developed West*, London: Allen & Unwin.

Linz, J. and Stepan, A. (1992) 'Political identities and electoral consequences: Spain, the Soviet Union, and Yugoslavia', *Daedalus*, 121 (2).

Linz, J. and Stepan, A. (1996) *Problems of Democratic Transition and Consolidation: Southern Europe, South America, and Post-Communist Europe*, Baltimore and London: The Johns Hopkins University Press.

Llobera, J. (1989) 'Catalan national identity: the dialectics of past and present', in E. Tonkin, M. Chapman and M. McDonald (eds) *History and Ethnicity*, London: Routledge.

Llobera, J. (1994) 'Durkheim and the national question', in W.S.F. Pickering and H. Martins (eds) *Debating Durkheim*, London: Routledge.

Llobera, J. (1994) *The God of Modernity: The Development of Nationalism in Western Europe*, Oxford: Berg.

Ludden, D. (ed.) (1996) *Contesting the Nation: Religion, Community and the Politics of Democracy in India*, Philadelphia: University of Pennsylvania Press.

Lynch, P. (1996) *Minority Nationalism and European Integration*, Cardiff: University of Wales Press.

Lyons, F.S.L. (1979) *Ireland since the Famine*, London: Fontana.

MacCormick, N. (1994) 'What place for nationalism in the modern world?', in David Hume Institute, *In Search of New Constitutions*, Edinburgh University Press, 2 (1).

MacCormick, N. (1995) 'Sovereignty: myth and reality', *Scottish Affairs*, 11.

MacCormick, N. (1996) 'Liberalism, nationalism and the post-sovereign state', *Political Studies*, XLIV.

McClintock, A. (1993) 'Family feuds: gender, nationalism and the family', *Feminist Review*, 45.

McClintock, A. (1996) '"No longer in a future heaven": nationalism, gender and race', in G. Eley and R.G. Suny (eds) *Becoming National*, Oxford: Oxford University Press.

McCrone, D. (1992) *Understanding Scotland: The Sociology of a Stateless Nation*, London: Routledge.

McCrone, D. (1997) 'Opinion polls in Scotland, July 1996–June 1997', *Scottish Affairs*, 20.

McCrone, D., Morris, A. and Kiely, R. (1995) *Scotland – the Brand: The Making of Scottish Heritage*, Edinburgh: Edinburgh University Press.

McDonald, M. (1989) *We are not French! Language, Culture and Identity in Brittany*, London: Routledge.

MacDougall, H. (1982) *Racial Myth in English History: Trojans, Teutons and Anglo-Saxons*, Montreal: Harvest House, London: University Press of New England.

McGrew, A. (1992) 'A global society?', in S. Hall *et al.* (eds) *Modernity and its Futures*, Cambridge: Polity Press.

Malcolm, D. (1994) *Bosnia: A Short History*, London: Macmillan.

Malesevic, S. (1997) 'Chetniks and Ustashas: delegitimization of an ethnic enemy in the Serbian and Croatian war-time cartoons', in C. Lowney (ed.) *Identities in Change*, Vienna: Institute for Human Sciences.

Mann, M. (1984) 'The autonomous power of the state: its origins, mechanisms and results', in *Archives Européens de Sociologie*, XXV.

Mann, M. (1986) *The Sources of Social Power, Vol. 1: A History of Power from the Beginning to A.D. 1760*, Cambridge: Cambridge University Press.

Mann, M. (ed.) (1990) *The Rise and Decline of the Nation-State*, Oxford: Blackwell.

Mann, M. (1992) 'The emergence of modern European nationalism', in J. Hall and I.C. Jarvie (eds) *Transition to Modernity*, Cambridge: Cambridge University Press.

Mann, M. (1993a) 'Nation-states in Europe and other continents: diversifying, developing, not dying', *Daedalus*, 122 (3).

Mann, M. (1993b) *The Sources of Social Power, Vol. 2: The Rise of Classes and Nation-States, 1760–1914*, Cambridge: Cambridge University Press.

Mann, M. (1995) 'A political theory of nationalism and its excesses', in S. Periwal (ed.) *Notions of Nationalism*, Budapest: Central European University Press.

Mann, M. (1997) 'Has globalization ended the rise and rise of the nation-state?', *Review of International Political Economy*, 4 (3).

Marquand, D. (1988) *The Unprincipled Society*, London: Fontana.

Marquand, D. (1993) 'The twilight of the British state? Henry Dubb versus sceptred awe', *Political Quarterly*, 64 (2).

Marx, K. (1959) 'The Eighteenth Brumaire of Louis Bonaparte', in L. Feuer (ed.) *Marx and Engels: Basic Writings in Politics and Philosophy*, New York: Doubleday.

Mattossian, M. (1994) 'Ideologies of delayed development', in J. Hutchinson and A.D. Smith (eds) *Nationalism*, Oxford: Oxford University Press.

Meehan, E. (1993) 'Citizenship and the European Community', *Political Quarterly*, 64 (2).

Melucci, A. (1989) *Nomads of the Present: Social Movements and Individual Needs in Contemporary Society*, London: Hutchinson Radius.

Mercer, K. (1990) 'Welcome to the jungle: identity and diversity in post-modern politics', in J. Rutherford (ed.) *Identity: Community, Culture, Difference*, London: Lawrence & Wishart.

Middlemas, K. (1979) *Politics in Industrial Society: The Experience of the British System Since 1911*, London: Deutsch.

Miles, R. (1993) *Racism after 'Race Relations'*, London: Routledge.

Miller, D. (1995) *On Nationality*, Oxford: Clarendon Press.

Milward, A. (1992) *The European Rescue of the Nation-State*, London: Routledge.

Minogue, K. (1996) 'Ernest Gellner and the dangers of theorising nationalism', in J.A. Hall and I. Jarvie (eds) *The Social Philosophy of Ernest Gellner*, Amsterdam: Rodopi.

Mommsen, W. (1990) 'The varieties of the nation-state in modern history: liberal, imperialist, fascist and contemporary notions of nations and nationality', in M. Mann (ed.) *The Rise and Decline of the Nation-State*, Oxford: Blackwell.

Moreno, L. (1995) 'Multiple ethnoterritorial concurrence in Spain', *Nationalism and Ethnic Politics*, 1 (1).

Moreno, L. and Arriba, A. (1996) 'Dual identity in autonomous Catalonia', *Scottish Affairs*, 17.

Morton, G. (1994) *Unionist Nationalism: The Historical Construction of Scottish National Identity, Edinburgh, 1830–1860*, Ph.D. thesis, Edinburgh University.

Morton, G. (1996) 'Scottish rights and "centralisation" in the mid-nineteenth century', *Nations and Nationalism*, 2 (2).

Morton, G. (1998a) 'The Most Efficacious Patriot: the heritage of William Wallace in nineteenth-century Scotland', *The Scottish Historical Review* (forthcoming).

Morton, G. (1998b) *Unionist-Nationalism: Governing Urban Scotland, 1830–1860*, East Linton: John Tuckwell Press (forthcoming).

Nairn, T. (1975) 'Nationalism of the elect and nationalism of the damned', mimeo.

Nairn, T. (1977) *The Break-Up of Britain*, London: New Left Books.

Nairn, T. (1993) 'Demonising nationalism', *London Review of Books*, 25 February.

Nairn, T. (1994) 'Beyond Reason? Ethnos or Uneven Development', *Scottish Affairs*, 8.

Nairn, T. (1995) 'Upper and lower cases', *London Review of Books*, 24 August.

Nairn, T. (1997) *Faces of Nationalism*, London: Verso.

O'Brien, C. Cruise (1994) *Ancestral Voices*, Dublin: Poolbeg Press.

O'Leary, B. (1996) 'On the nature of nationalism: an appraisal of Ernest Gellner's writings on nationalism', in J.A. Hall and I. Jarvie (eds) *The Social Philosophy of Ernest Gellner*, Amsterdam: Rodopi.

Østergård, U. (1992) 'Peasants and Danes: the Danish nationality and political culture', *Comparative Studies in Society and History*, 34 (1).

Pandey, G. (1992) *The Construction of Communalism in Colonial North India*, Oxford: Oxford University Press.

Paterson, L. (1991) 'Ane end of ane auld sang: sovereignty and the renegotiation of the Union', in A. Brown, and D. McCrone (eds) *Scottish Government Yearbook*, Edinburgh: Edinburgh University Press.

Paterson, L. (1994) *The Autonomy of Modern Scotland*, Edinburgh: Edinburgh University Press.

Pearson, R. (1995) 'The making of '89: nationalism and the dissolution of Communist Eastern Europe', *Nations and Nationalism*, 1 (1).

Pi-Sunyer, O. (1985) 'Catalan nationalism: some theoretical and historical considerations', in E. Tiryakian and R. Rogowski (eds) *New Nationalisms of the Developed West*, London: Allen & Unwin.

Plamenatz, J. (1976) 'Two types of nationalism', in E. Kamenka (ed.) *Nationalism: The Nature and Evolution of an Idea*, London: Edward Arnold.

Pocock, P. (1975) 'British history: a plea for a new subject', *Journal of Modern History*, 4.

Poggi, G. (1978) *The Development of the Modern State*, London: Hutchinson.

Poggi, G. (1983) *Calvinism and the Capitalist Spirit: Max Weber's Protestant Ethic*, London: Macmillan.

Poggi, G. (1990), *The State: Its Nature, Development and Prospects*, Cambridge: Polity Press.

Portes, A. and MacLeod, D. (1996) 'What shall I call myself? Hispanic identity formation in the second generation', *Ethnic and Racial Studies*, 19 (3).

Quebec, Government of (1995) *Bill Respecting the Future of Quebec, Including the Declaration of Sovereignty and the Agreement of June 12, 1995*, National Assembly, first session, 35th legislature.

Raissiguier, C. (1995) 'The construction of marginal identities: working class girls of Algerian descent in a French school', in M.H. Marchand, and J.L. Parpart (eds) *Feminism, Post-Modernism and Development*, London: Routledge.

Renan, E. (1882) 'What is a nation?', reprinted in H.K. Bhabha (ed.) (1990) *Nation and Narration*, London: Routledge.

Rodkin, P. (1993) 'The psychological reality of social constructions', *Ethnic and Racial Studies*, 16 (4).

Said, E. (1993) *Culture and Imperialism*, London: Chatto & Windus.

Said, E. (1995) *Orientalism: Western Conceptions of the Orient*, Harmondsworth: Penguin.

Samary, C. (1995) *Yugoslavia Dismembered*, New York: Monthly Review Press.

Samuel, R. (ed.) (1992) *Patriotism: The Making and Unmaking of British National Identity*, London: Routledge.

Sarkar, S. (1996) 'Indian nationalism and the politics of Hindutva', in D. Ludden (ed.) *Contesting the Nation: Religion, Community and the Politics of Democracy in India*, Philadelphia: University of Pennsylvania Press.

Sassoon, D. (1997) *One Hundred Years of Socialism: The West European Left in the Twentieth Century*, London: Fontana Press.

Schama, S. (1996) *Landscape and Memory*, London: Fontana Press.

Schlesinger, P. (1991) *Media, State and Nation: Political Violence and Collective Identities*, London: Sage.

Schlesinger, P. (1992) '"Europeanness" – a new cultural battlefield?', *Innovation*, 5 (1).

Schlesinger, P. (1997) 'From cultural defence to political culture: media, politics and collective identity in the European Union', *Media, Culture and Society*, 19 (3).

Schnapper, D. (1997) 'The European debate on citizenship', *Daedalus*, 126 (3).

Scruton, R. (1990) 'In defence of the nation', in J. Clark (ed.) *Ideas and Politics in Modern Britain*, London: Macmillan.

Seers, D. (1983) *The Political Economy of Nationalism*, Oxford University Press.

Sekulic, D., Massey, G. and Hodson, R. (1994) 'Failed sources of a common identity in the former Yugoslavia', *American Sociological Review*, 59 (1).

Seligman, A. (1995) 'Animadversions upon civil society and civic virtue in the last decade of the 20th century', in J. Hall (ed.) *Civil Society*, London: Polity Press.

Seton-Watson, H. (1977) *Nations and States: An Enquiry into the Origins and the Politics of Nationalism*, London: Methuen.

Shils, E. (1995) 'Nation, nationality, nationalism and civil society', *Nations and Nationalism*, 1 (1).

Silber, L. and Little, A. (1995) *The Death of Yugoslavia*, Harmondsworth: Penguin.

Skocpol, T. (1977) 'Wallerstein's world capitalist system: a theoretical and historical critique', *American Journal of Sociology*, 82 (5).

Smith, A. (1981) *The Ethnic Revival*, Cambridge: Cambridge University Press.

Smith, A. (1986) *The Ethnic Origins of Nations*, Oxford: Blackwell.

Smith, A. (1988) 'The Myth of the "modern nation" and the myths of nations', *Ethnic and Racial Studies*, 11 (1).

Smith, A. (1991) *National Identity*, Harmondsworth: Penguin.

Smith, A. (1994) 'The politics of culture: ethnicity and nationalism', in T. Ingold (ed.) *Companion Encyclopedia of Anthropology*, London: Routledge.

Smith, A. (1996a) 'Opening statement: nations and their pasts', *Nations and Nationalism*, 2 (3).

Smith, A. (1996b) 'Memory and modernity: reflections on Ernest Gellner's theory of nationalism', *Nations and Nationalism*, 2 (3).

Smith, A. (1996c) *Nations and Nationalism in a Global Era*, Cambridge: Polity Press.

Smith, D. and Blanc, M. (1996) 'Citizenship, nationality and ethnic minorities in three European nations', *International Journal of Urban and Regional Research*, 20 (1).

Smith, G. (1996) 'The resurgence of nationalism', in G. Smith (ed.) *The Baltic States: The national self-determination of Estonia, Latvia and Lithuania*, London: Macmillan.

Smout, T.C. (1994) 'Perspectives on the Scottish identity', *Scottish Affairs*, 6.

Stargardt, N. (1995) 'Origins of the constructionist theory of the nation', in S. Periwal (ed.) *Notions of Nationalism*, Budapest: Central European University Press.

Stargardt, N. (1996) 'Gellner's nationalism: the spirit of modernisation?' in J.A. Hall and I. Jarvie (eds) *The Social Philosophy of Ernest Gellner*, Amsterdam: Rodopi.

Stevenson, J. (1984) *British Society, 1914–45*, Harmondsworth: Penguin.

Sullivan, J. (1988) *Eta and Basque Nationalism: The Fight for Euskadi, 1890–1986*, London: Routledge.

Szporluk, R. (1988) *Communism and Nationalism: Karl Marx versus Friedrich List*, Oxford: Oxford University Press.

Tamamoto, M. (1995) 'Reflections on Japan's Postwar State', *Daedalus*, 124 (2).

Tamir, Y. (1993) *Liberal Nationalism*, Princeton: Princeton University Press.

Taylor, M. (1992) 'John Bull and the iconography of public opinion in England, c.1712–1929', *Past and Present*, 134.

Taylor, P. (1993) 'The meaning of the North: England's "foreign country" within?', *Political Geography*, 12 (2).

Tilly, C. (1992) *Coercion, Capital and European States, AD 990–1992*, Oxford: Blackwell.

Tiryakian, E. and Rogowski, R. (eds) (1985) *New Nationalisms of the Developed West*, London: Allen & Unwin.

Tonkin, E., Chapman, M. and McDonald, M. (eds) (1989) *History and Ethnicity*, London: Routledge.

Touraine, A. (1981) 'Une Sociologie sans Société', *Revue Française de Sociologie*, 22 (1).

Treanor, P. (1997) 'Structures of nationalism', *Sociological Research Online*, 2 (1).

Van de Veer, P. (1994) *Religious Nationalism: Hindus and Muslims in India*, London: University of California Press.

Varshney, A. (1993) 'Contested meanings: India's national identity, Hindu nationalism, and the politics of anxiety', *Daedalus*, 122 (3).

Verdery, K. (1993) 'Whither "Nation" and "Nationalism"?', *Daedalus*, 122 (3).

Walby, S. (1993) 'Women and nation', *Feminist Review*, 45.

Walby, S. (1996) 'Woman and nation', in G. Balakrishnan (ed.) *Mapping the Nation*, London: Verso.

Wallace, W. (1995) 'Rescue or retreat? The nation state in Western Europe, 1945–1993', in J. Dunn (ed.) *Contemporary Crisis of the Nation State?*, Oxford: Blackwell.

Wallerstein, I. (1974) *The Modern World-System: Capitalist Agriculture and the Origins of the European World-Economy in the 16th century*, New York: Academic Press.

Wallerstein, I. (1979) *The Capitalist World-Economy*, Cambridge: Cambridge University Press.

Wallerstein, I. (1980) 'One man's meat: the Scottish great leap forward', *Review*, 3 (4).

Wandycz, P.S. (1992) *The Price of Freedom: A History of East-Central Europe from the Middle Ages to the Present*, London: Routledge.

Weber, E. (1977) *Peasants into Frenchmen: The Modernisation of Rural France, 1870–1914*, London: Chatto & Windus.

Weber, M. (1966) *General Economic History*, New York: Collier Books.

Weber, M (1978) *Economy and Society*, Berkeley: University of California Press.

Williams, G. (1980) *When was Wales?*, BBC Radio Wales, annual lecture.

Williamson, E (1992) *The Penguin History of Latin America*, Harmondsworth: Penguin.

Woodward, S. (1995) *Balkan Tragedy: Chaos and Dissolution after the Cold War*, Washington, DC: Brookings Institution.

Worsley, P. (1984) *The Three Worlds: Culture and World Development*, London: Weidenfeld & Nicolson.

Yuval-Davis, N. (1993) 'Gender and nation', *Ethnic and Racial Studies* 16 (4).

Yuval-Davis, N. (1997) *Gender and Nation*, London: Sage.

Zubaida, S. (1989) 'Nations: old and new. Comments on Anthony D. Smith's "The myth of the 'modern nation' and the myth of nations"', *Ethnic and Racial Studies*, 12 (3).

INDEX